Getting the most from Windows Me

Other Books of Interest

BP454 Windows 98 assistant
BP455 Windows 98 hard disc and file management
BP456 Windows 98 explained
BP457 Windows 98 applets explained
BP458 Tune up Windows 98
BP459 Windows 98 communications
BP466 Understanding Windows 98 registry
BP469 Simple networking with Windows 98
BP471 Microsoft Office 2000 explained
BP472 Microsoft Word 2000 explained
BP473 Microsoft Excel 2000 explained
BP474 Microsoft Access 2000 explained
BP476 Microsoft Powerpoint 2000 explained
BP478 Microsoft Works 2000 explained
BP485 A practical introduction to Microsoft Works 2000
BP489 Basic Microsoft Office 2000 skills
BP490 Web pages using Microsoft Office 2000
BP491 Windows 2000 explained
BP493 Windows Me explained
BP494 Basic Internet skills
BP495 Easy Windows troubleshooting
BP502 Windows Me Multimedia explained

* * * * *

Getting the most from Windows Me

Jim Gatenby

BERNARD BABANI (publishing) LTD
The Grampians
Shepherds Bush Road
London W6 7NF
England

www.babanibooks.com

Please Note

Although every care has been taken with the production of this book to ensure that any projects, designs, modifications and/or programs, etc., contained herewith, operate in a correct and safe manner and also that any components specified are normally available in Great Britain, the Publishers and Author do not accept responsibility in any way for the failure (including fault in design) of any project, design, modification or program to work correctly or to cause damage to any equipment that it may be connected to or used in conjunction with, or in respect of any other damage or injury that may be so caused, nor do the Publishers accept responsibility in any way for the failure to obtain specified components.

Notice is also given that if equipment that is still under warranty is modified in any way or used or connected with home-built equipment then that warranty may be void.

First Published - April 2001

British Library Cataloguing in Publication Data:

A catalogue record for this book is available from the British Library

ISBN 0 85934 496 7

Cover Design by Gregor Arthur

Printed and bound in Great Britain by The Guernsey Press

About this Book

This book builds on the author's earlier titles, such as "Windows 98 hard disc and file management", and also embraces the many new features built into Windows Me. These include System Restore, Compressed Folders, the Home Networking Wizard and Internet Connection Sharing. The new Windows Media Player 7 is packed with features to enhance the playing and management of audio and video files, including those downloaded from the Internet in the popular MP3 compressed audio format.

The book is aimed at the user new to Windows Me, who wishes to manage their computer efficiently, while making the most of the novel features introduced by Windows Me. The first part of the book describes the way your work can be saved in an organized set of personal folders instead of haphazard, unstructured saving destinations. To keep the computer running in peak condition, Windows Me provides a number of maintenance tools such as ScanDisk and Disk Defragmenter, which should be used regularly. These are described, together with System Restore, a new feature which returns a faulty computer to a previous configuration known to be healthy.

Disaster often strikes in the form of viruses and accidental deletion of data. Peace of mind can be achieved with sensible backup procedures and the use of good anti-virus software. The arrival of affordable re-writable CD drives provides a high capacity backup medium which is cheap, fast and easy to use. These important topics are covered in depth and, to cover the worst case scenario, the fitting of a new hard disc drive is also described, including the use of disc imaging software to transfer the entire contents of an old hard disc onto a new one.

Escalating use of the Internet required third party software to compress files so that they could be downloaded more quickly. Windows Me now contains its own facility, Compressed Folders, which also manages the economical archiving of data.

The Direct Cable Connection is a component of Windows Me, allowing two computers to be connected with only a simple cable costing a few pounds. It is the cheapest way for two computers to share data and printers, etc. The popular LapLink communications and file transfer software is also covered, including connection by fast USB ports.

Connecting two or more computers to form a *network* can be very cost-effective in terms of shared resources and data. However, in the past this was a highly technical job requiring specialist knowledge. The Home Networking Wizard introduced with Windows Me makes this a much easier task and shields the user from the most obscure jargon. All you need is a cheap network card for each machine and cable(s) to connect them. Once connected you can share software and printers, copy data files and send messages between machines. As more homes and small businesses acquire two or more computers, the ability to network and also connect to the Internet is becoming essential. The Internet Connection Sharing feature in Windows Me enables several computers on a network to share a single Internet connection consisting of one modem and a telephone line.

Later chapters cover the above networking topics before describing the method of fitting a modem to your computer. Also discussed are faster and more expensive methods of connection such as ISDN, ADSL and Cable Modems. Points to consider when choosing an Internet Service Provider are then listed, followed by a step-by-step description of the process of getting on-line to the Internet.

The final chapter describes Windows Media Player 7 and its many features for managing and playing audio and video files. Software such as Windows Media Player will become increasingly important in the future when broadband Internet connections allow fast downloading and streaming of audio files and video on demand. Also covered are other features of Windows Media Player such as the Internet Radio Tuner, copying CDs to a hard disc and transferring audio files to portable MP3 devices.

About the Author

Jim Gatenby trained as a Chartered Mechanical Engineer and initially worked at Rolls-Royce Ltd using computers in the analysis of performance. He obtained a Master of Philosophy degree in Mathematical Education by research at Loughborough University of Technology and taught mathematics and computing to 'A' Level for many years. His most recent posts have included Head of Computer Studies and Information Technology Coordinator. During this time he has written many books in the fields of educational computing and Microsoft Windows.

The author has considerable experience of teaching students of all ages and abilities, in school and in adult education. For several years he successfully taught the well-established CLAIT course (Computer Literacy and Information Technology) from Oxford Cambridge and RSA Examinations, as well as GCSE and National Curriculum Information Technology courses.

Trademarks

Contents

3

Backup Activities 51

4

Backup Software 75

1

Managing Files and Folders

Introduction

This section gives an overview of the way Windows Me can be used to organise your work into a hierarchy of files and folders. The term *file*, in this context, refers to a single piece of work stored on the hard disc. The piece of work may be a letter or report, a spreadsheet, a drawing or a set of records in a database.

In the same way that loose papers in the traditional office are organised into *folders*, computer files are grouped into metaphorical folders on the hard disc. This makes it easier to find a particular piece of work. Disc management tasks such as copying or deleting groups of files become much simpler. Folders are a graphical representation of the text-based *directories* used in earlier systems. Windows Me has two component programs which can be used for managing files and folders; Windows Explorer and My Computer.

The Windows Explorer

Explorer can be opened using **Start**, **Programs**, **Accessories** and **Windows Explorer**. However, a quicker method is to click the right mouse button over the **Start** button, then select **Explore**.

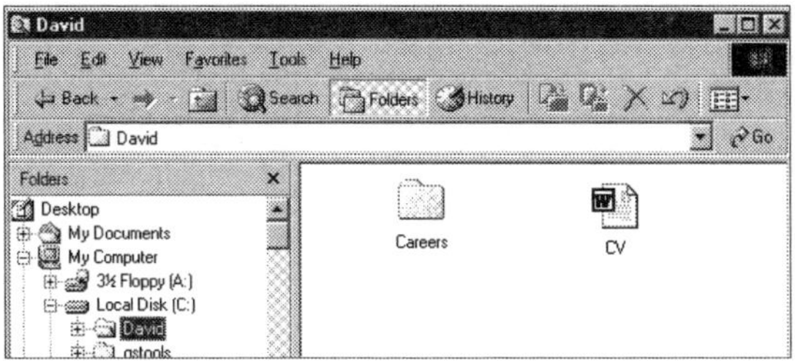

Windows Explorer is particularly useful for viewing the hierarchical or branching structure of the various discs and their folders. Folders can be opened up to reveal the *subfolders* and files within.

My Computer

This is launched by double clicking its icon on the Windows Desktop. **My Computer** gives an immediate view of the different disc storage devices and the **Control Panel**.

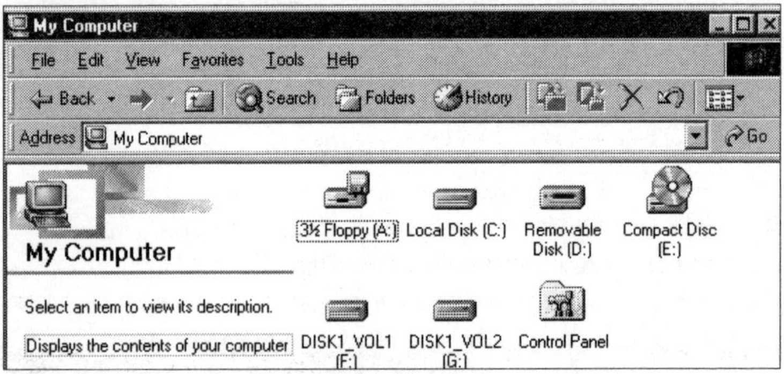

Double-clicking on the icon for a disc drive, such as drive **C:** reveals the folders and files on the disc and statistics for the amount of space used. In addition to file management tasks, My Computer is also used for setting up new hardware and software, via the Control Panel.

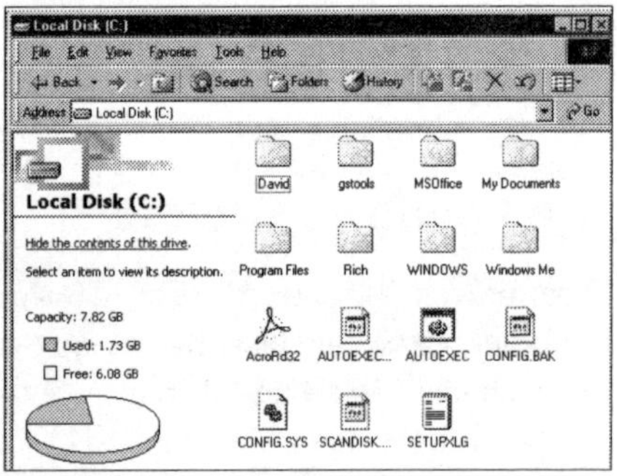

Both the Windows Explorer and My Computer can be used for managing files and folders, either by "dragging" and "dropping" with the mouse or by using the menus accessed from **File** and **Edit**. These tasks are covered in detail in later sections of this book.

Folder Options

Windows Me provides a number of alternative ways of displaying folders in My Computer and the Windows Explorer. These include displaying the contents of folders in the style of an Internet browser as shown below, with **Back** and **Forward** buttons to enable movement between windows, and an **Address** bar.

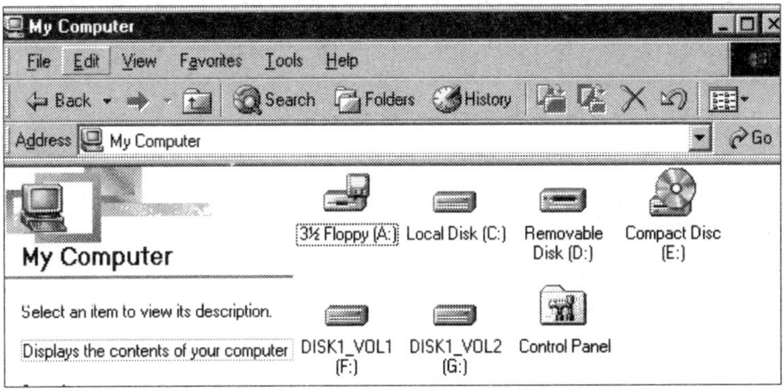

You can customize the folders by selecting **Tools** and **Folder Options...** from the menu bar across the top of My Computer and the Windows Explorer.

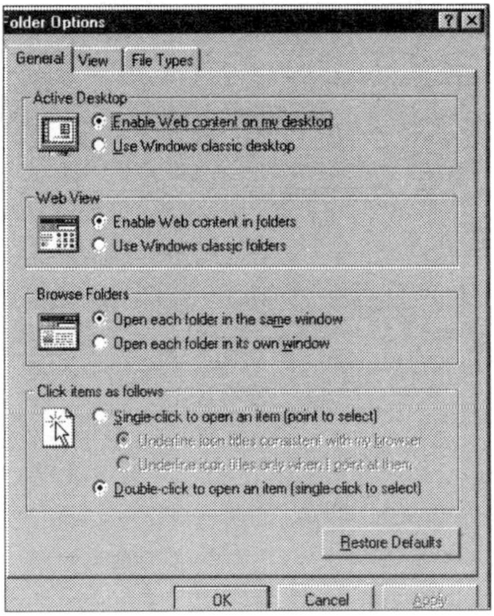

Selecting **Enable Web content...** will give the Internet type screens just described. Selecting **Use Windows classic...** will revert to the normal Windows Me layout. You can also choose between single or double click mouse operations to open a folder.

The Folder "My Documents"

Windows Me is designed to simplify the organisation of your work into folders. When Windows Me is first installed on your computer, a folder is automatically created called **My Documents**, normally located on the **C:** drive. When you save a new piece of work, it is be placed, by default, into **My Documents**. Experienced users create folders of their own with meaningful names, then select the required folder before saving their work. This makes it easier to locate and retrieve files at a later date. Creating your own folders is discussed shortly, but **My Documents** is useful when you first start saving your work on the computer. **My Documents** is often used as the default folder when files are downloaded to your hard disc from the Internet. (The default folder is suggested automatically at the start of the downloading process although you can override this by selecting a folder of your choice).

Opening up the folder **My Documents** on my particular computer, as shown in the window below, illustrates that a folder can contain various types of object, identified by their different icons.

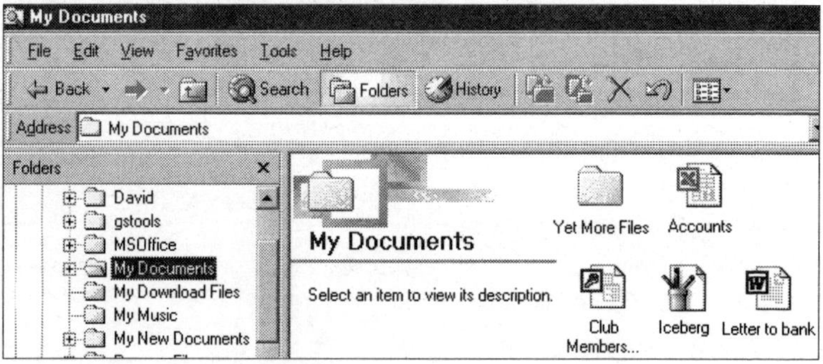

In the right hand panel entitled **My Documents**, the icons represent a subfolder "**Yet More Files**", an Excel spreadsheet file named "**Accounts**", an Access database file called "**Club Membership List**", a drawing file from Paint entitled "**Iceberg**" and finally a letter produced in Word 2000.

The Hierarchy of Folders

The previous window showing the folder **My Documents** also contains another folder within it - a "subfolder". The Windows Explorer displays the branching or hierarchical structure of folders and subfolders.

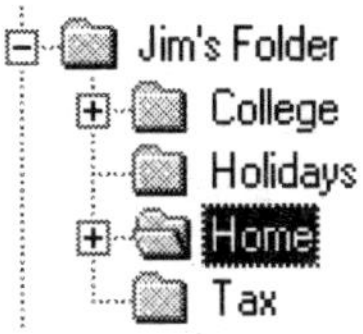

Shown on the left is **Jim's Folder** with 4 subfolders branching off. The **+** sign indicates that a folder contains more folders within it.

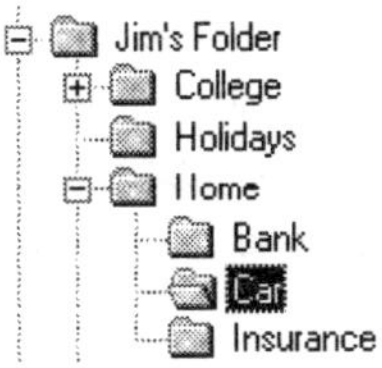

Clicking on the **+** sign against the folder **Home** reveals three subfolders, **Bank**, **Car** and **Insurance**. (Clicking the **-** sign to the left of **Home** hides the subfolders **Bank**, **Car** and **Insurance**).

The files contained in the folder **Car** are revealed in the Windows Explorer by clicking on the folder icon. The **Size** and **Type** of file are displayed when you select **View** and **Details** from the Explorer menu.

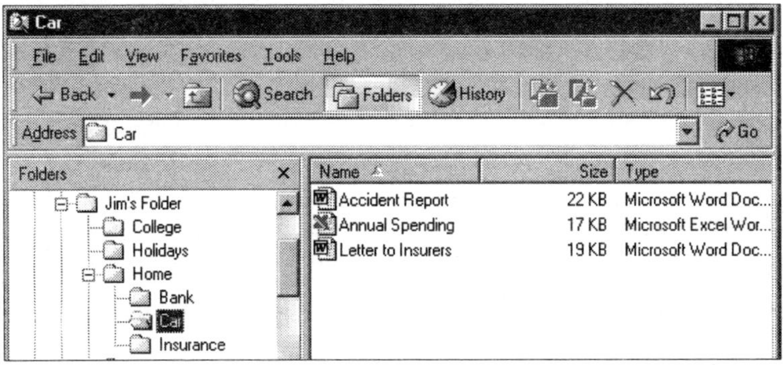

It can be seen that the folder **Car** contains 3 files, consisting of two Word documents and an Excel spreadsheet. Note that Windows Me, like Windows 98 before it, allows files to be saved with long filenames such as "**Letter to Insurers**".

Files in Detail

There are two main types of file on your computer: *software files* and *data files*.

Software Files

The software used to run your computer is made up of many different *program files* designed to carry out specific tasks. The *systems software*, such as the Windows Me operating system, is used to control all of the basic functions of the computer and to provide the interface with the user. The systems software is essential no matter what purpose you intend to use the computer for.

The *applications software* (such as Microsoft Office or Internet Explorer) includes the programs you buy and install to carry out a task such as word processing, drawing or accounts work. Program files have filename extensions like **.exe** (discussed shortly).

The non-expert user should never attempt to modify or move program files, as this will almost certainly cause major problems.

Data Files

These files are the work you produce and save on the hard disc. A data file may be a word processing document, database records, spreadsheets, pictures, photographs or music. Initially you will be concerned with creating and naming new files but later you will need to perform tasks such as copying, moving, renaming and deleting files. You may also create new folders to organize your data files efficiently.

Types of Data File

When a file is created, e.g. by saving in one of the applications, such as Microsoft Word 2000, an icon is attached to the filename to indicate the type of file, as shown below:

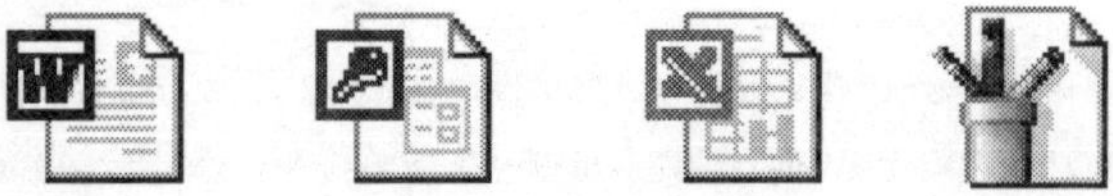

Word **Access** **Excel** **Paint**

Filename Extensions

Although Windows Me doesn't normally display them, files are automatically saved with a 3-letter extension after the filename, which identifies the file type. For example, some program files are saved with the **.exe** extension. In the text-only MSDOS operating system which preceded the various icon-based Windows systems, files were listed in directories with filenames such as **myfile.doc** or **program.exe**. Since there were no icons in these early systems, the extension was necessary to show the type of file.

You can switch on the filename extensions in Windows Me by highlighting the required folder in Explorer or My Computer, then selecting **Tools**, **Folder Options...** and the **View** tab. To display the file extensions remove the tick in the box to the left of **Hide file extensions ....**

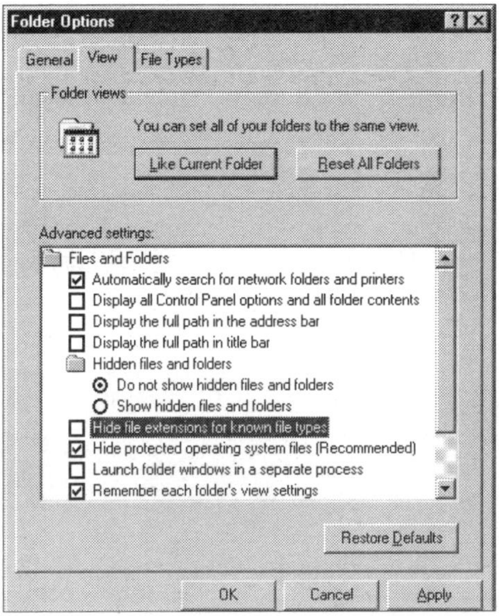

After switching on the filename extensions as described above, the full details of the files can be displayed in the Windows Explorer or My Computer, as shown on the next page.

Name	Size	Type	Modified
Accounts.xls	14 KB	Microsoft Excel Worksheet	10/24/2000 10:41 AM
Letter to bank.doc	19 KB	Microsoft Word Document	10/24/2000 10:49 AM
Club Membership List.mdb	120 KB	Microsoft Access Application	10/24/2000 10:48 AM
Iceberg.bmp	901 KB	Bitmap Image	10/24/2000 10:52 AM

Shown above are the filename extensions **.xls**, **.doc**, **.mdb**, and **.bmp** representing files produced in Excel, Word, Access and Paint respectively.

To display all of the information shown above you need to switch on **View** and **Details** from the Explorer (or My Computer) menu bar. You may need to stretch the columns to see all of the details, by dragging the small vertical bars e.g. between **Name** and **Size**, etc.

The **Folder Options/View** dialogue box shown below and on the previous page also allows you to completely hide particular types of file, such as **operating system files** or those with certain attributes, such as **Hidden**. (File attributes are discussed in the next section). The filenames of hidden files will therefore not be listed in the Windows Explorer or My Computer. This is a good idea since it makes it harder to delete important system files essential for the operation of the computer.

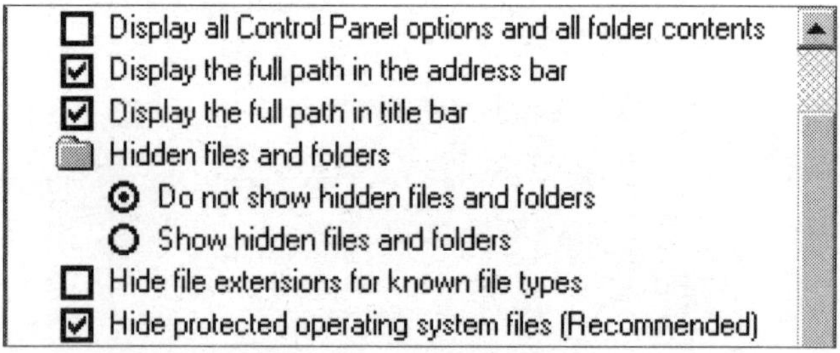

Switch on **Display the full path ...** in both boxes above if you want to see something like **C:\My Documents**, for example, rather than simply **My Documents**. This option can be set for both the title bar and the address bar in Windows Explorer and My Computer, as shown above.

File Properties

When a file is saved, it is automatically given certain properties and attributes. The user may view and perhaps change these properties in My Computer or the Windows Explorer. To view a file's properties, highlight the filename by moving the cursor over it. The filename should be surrounded by a coloured background. Now click the *right* button; a menu appears which includes, amongst others, the option to display the file **Properties.** (You can also access **Properties** using **File** on the menu bar across the top of the Explorer or My Computer window).

Selecting **Properties** allows you to view the file details and change the file attributes if necessary.

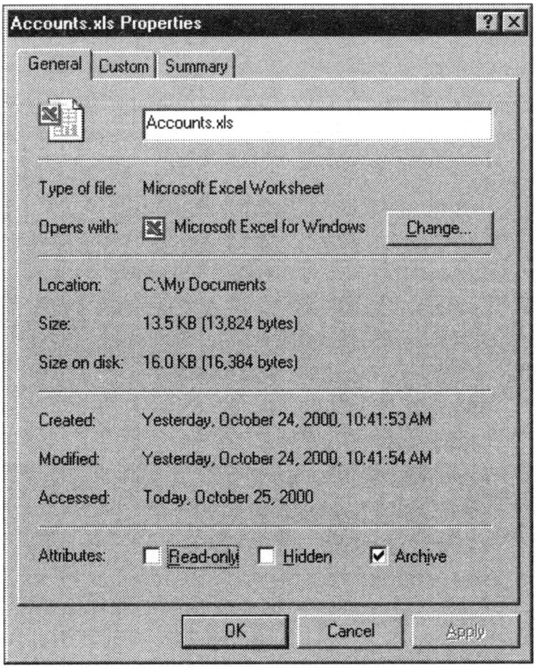

The **Properties** dialogue box above shows the icon attached to the file by Windows Me - in this case denoting an Excel worksheet i.e a file with the **.xls** extension.

File Attributes

At the bottom of the properties dialogue box are the file attributes **Read-only**, **Hidden** and **Archive**.

Switching these attributes on with a tick in the adjacent box has the following effects:

Read-Only

You can view the contents of the file but the file cannot be altered or deleted. This attribute would be switched on to protect important files which you don't want deleted (either accidentally or deliberately).

Hidden

Confidential files can be protected by switching this attribute on. Anyone else using the computer will not be aware of the existence of hidden files. The filename will not appear when you view the contents of folders using the Windows Explorer or My Computer or when you do **File** and **Open...** to reveal a list of files in an application such as Word. To open a hidden file, you need to know the filename and type it in during a **File** and **Open...** operation.

To make sure your "hidden" files really are hidden you need to tell My Computer or the Windows Explorer to hide them as discussed previously. This is done by selecting **Tools**, **Folder Options...** and the **View** tab. Then switch on the option **Do not show hidden files and folders**.

Archive

This is used by special backup programs which are set to make regular duplicate copies of important files. If the archive attribute is ticked, the file will be included in the next backup operation.

Working with Files and Folders

This section deals with the common tasks involved in organizing and maintaining your folders and the files you have produced in Word, Excel, Access, etc. These tasks include copying, moving, deleting and renaming files and folders.

Before files and folders can be examined or manipulated they must be selected or highlighted then opened with the mouse. Windows Me allows you to perform these tasks using either a single click or double click of the left hand mouse button. This option can be set in the **Folder Options** dialogue box mentioned earlier. This is accessed by selecting **Tools**, **Folder Options...** and the **General** tab from the menu bar in the Windows Explorer or My Computer.

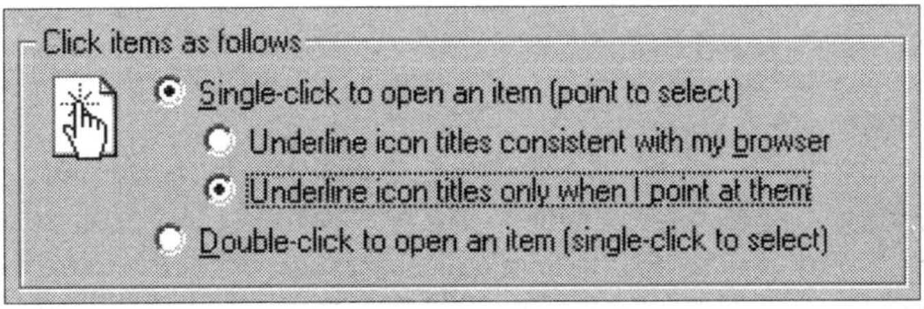

After you switch on the radio buttons of your choice as shown above, click **Apply** and **OK** for your selection to take effect. Then, depending on the option you have chosen, you will be able to use either a single or double click of the left mouse button to carry out the following operations:

- Open a folder to reveal any files or subfolders.
- Start a program such as My Computer from its icon on the Windows Desktop.
- Open an application file running in its associated program.

The last operation is explained in more detail on the next page.

Consider the four sample files shown below in the Windows Explorer.

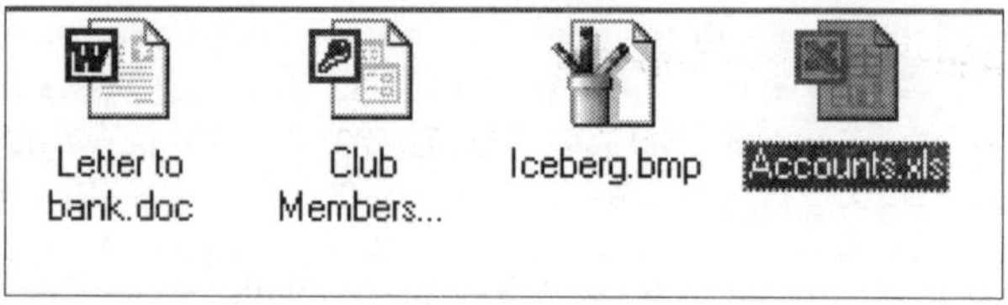

The associated program for each file is the program in which the file was created. In the above example, the **Iceberg** file is associated with Microsoft Paint and the **Accounts** spreadsheet is associated with Microsoft Excel.

For example, highlight the spreadsheet **Accounts** file in the Windows Explorer or My Computer. Then, depending on the mouse clicking option set in **Tools**, **Folder Options...**, **General** as described earlier, either click or double click over the icon or the filename. The spreadsheet program Microsoft Excel will start up, with the **Accounts** file open in its window.

Right-clicking

A quick way to access the menus (as an alternative to **File** and **Edit** on the menu bars) is to click the right mouse button over a file or (folder) in the Windows Explorer or My Computer. This produces the menu shown left. Right clicking on a gap on the Windows Taskbar on the bottom of the screen brings up a menu for "tiling" the screen windows. This enables folders to be displayed side-by-side and makes it easy to copy files between folders using "drag and drop". (Discussed shortly). Right-clicking the icon for a hard disc drive in My Computer is useful to examine the free space on the disc and to access the disc maintenance tools. (Described later in this book).

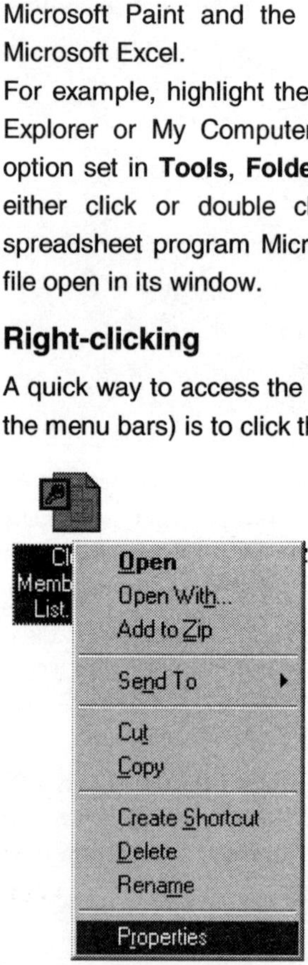

Saving Files in a Specified Location

Selecting the Destination Disc

A file is created every time you save a piece of work in an application such as Word, Excel or Paint. Using **File** and **Save As...** you can select the location where you want to save the work. The computer shown below shows the **C:** drive (primary hard disc drive), the floppy disc drive **A:** and the removable hard disc (ZIP disc) drive **D:**. Drive **E:** on this computer contains a re-writeable Compact Disc (CD-RW), which can be used for saving files. Drives **F:** and **G:** represent two partitions on a secondary hard disc drive. This was the original hard disc which was retained when a new and larger **C:** drive was fitted to the computer.

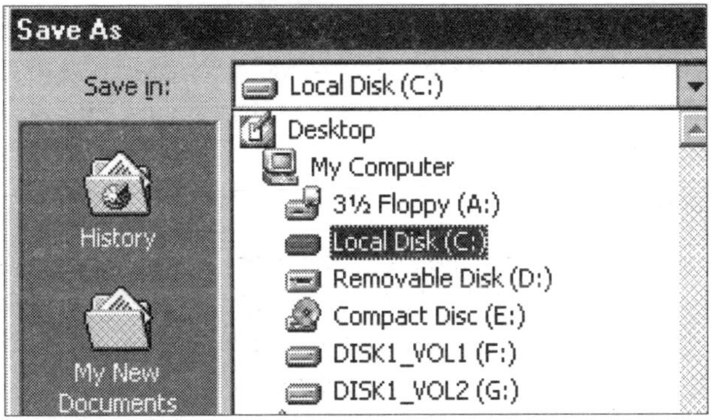

Initially most work will be saved on the primary hard disc drive (drive **C:** in this case). However, if it is necessary to make a backup copy of files, the floppy drives, ZIP disc or writeable CD may be used.

Selecting the Folder

When you have selected the disc on which to save your work, you then select the folder in which it is to be placed. Click or double click on the required disc drive to display the folders on the disc. It may be necessary to open a main folder followed by several subfolders to select the required save location.

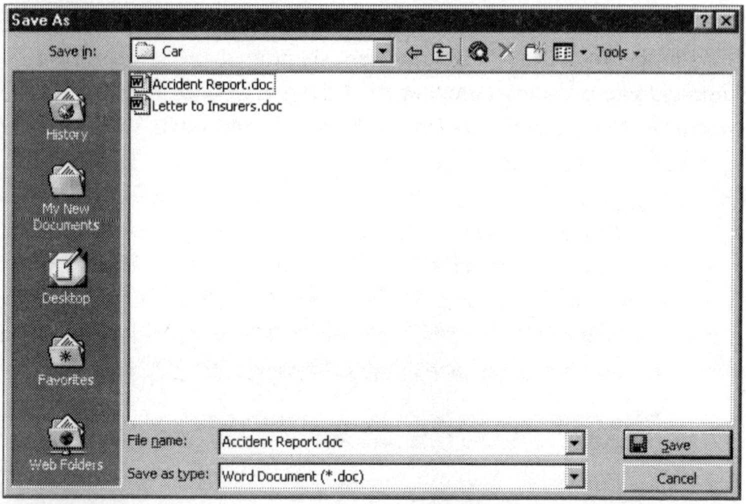

Adding the Filename

At this point you make up the name you wish to give to the file and enter it in the **File name:** bar at the bottom of the window. Windows Me permits long filenames (up to 255 characters). So you can give the file a meaningful name which should help you to find it at a later date.

Selecting the File Type

When you save a file in Word or Excel, etc., the file type will be automatically set as a Word Document (**.doc**) or whatever, depending on the program associated with the file. This is shown in the **Save as type:** bar at the bottom of the **Save As** window shown above. However, it is possible to specify a different file type by clicking the down arrow on the right of **Save as type:** bar. This reveals a choice of file formats in which the document can be saved.

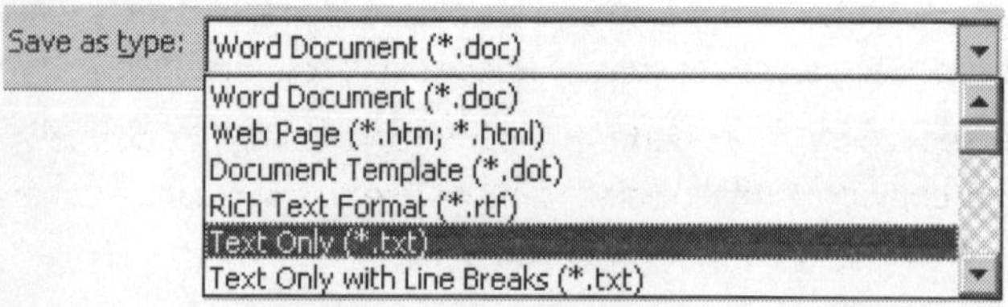

The ability to save files in different formats makes it easier to transfer files between computers running different software. For example, saving a file in the **Text Only (*.txt)** file type will produce a file which can be imported into a variety of software. This enables files produced using Microsoft Word, say, to be imported into computers using a different brand of word processor.

Options for Saving

Applications such as Word and Excel contain a range of options for saving files. For example, in Microsoft Word, selecting **File**, **Save As...**, then **Tools** and **General Options...** displays the following dialogue box:

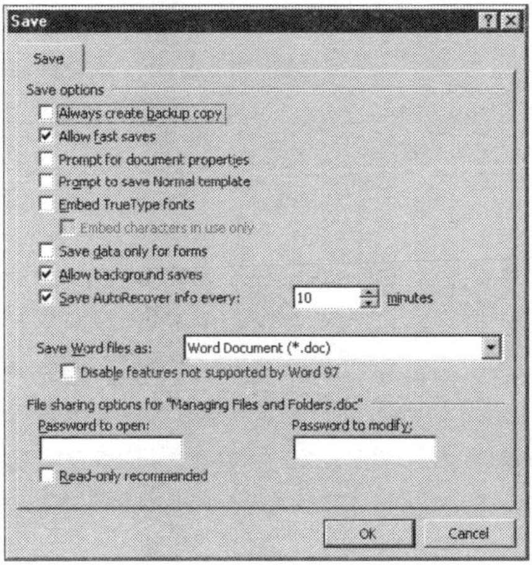

The option **Always create backup copy** makes a duplicate of the document being saved. The backup has the file extension **.WBK** and is placed in the same folder as the main copy of the file. **Allow fast saves** only records the changes to a file. **Save AutoRecover info every:** allows you to recover your work on restarting Word after a power failure or machine crash, etc. The **Save** dialogue box also allows you to apply a password to prevent anyone else looking at the files.

While producing an important document, it's a good idea to make a backup copy on a floppy disc. Simply use the **Save As...** option and select **3½ Floppy (A:)** as the destination.

Creating Folders

The Windows Explorer and My Computer can both be used to create new folders in which to organize your work. The Windows Explorer has been used in this example.

Suppose I want to start a new folder, **Building Project**, to hold files on some home improvements. I want to create the new folder within my existing folder **Home** which itself resides in **Jim's Folder** at the top level of the hierarchy on the **C:** drive.

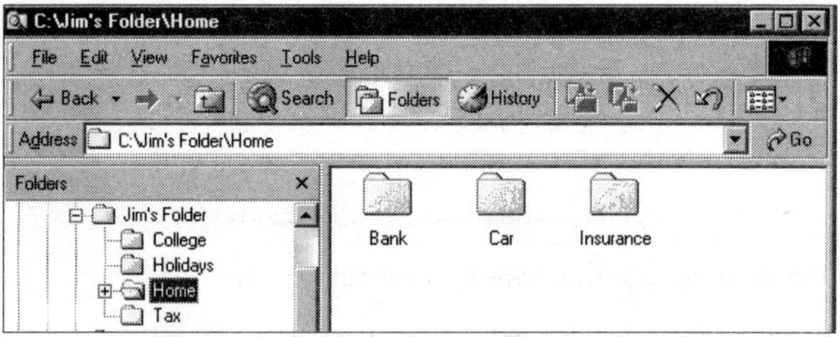

Start the Windows Explorer after right clicking over the **Start** button. Highlight the **Home** folder into which the new folder is to be located. Select **File**, **New** and **Folder** and a **New Folder** will appear as shown below. Alternatively you can press the right hand mouse button over an empty part of the Explorer right hand window, then select **New** and **Folder** from the menu which appears.

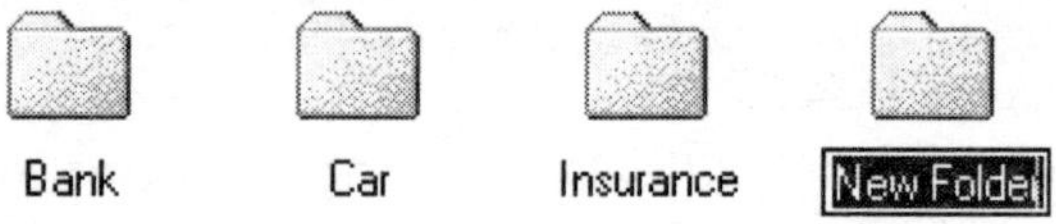

As can be seen above, the **New Folder** has been placed alongside of the existing folders in the **Home** folder. The flashing cursor is used to delete the default name **New Folder** and replace with the chosen filename (**Building Project** in this example) as shown on the next page.

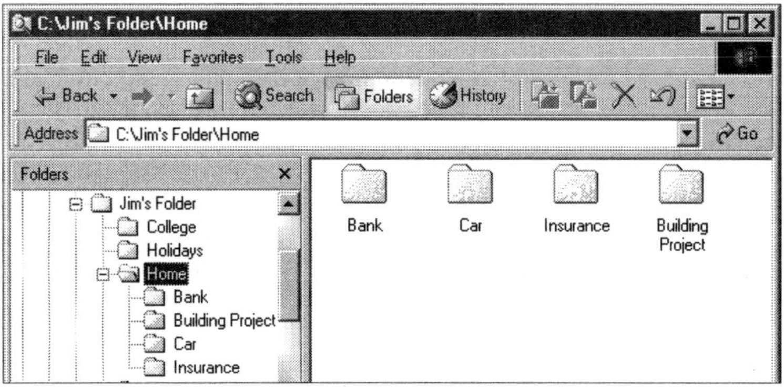

The left hand panel above shows the new folder **Building Project** in the list of folders in the **Home** folder, which is itself in **Jim's** Folder. The full *path name* of a file in the **Building Project** folder would be:

C:\Jim's Folder\Home\Building Project

This is shown in the Windows Explorer window below:

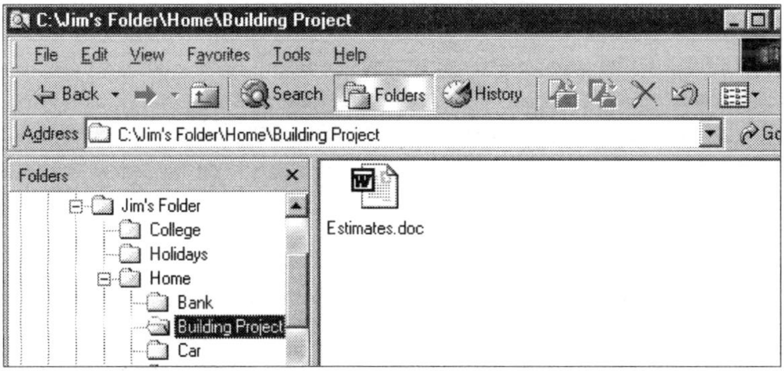

You can place new folders anywhere in your hierarchy of folders. Simply highlight the required "parent" folder which is to host the new folder, before selecting **File**, **New** and **Folder**. To place a new folder at the highest level of the hierarchy, open the Windows Explorer and make sure that your **C:** drive (or whatever) is highlighted before selecting **File**, **New** and **Folder**.

Renaming Files and Folders

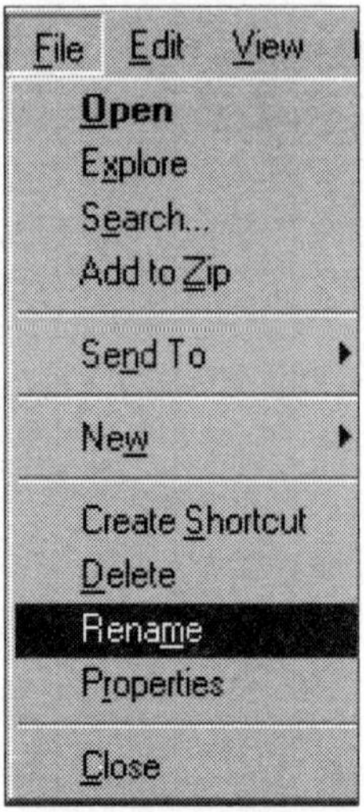

This work can be carried out equally well in the Windows Explorer or in My Computer. A folder or file can be renamed by right clicking over its icon in My Computer or the Windows Explorer then selecting **Rename** from the menu which appears (shown on the right). Alternatively the folder or filename can be highlighted, followed by selection of **File** and **Rename** from the menu bar across the top of the Explorer or My Computer window.

The folder name or filename appears in a rectangle with a flashing cursor. Rename the folder or file by deleting the existing name and typing in the new one, then press **Enter**.

Deleting Files and Folders

Highlight the file or folder in the Windows Explorer or My Computer then press the **Delete** key. Or you can select **Delete** from the **File** menu. (The **File** menu can be invoked from the menu bar or by right clicking over the file or folder). When you delete a folder then all of the subfolders and files contained within are also be deleted i.e. moved to the Recycle Bin. Unlike some earlier systems, Windows Me doesn't require a folder to be empty before it can be deleted.

If you make a mistake and delete the wrong folders or files, you can use the **Undo Delete** option in the **Edit** menu (provided you spot the mistake straight away.) Alternatively click the **Undo** icon on the Explorer bar of the Windows Explorer or My Computer (shown on the left).

Fortunately files and folders are not lost forever when they are deleted. Windows Me merely transfers them to its **Recycle Bin**. Files and folders in the Recycle Bin can then be either permanently deleted from the hard disc or they can be restored to their original location. The Recycle Bin is described on the next page.

The Recycle Bin

The Recycle Bin is invoked by clicking its icon on the Windows Desktop. It is effectively a folder into which all deleted files are initially sent. An easy way to delete files (in the Windows Explorer or My Computer) is to drag the icon for the file or folder and drop it over the Recycle Bin icon on the Windows Desktop.

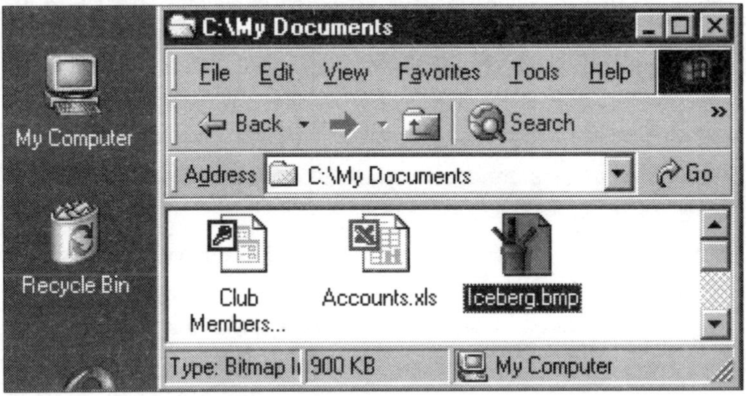

You can view the contents of the Recycle Bin at any time by clicking its icon on the Windows Desktop.

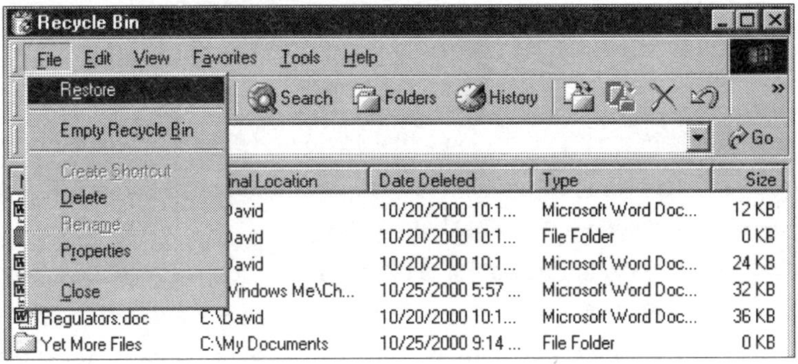

Files which have been "deleted" remain in the Recycle Bin until you decide to empty it. This is done by selecting **File** then **Empty Recycle Bin** off the menu bar at the top of the Recycle Bin window. The Recycle Bin should be emptied regularly since files in the Recycle Bin are still taking up disc space. Individual files can also be highlighted and deleted.

Should you wish to reinstate files which have been consigned to the bin, open up the Recycle Bin window by clicking its icon on the Windows Desktop. Then highlight the files to be restored and select **File** and **Restore** from the menu bar for the Recycle Bin. The files will be restored to their original locations.

Moving and Copying Files and Folders

The following tasks are described in the context of files, but the notes apply equally to folders.

Moving a file deletes the file from its original location and places it in a new one.

Copying a file places a replica of the file in a new location and leaves the original edition of the file in the original location.

Files may be copied or moved between different locations on the same hard disc, between two hard discs in the same computer or between different media such as hard and floppy discs. It is common practice to make backup copies of important files by copying onto floppy discs, ZIP discs, writeable or rewriteable CD-ROMs and special backup tapes.

A common copying method is to drag the file or folder and drop it over the new location. Different results are obtained depending on whether you are dragging and dropping to the same or a different medium:

- The file is ***moved*** if it is dragged and dropped into a different location on the *same* hard disc.
- The file is ***copied*** if it is dragged and dropped onto a different disc drive.
- To ***copy*** files within the same hard disc the **Control** key must be held down while dragging with the left hand mouse button.

Dragging and Dropping

Files and folders can be copied in the Windows Explorer. You can copy between different locations on the main hard disc drive **C:** or to and from any other drives such as the floppy disc, ZIP disc, rewriteable (CD-RW) or secondary hard disc drives. Invoke the Windows Explorer and make sure the folders or files you wish to copy or move are visible in the right hand panel.

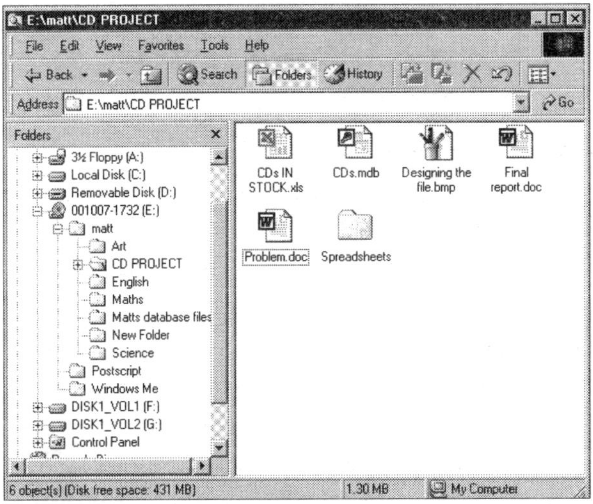

Now highlight the file(s) or folder(s) to be copied or moved. (To copy or move multiple files and folders simultaneously, hold down the **Ctrl** key while highlighting with the mouse.) Next hold down the left hand button and drag the highlighted files and/or folders to their destination in the left hand panel. Release the mouse button to drop the files into the new location. As described on page 22, dragging with the *right* mouse button gives a choice between **copying** and **moving** the files, when the right button is released.

This method would typically be used to copy some files onto a floppy disc or CD to transfer them to another computer. The same method would be used to drag and drop the files onto the new computer.

Using the Right Hand Mouse Button to Copy or Move Files

If you drag the icon for a file or folder using the *right* button on the mouse, then release the button to drop the file over its new location, the menu shown on the right appears. This allows you to select whether the file is to be moved or copied. This is probably the easiest and safest way of copying or moving files.

You can also copy and move files in the Windows Explorer or My Computer by using the **Edit** menus in the respective windows. Select the file(s) then use **Edit** and either **Copy** or **Cut** in the first (source) window followed by **Edit** and **Paste** in the destination window.

WARNING !

It is extremely easy to move files and folders around a hard disc. Many files are pronounced lost or deleted or "wiped" when in fact they have inadvertently been moved to a different location.

The notes in this book on the copying, moving, deleting and renaming of files apply only to the **data** files and folders which **you have created**.

Under no circumstances should you attempt to move, copy, delete or rename any of the **program files** or folders in Windows, Office, Word, Excel, Access or any of the other applications. The computer expects to find the programs in specific locations and the effect of organizing **program files** into your own folders will be to render the computer useless.

Displaying Windows

It is sometimes convenient to arrange for two or more windows to be displayed on the screen at the same time in My Computer. First you need to make sure that each folder opens up in its own window. This is set in **Tools** and **Folder Options...** and the **General** tab, as shown below.

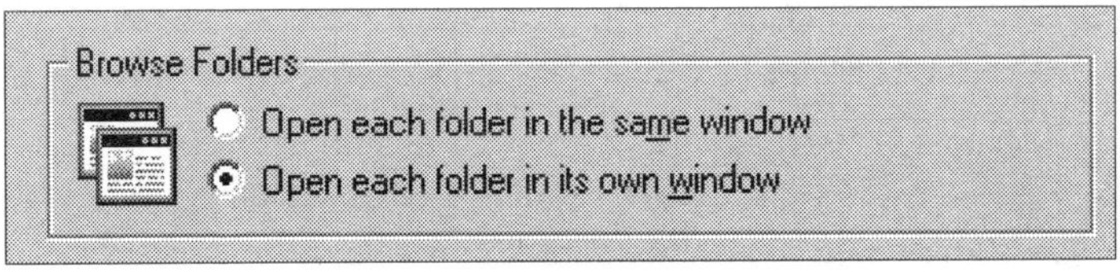

Make sure **Open each folder in its own window** is switched on as shown above then click **Apply** and **OK**.

Now open, in turn, each of the folders to be used in the copying or moving operation. At first the windows may not be clearly visible as they are in the *cascade* format, one behind another. Clicking anywhere on a folder brings it to the top of the cascade.

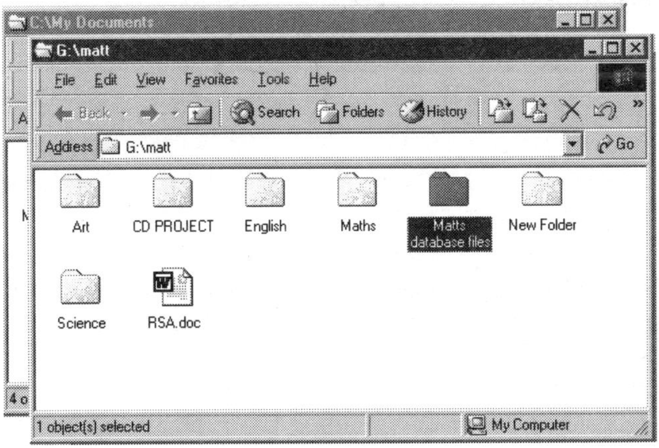

We now need to change from the cascade arrangement to the *tiling* display shown on the next page.

Tiling Windows

In this arrangement the windows are displayed in their entirety. To select tiling, move the cursor over an empty part of the Taskbar at the bottom of the Windows screen and click the right mouse button.

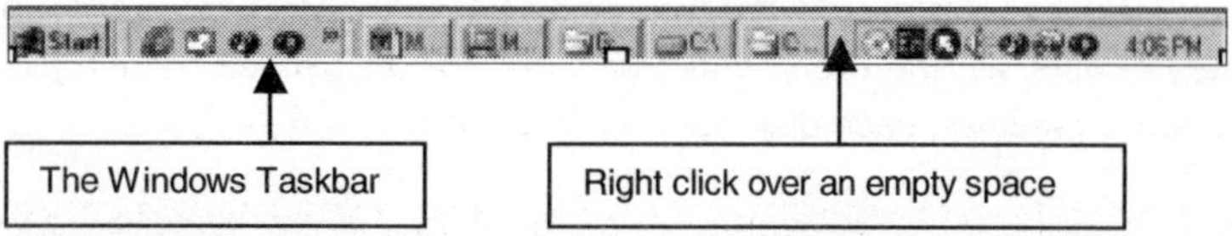

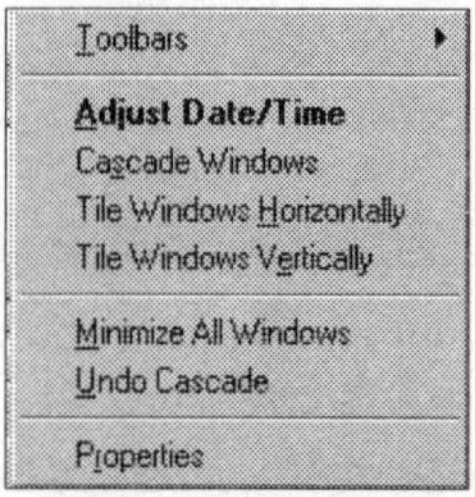

The menu on the left appears. If you select **Tile Windows Vertically** any windows which are currently open will be displayed in the arrangement shown below. To return to the cascade arrangement right click again over an empty space on the Windows Taskbar and select **Cascade Windows** from the menu.

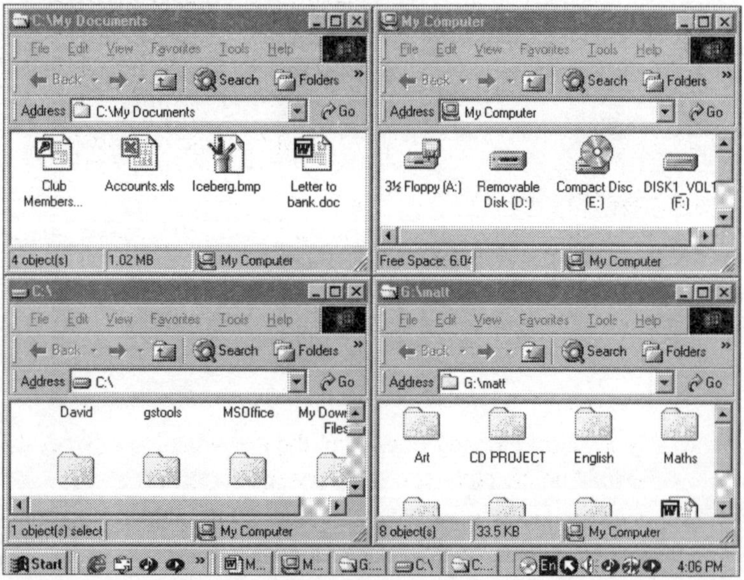

Copying Extracts Between Files Open in Programs

The Tile display makes it easy to copy and move files and folders between folders which may be on the same or different discs. The same idea can be used to copy an extract from a document or drawing running in a window in one program and paste into another program. In the example below, Word and Paint are simultaneously running in separate windows, each displaying an open file.

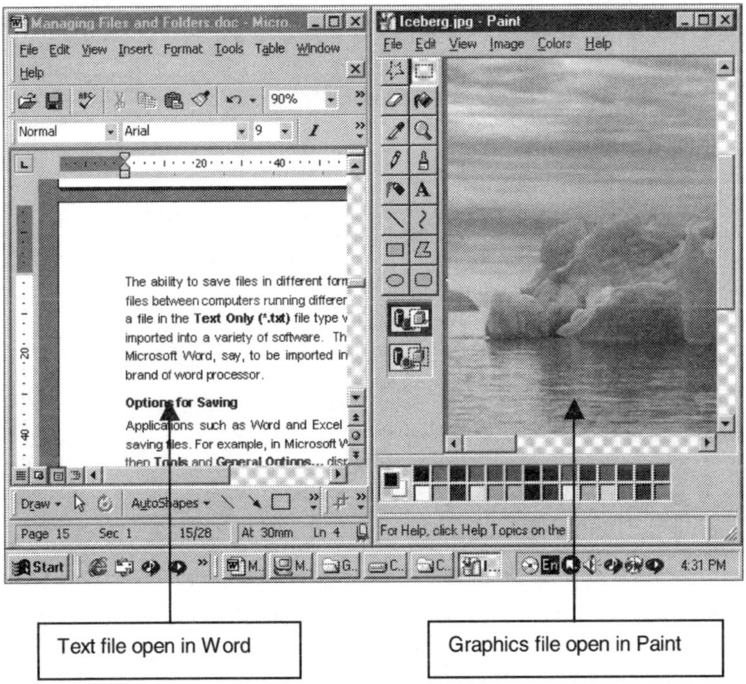

- First select or highlight the extract which is to be copied.
- Next select **File** and **Copy** from the menu bar. This places the extract on the *clipboard* - a temporary storage area.
- Now change to the second window and place the cursor at the point where the extract is to be inserted.
- Select **File** and **Paste** to place the extract in its new position.

Finding Files and Folders

Even if your work is organized into a system of clearly labelled folders, there are still occasions when you need help to locate files and folders. Windows Me provides a search facility which scans selected disc drives then provides a list of any locations where the required files or folders have been found. You can initiate the search process from the menus using **Start**, **Search** and **For Files and Folders....**

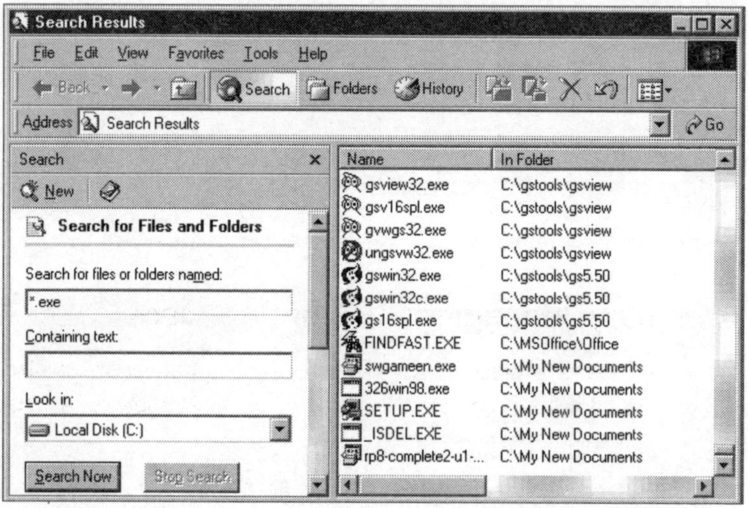

The first bar entitled **Search for files or folders named:** allows you to enter the name of a file or folder to be found. Alternatively you can use the *wildcard* asterisk (*) to replace any letters you are not sure of or do not want to type. In the example above, ***.exe** will search for all files which end in the **.exe** extension. The second bar **Containing text:** searches the contents of the files rather than the file and folder names. The **Look in:** bar allows you to select which disc drives are to be searched. After clicking **Search Now**, the discs are scanned and eventually, if successful, the results are displayed in the right panel as shown above.

Creating a Shortcut Icon on the Windows Desktop

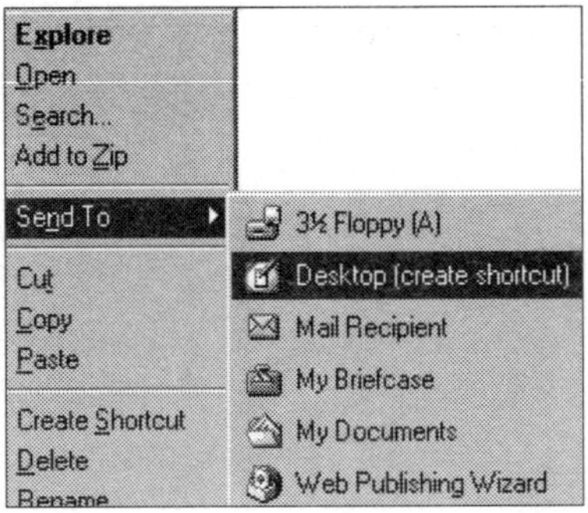

To save time when opening up frequently used files and folders, you can place a shortcut icon on the Windows Desktop. First highlight the file or folder in the Windows Explorer or My Computer. Now right click over the file or folder and select **Send To** and **Desktop (create shortcut)** from the menu shown right. The file or folder can now be accessed by clicking its shortcut icon on the Windows Desktop. There is a menu option to **Rename** the shortcut obtained by right clicking over the shortcut icon.

Summary: Managing Files and Folders

- A file is a piece of work which has been saved on a disc. Windows Me permits filenames of up to 255 letters, so that meaningful names can be used.
- Files are created when you save your work in applications such as Word and Excel. These are generally referred to as documents or data files. Different applications produce different types of file identified with their own filename *extension* such as **.doc** or **.xls**.
- The programs or applications which you run, such as Word and Excel, contain many special files. These are known as program files (with extensions such as **.exe**) and these files must not be moved, modified or deleted by the user.
- Windows Me has been designed to allow the user to organise files easily into folders and subfolders. Use the folder My Documents, provided by Windows, to save your work until you create your own hierarchy of folders and subfolders.

- Files have attributes which may be changed by the user. These include **Read Only** to prevent the file from being accidentally deleted, and **Hidden** to disguise the presence of the file. The **Archive** attribute marks the file as needing to be backed up.
- Both My Computer and the Windows Explorer provide facilities to manage your work including creating folders, copying, moving, deleting and renaming files and folders.
- The **Save As...** option, in applications such as Word and Excel, allows you to specify a saving location for the file, including a particular folder or subfolder and different disc drives like the hard disc, floppy disc, ZIP drive or CD-ROM.
- Files which are deleted are sent to the Windows Me Recycle Bin. Files in the Recycle Bin can either be restored to their original locations or permanently deleted to save disc space.
- Most file and folder tasks can be accomplished by simple mouse operations such as "dragging" and "dropping" or by selecting options from the **File** and **Edit** menus.
- The safest way to manipulate files and folders is to drag and drop using the right hand button then select the required copy or move operation from the small menu which appears.
- Care should be taken when moving files: program files should never be moved. Accidental moving of files (when copying is intended) may result in the loss of important work.
- The Windows **Search** option allows you to search for files and folders using the full name of the file or folder. You can also use part of the name and one or more wildcard characters (*) to replace any unknown letters. Any files which contain a certain piece of text can also be found.
- A shortcut icon can be placed on the Windows Desktop, giving direct access to a frequently used file or folder. This is quicker than locating the file or folder in Windows Explorer or My Computer.

2

Hard Disc Care

Introduction

Hard disc drives are incredibly reliable for mechanical devices which rotate at several thousand rpm. Out of a few hundred machines with which I have been acquainted over recent years, only a handful have needed a replacement hard disc unit. However, the integrity of the program and data files stored on the magnetic surfaces of hard discs is a different matter. Apart from the risk of viruses (covered in detail in a later chapter), the software on the hard disc can be corrupted in a number of ways. It is therefore not unusual to have to carry out software repairs or even a complete formatting and re-installation of the program and data files on the hard disc.

Some of these problems can be avoided by careful maintenance or good "housekeeping". For example, as a hard disc drive becomes full, the computer gradually runs more slowly before finally grinding to a halt, when there is no room left to store the temporary files needed to run large applications.

Improvements in performance and reliability form a major part of the evolution from Windows 95 through Windows 98 to Windows Me. Windows Me provides a battery of utilities for maintaining your computer. Some of them were available in earlier versions of Windows, while others had to be purchased from third-party software companies.

The following pages contain a brief summary of the Windows Me utilities provided for maintaining your hard disc. Later pages give more details of the way some of the major utilities can be used.

The Maintenance Wizard

This schedules the hard disc utilities, **ScanDisk**, **Disk Defragmenter** and **Disk Cleanup**. The **Maintenance Wizard**, accessed off **Start**, **Programs**, **Accessories** and **System Tools**, can be used to set the utilities to run at any time on any day of the week.

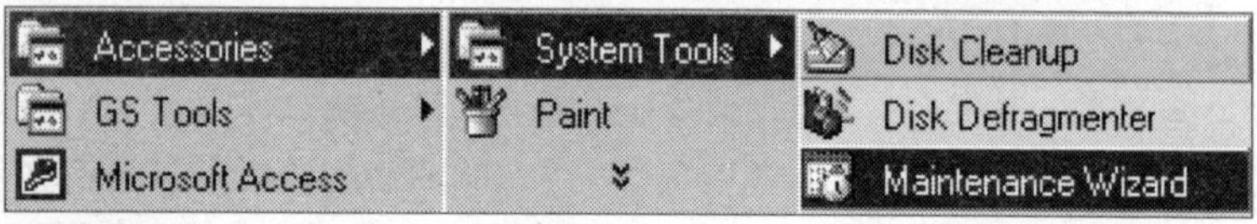

ScanDisk

This checks errors in files and on the physical surface of the disc and makes repairs if necessary. ScanDisk is run automatically on startup after every occasion when the computer is shut down incorrectly. For example, when the machine crashes or is switched off when files and applications are still open.

Disk Defragmenter

Defragmenter rearranges commonly used programs and their essential files so that they are all in close proximity (said to be "contiguous" or touching). This makes the applications run faster.

Disk Cleanup

Your hard disc can become cluttered with files which are no longer serving a useful purpose. This includes files which you no longer use and temporary files automatically created by the system. In earlier versions of Windows these files must be removed manually using the Windows Explorer or My Computer as described elsewhere in this book. Alternatively you can buy third-party software such as QuarterDeck CleanSweep to identify and remove rarely used files.

Windows Me introduces Disk Cleanup to increase disc space by removing redundant files, such as temporary files and those created when "surfing" the Internet. Without a healthy amount of free space your computer will perform badly or not at all.

You are prompted to use Disk Cleanup when the free space on your hard disc becomes very low.

Although the previous utilities are scheduled for automatic regular use by the Maintenance Wizard, they can also be invoked individually in the usual way from the menus using **Start**, **Programs**, **Accessories** and **System Tools**.

In addition to the 3 maintenance utilities ScanDisk, Disk Defragmenter and Disk Cleanup which are combined in the Maintenance Wizard, Windows Me contains several other utilities to maintain the system, including the Registry Checker, Windows Update and System Restore.

The Registry Checker

The registry is a database containing the personal settings for your computer and the software you have installed. Registry Checker automatically keeps backup copies of the registry. Each time the computer is started, the registry is checked. If there are any problems, these are fixed, either by using a backup copy or by effecting a repair. You can carry out a check of the registry at any time by invoking **Registry Checker** from the **System Information**, **Tools** menu in **Programs**, **Accessories**, **System Tools**.

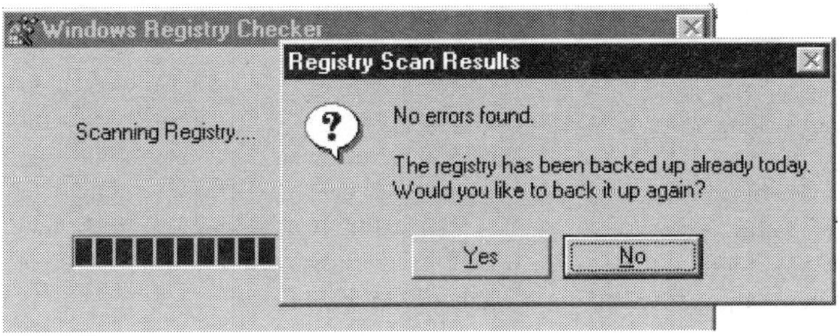

Windows Update

To use Windows Update you must be connected to the Internet, since its resources are drawn from a Web site. You can start Windows Update after clicking the **Start** button on the Windows Me Taskbar.

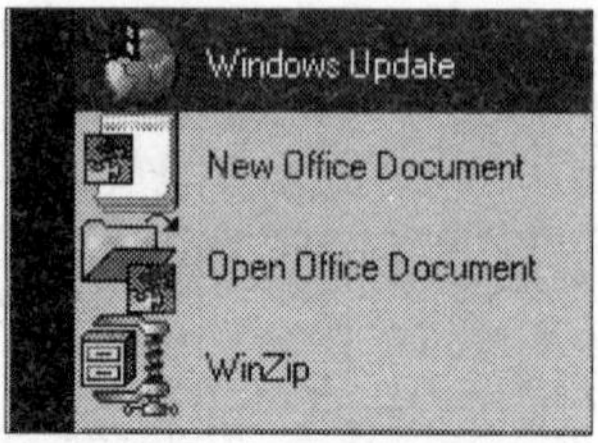

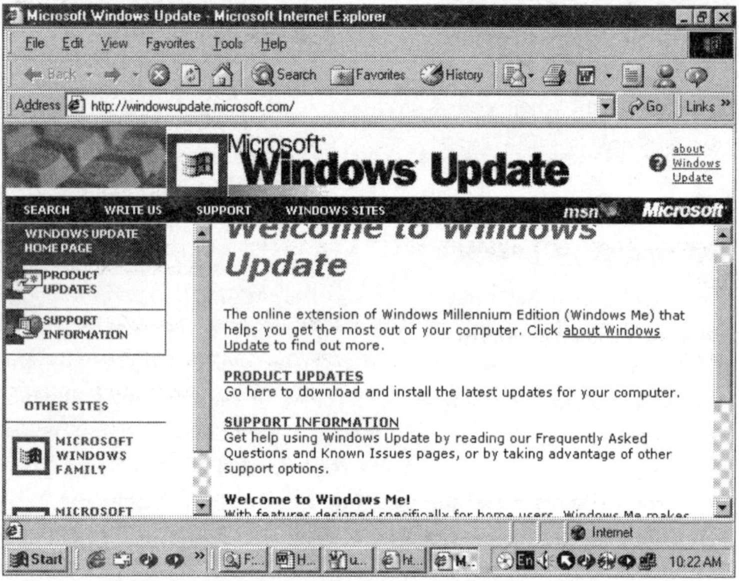

Once on-line to the Internet site, your hard disc is examined to see what software packages and device drivers are installed. If later versions do exist, you can choose to download them from the Internet and install them on your machine's hard disc. You can also use Windows Update to obtain technical support including answers to Frequently Asked Questions.

System Restore

This is a new feature built into Windows Me, although similar programs were previously available for purchase from third party companies. The purpose of System Restore is to allow you to repair your system if any of the important system settings are corrupted. This might happen if you have problems installing a new piece of software or hardware, for example. The idea is that you take regular snapshots of the critical settings. Then if things go wrong you can retrieve a previous configuration which you know to be correct. The snapshots or **restore points** are taken automatically by the system at regular intervals. Alternatively you can create a restore point when you are about to install new software or hardware or make some other change to the system. You can start **System Restore** from **Start**, **Programs**, **Accessories**, **System Tools** and **System Restore** as shown right.

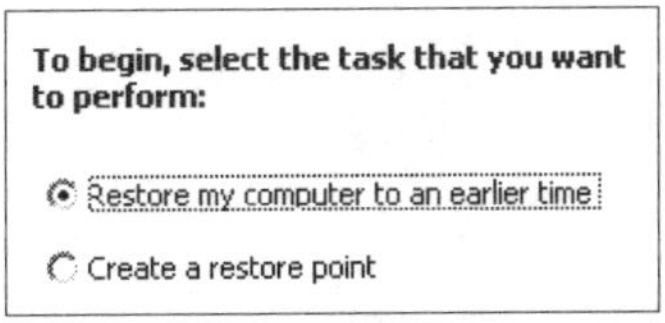

You are given a choice to either use a previous restore point or create a new one. Click **Next** and you are presented with one of two screens. If you opted to use an existing restore point, then you are given a calendar from which to choose a previous configuration which you know to be good. The dates when restore points were created are shown in bold.

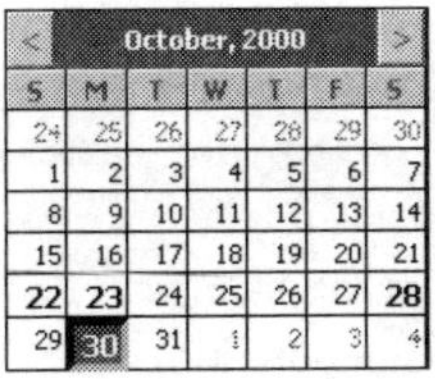

October, 2000
S M T W T F S
24 25 26 27 28 29 30
1 2 3 4 5 6 7
8 9 10 11 12 13 14
15 16 17 18 19 20 21
22 23 24 25 26 27 28
29 30 31 1 2 3 4

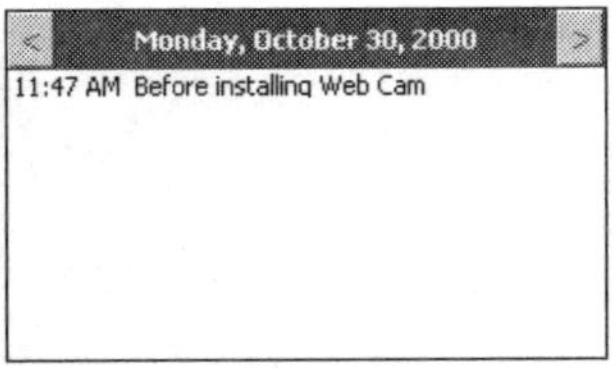

Click **Next** to restore the selected configuration.

If you choose to create your own restore point, you are asked to supply a meaningful name. The date and time are added automatically.

The Need for Hard Disc Free Space

Constantly deleting files and saving new ones causes the hard disc to become *fragmented*. Any remaining space may be scattered, requiring extra travel by the disc read/write heads which perform the saving and retrieving of files.

When Windows Me is working away on memory hungry applications, it uses part of the hard disc to supplement the memory or RAM chips (SIMMs). This "virtual memory" takes the form of a *temporary swap file* on the hard disc. The size of the swap file increases and decreases automatically according to the demands of the applications being run, within the limitation of the available free disc space.

You can look at the virtual memory of your computer by selecting **Start, Settings**, **Control Panel** then clicking on the **System** icon. From the **System Properties** window box select the **Performance** tab. At the bottom right of this window, there is a button to launch the **Virtual Memory** dialogue box shown below.

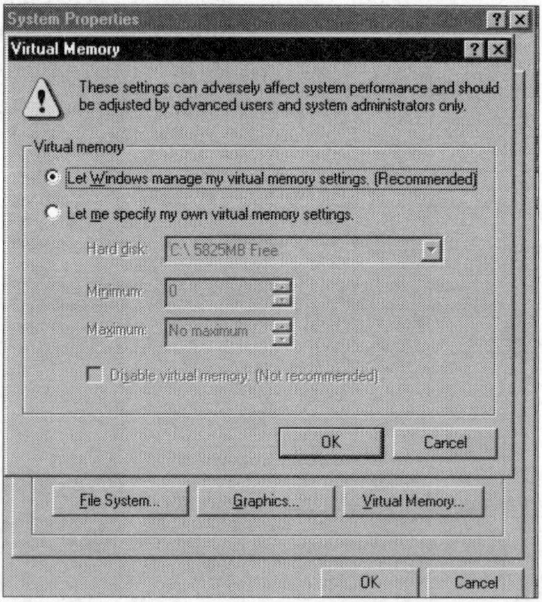

The Virtual Memory dialogue box on the previous page allows you to specify the size of the swap file or to allow Windows Me to manage it for you. It is recommended that you allow Windows Me to determine the size of the virtual memory. Without sufficient virtual memory your computer may run very slowly or even crash.

The size of the virtual memory is limited to the available hard disc space. Machines short on memory in the form of RAM will need to rely more heavily on virtual memory. This will be indicated by frequent flashing of the hard disc light. In this situation, as data needs to be moved in and out of the swap file regularly, any fragmentation will further impair the performance of the computer.

Defragmenting the hard disc and therefore the swap file, together with maximising the disc free space are essential to the efficient running of your computer. Using Disk Defragmenter is discussed later in this chapter.

Examining Your Hard Disc

You can view the properties of your hard disc by highlighting the **C:** drive (or **D:** or whatever) in **My Computer** and selecting **File** and **Properties**. Alternatively right click over the disc drive in My Computer and select **Properties** form the resulting menu.

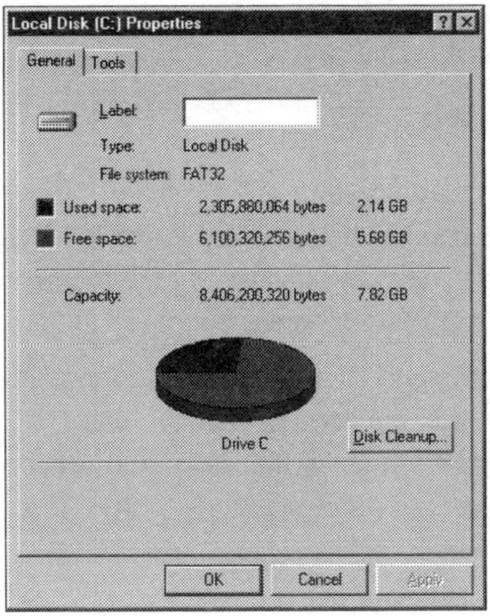

Apart from showing the amounts of used and free space and the disc capacity, the window contains a button to start the **Disk Cleanup** feature described in detail later in this chapter.

If you click the **Tools** tab on the previous **Properties** window, you are presented with details of when you last carried out essential maintenance tasks on your hard disc.

Error-checking status: refers to the last time you used **ScanDisk** and if necessary this can be launched by clicking the **Check Now...** button. Similarly you can improve a neglected and fragmented hard disc drive by clicking the **Defragment Now...**button.

It is often recommended that these important housekeeping tasks should be carried out on a regular basis. The Windows Me Maintenance Wizard enables the automatic scheduling of ScanDisk, Disk Cleanup and Disk Defragmenter.

You can also start the Maintenance Wizard at any time and it will run through the scheduled tasks immediately. However if you want to use ScanDisk, Disk Cleanup and Disk Defragmenter as separate programs they can be started from the System Tools menu. Using the tools individually is described on the following pages.

Using ScanDisk

ScanDisk can be started from **Start**, **Programs**, **Accessories** and **System Tools**. Or you can start it from My Computer as described on the previous page.

This brings up the ScanDisk dialogue box which allows you to choose either the **Standard** or **Thorough** test.

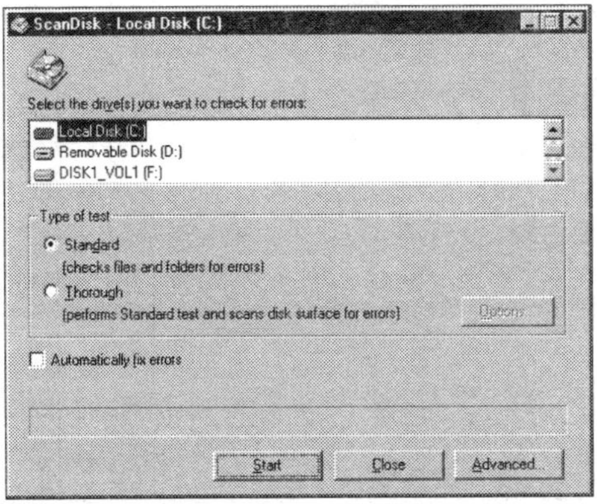

The standard test checks only the files on the disc drive, while the thorough test, which takes much longer, also checks for defects on the disc surface. There are options to select which disc to scan, including floppies, and any secondary hard discs fitted, and to fix errors automatically.

It is recommended that all other applications and any screen savers are disabled while ScanDisk is operating, since open files cannot be checked for errors. When the scan is complete, detailed results are presented as shown in the following **ScanDisk Results** box.

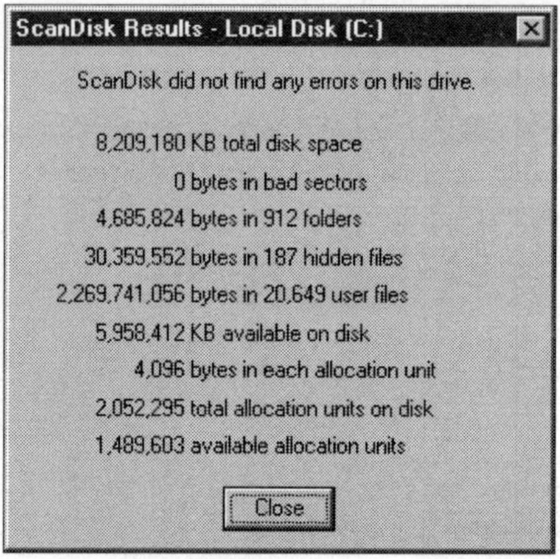

The results box in ScanDisk is optional and may be switched off in **Advanced**, **Display Summary**.

The **Options** dialogue box (**Thorough Test** only) allows the user to prescribe which areas of the disc are to be scanned and to switch off write testing of the disc.

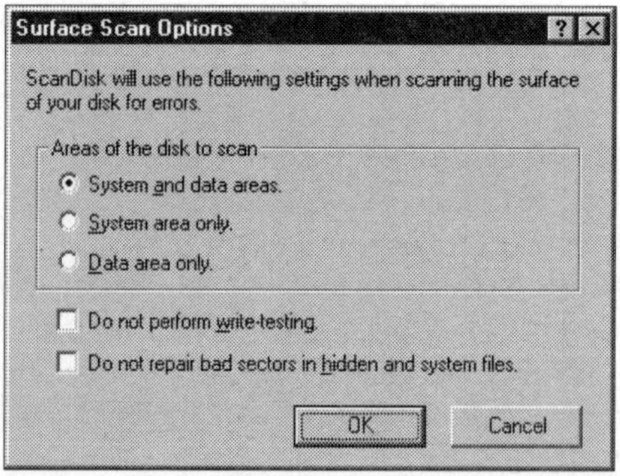

Using Disk Defragmenter

The purpose of defragmentation is to consolidate the files and spaces on a disc in order to reduce the time needed for read and write operations, so that programs run faster.

The Disk Defragmenter program can be started from **Start**, **Programs**, **Accessories** and **System Tools**.

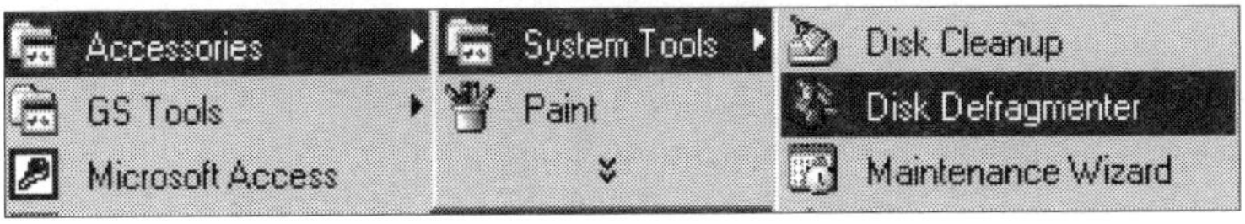

Or you can use My Computer to select the hard disc drive, **C:** for example, then use **File**, **Properties** and the **Tools** tab. You are presented with the **Properties** box shown previously, from which you can select **Defragment Now**.

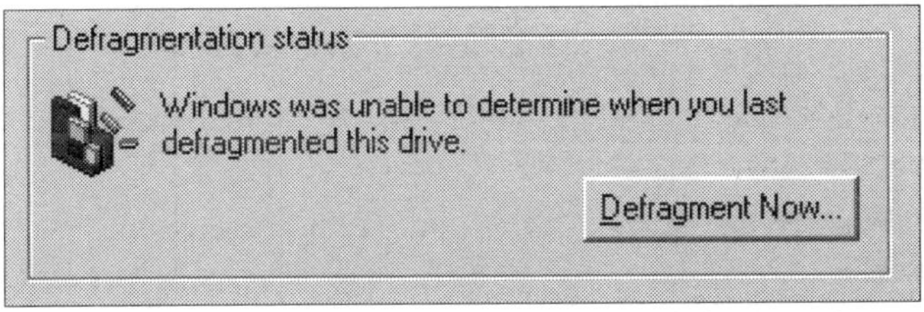

There is an option to select which drive to defragment. The drop down menu includes your hard disc, usually drive **C:**, and any additional hard drives installed.

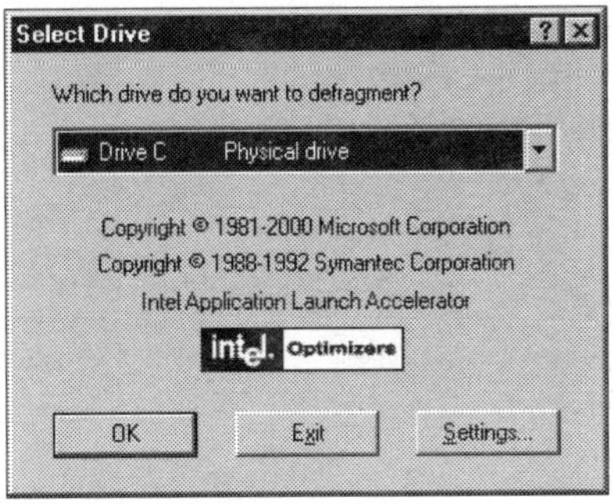

The **Settings** button presents the user with an option to re-arrange the files on the disc so that programs start faster. This is done by placing close together all files needed for a particular program.

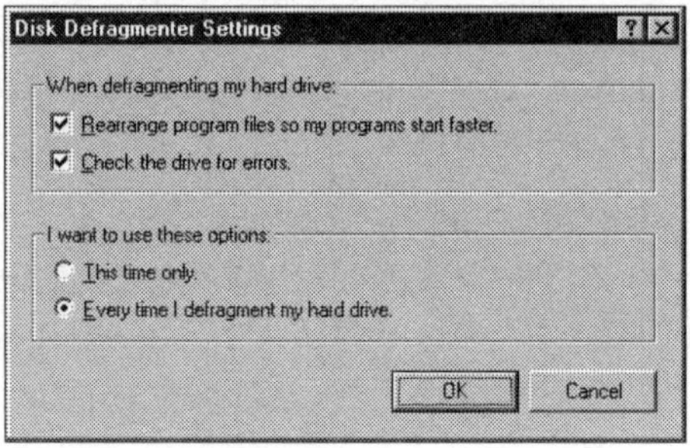

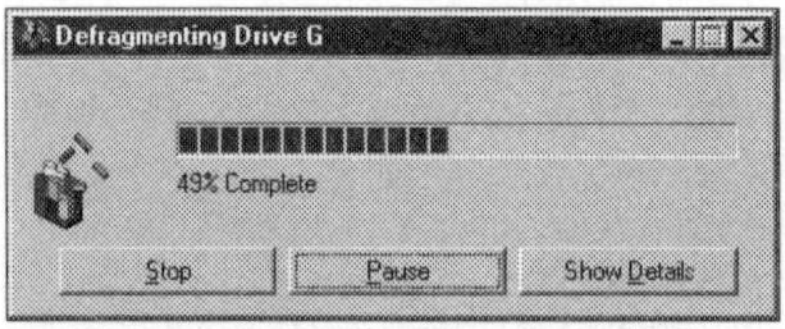

After you click **OK** to start defragmentation, the progress window keeps you informed. When the defragmentation is finished you are given the opportunity to leave the program or select another drive to defragment.

Using Disk Cleanup

This is the third member of the trio which make up the Maintenance Wizard. (The other two being ScanDisk and Disk Defragmenter).

The purpose of Disk Cleanup is to remove redundant files which are occupying valuable disc space. These include Temporary Internet Files - Web pages and graphics which Internet Explorer downloads to your hard disc. The purpose of the temporary Internet files is to save on-line time when you revisit the same Web site. However, in many cases the files may just be occupying valuable disc space.

Temporary files are also created by Windows Me applications such as Microsoft Word. These temporary files are supposed to be removed automatically by the system (if it is shut down properly) but for various reasons some of them may remain.

Disk Cleanup can be started from the menus using **Start**, **Programs**, **Accessories** and **System Tools**.

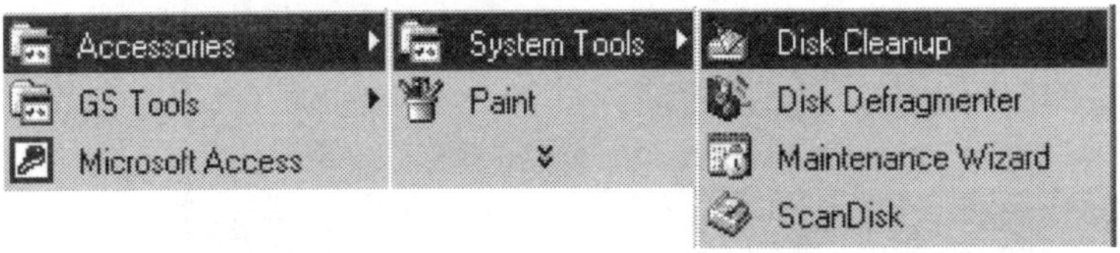

Alternatively, **Disk Cleanup** can be started from the **Properties**, **General** window obtained by pressing the right button over the **C:** drive (or whatever) in My Computer. The **Disk Cleanup** button is lower right.

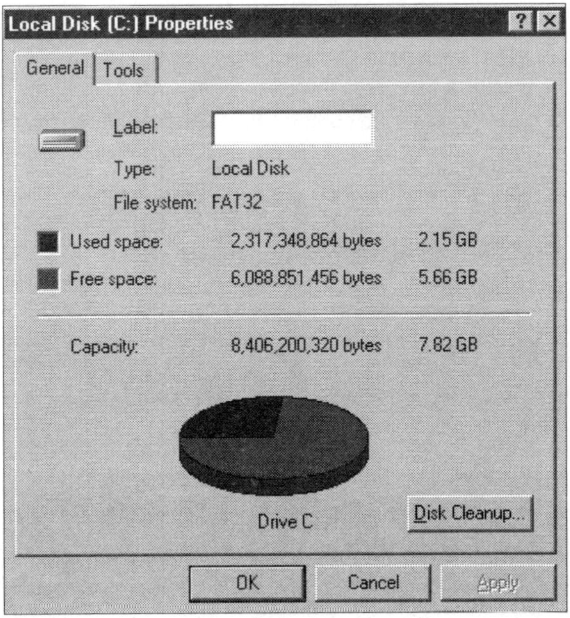

When Disk Cleanup is started, it calculates how much disc space can be saved and allows you to select which of the redundant files are to be deleted. This is shown on the next page.

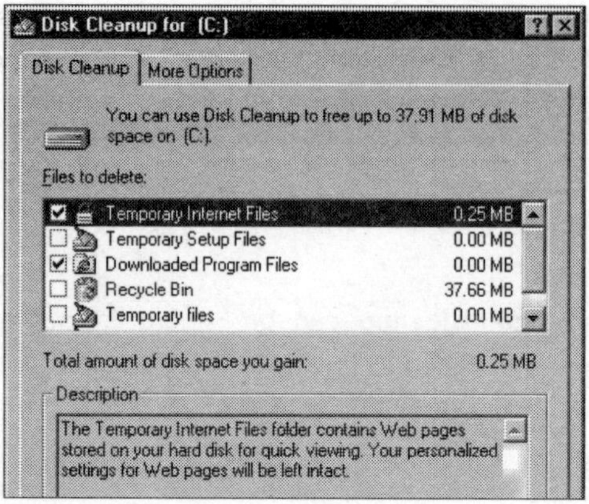

The **More Options** tab gives the user other suggestions for removing programs and Windows Me components which are no longer needed.

The first **Clean up...** button (shown on the previous page) allows you to delete unwanted Windows components in the **Windows Setup** dialogue box shown below.

The second **Clean up...** button (shown on the previous page) allows you to remove any unwanted installed programs.

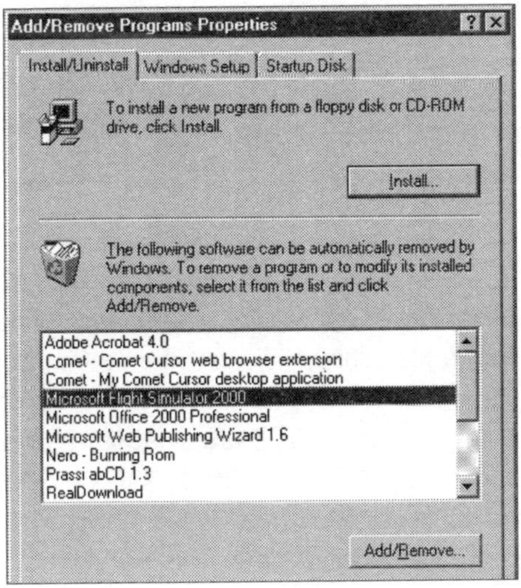

Highlight the program to be uninstalled and click the **Add/Remove...** button.

Please note that some programs have their own uninstall features built in and this is often provided as an option accessed from the **Start** and **Programs** menus.

The third **Clean up...** button (shown on page 42) allows you to increase the free disc space by reducing the amount of space allocated to the System Restore feature discussed earlier in this chapter.

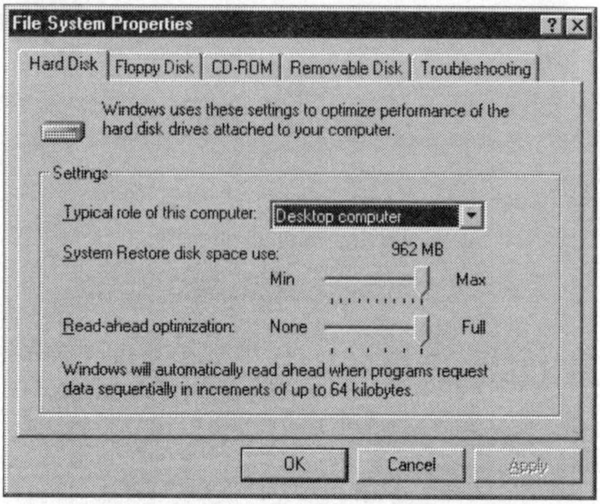

Briefly, System Restore saves regular snapshots or checkpoints of the important Windows Me settings. Then if the system is corrupted you can revert to one of the earlier configurations. You can reduce the amount of disc space available to **System Restore** by dragging to the left the slider shown above, under **962MB**. Although the free hard disc space will increase, fewer snapshots of the system will be saved and these will not go back as far in time. This will reduce your choice of checkpoints or system snapshots should you need to restore an earlier configuration.

Using the Maintenance Wizard

Regular scans, defragmenting and removal of redundant files are essential to the efficient running of your computer. So that you don't need to remember to do this job, you can automate the task using the Maintenance Wizard, which includes ScanDisk, Defragmenter and Disk Cleanup.

You can start the Maintenance Wizard from **Start**, **Programs**, **Accessories** and **System Tools**.

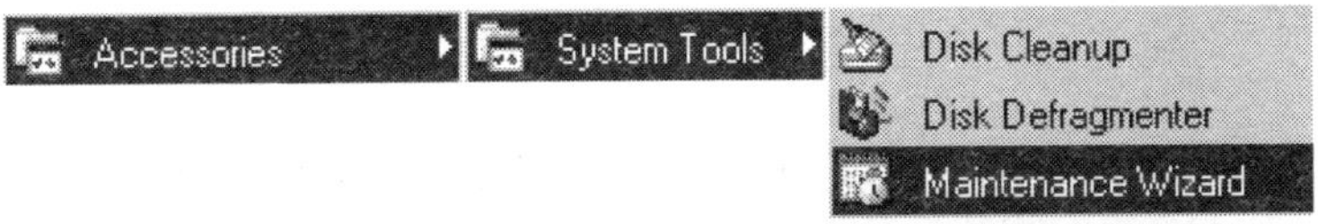

After selecting the Wizard you can choose to do the maintenance tasks now or you can opt to change the maintenance settings and schedule.

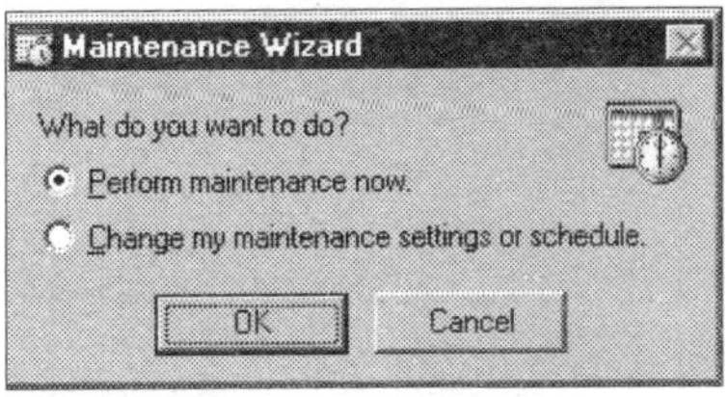

If you select the first option, the wizard starts to work through the disc maintenance programs, Disc Cleanup, ScanDisk and Defragmenter.

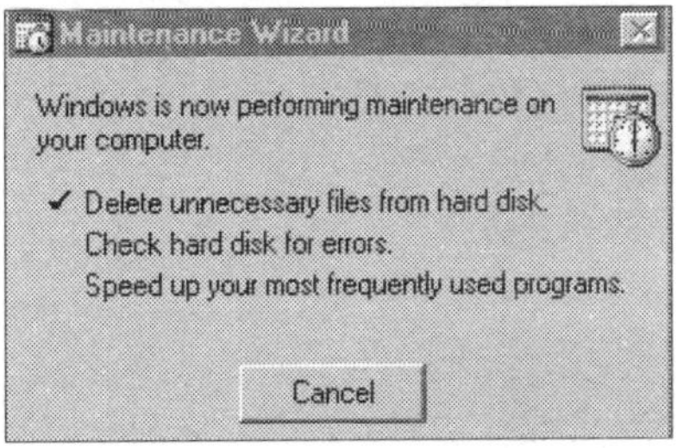

If you choose **Change my maintenance settings or schedule** as shown above, you are given the choice of either **Express** or **Custom**.

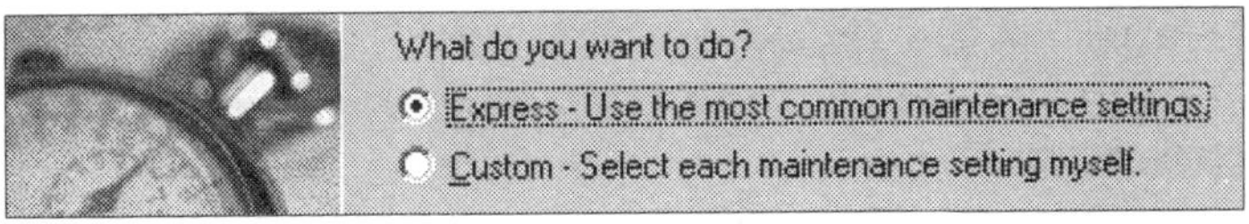

If you choose the **Express** option, a choice of times for the schedule is provided by the wizard.

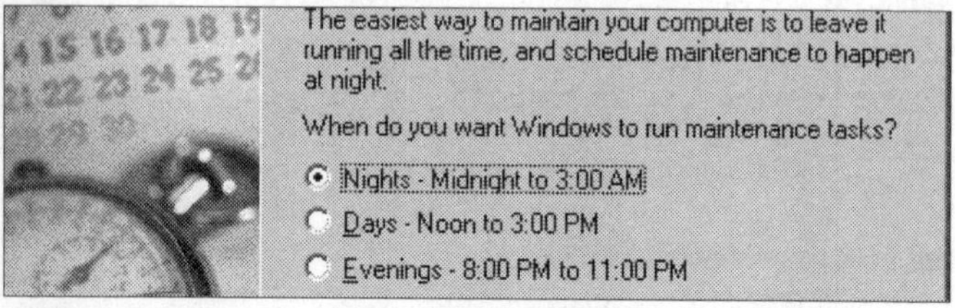

The easiest way to maintain your computer is to leave it running all the time, and schedule maintenance to happen at night.
When do you want Windows to run maintenance tasks?
Nights - Midnight to 3:00 AM
Days - Noon to 3:00 PM
Evenings - 8:00 PM to 11:00 PM

After selecting the time and clicking **Next**, the wizard presents the final window showing the tasks to be performed and allows you to run them on clicking **Finish**.

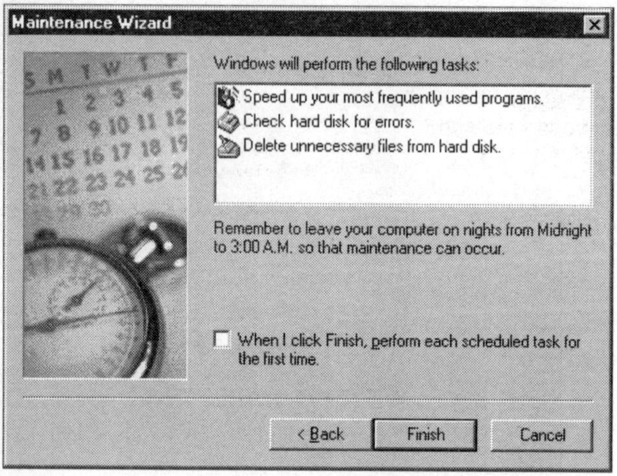

Maintenance Wizard
Windows will perform the following tasks:
Speed up your most frequently used programs.
Check hard disk for errors.
Delete unnecessary files from hard disk.
Remember to leave your computer on nights from Midnight to 3:00 A.M. so that maintenance can occur.
When I click Finish, perform each scheduled task for the first time.
< Back
Finish
Cancel

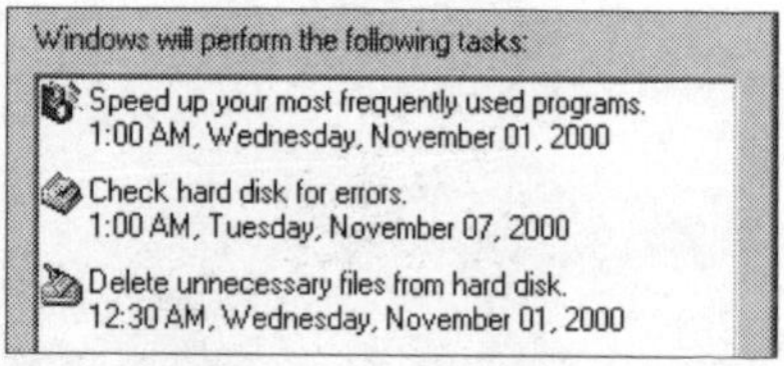

Windows will perform the following tasks:
Speed up your most frequently used programs.
1:00 AM, Wednesday, November 01, 2000
Check hard disk for errors.
1:00 AM, Tuesday, November 07, 2000
Delete unnecessary files from hard disk.
12:30 AM, Wednesday, November 01, 2000

If you choose the **Custom** option in the Maintenance Wizard you can choose which of the tools (ScanDisk, Defragmenter and Disk Cleanup) to include in the schedule and at what times to run them.

The tools scheduled by the Maintenance Wizard can also be accessed in the **Scheduled Tasks** folder opened from **Start**, **Programs**, **Accessories** and **System Tools**.

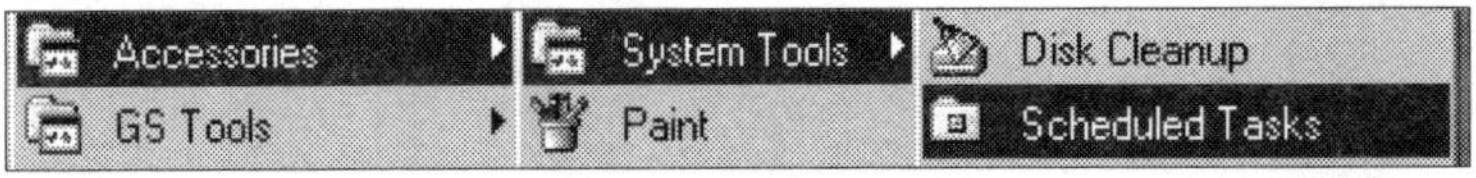

Alternatively you can open the Scheduled Tasks folder from its icon in the **Control Panel** (**Start**, **Settings**, **Control Panel**).

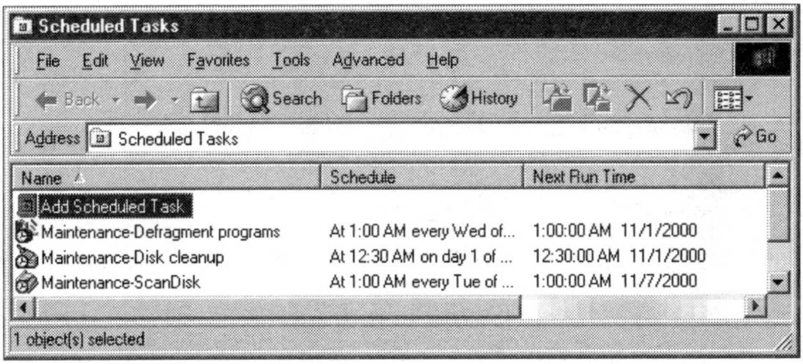

You can also schedule additional programs to run after clicking **Add Schedule Task**. Then browse through your hard discs to select the programs you wish to run at scheduled times.

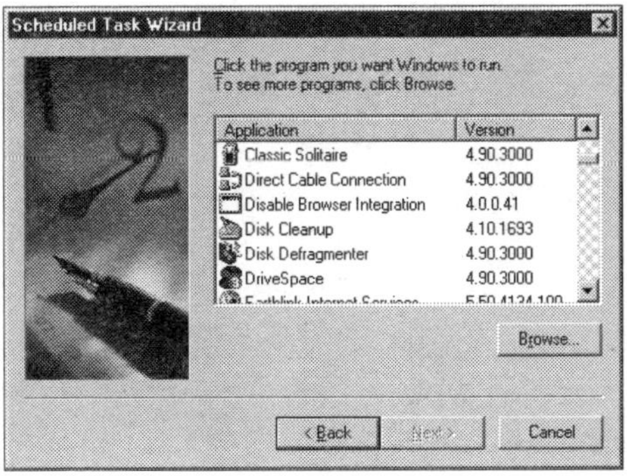

Removing Software

Some of this work was also described in the notes on **Disk Cleanup** but is repeated here because there are times when you only wish to remove a specific piece of software rather than a general tidying up of the hard disc.

Unfortunately it's not simply a case of deleting the folders bearing the name of the program in My Computer or the Windows Explorer. Programs usually have lots of other files and settings scattered about the system, apart from the files in their main folders. Failure to delete all of the associated files may cause problems or at least display some irritating error messages.

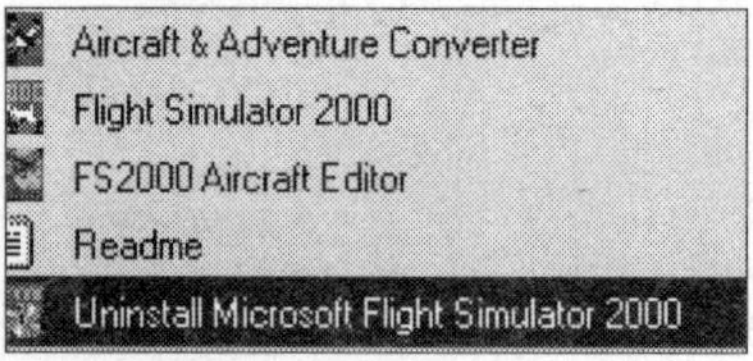

Many programs, such as Microsoft Flight Simulator for example, have an integral option to uninstall. This is accessed from **Start**, **Programs** then the name of the program. Selecting **Uninstall Microsoft Flight Simulator 2000** in the above menu should remove the program and all of its associated files.

Add/Remove Programs

If a program does not have its own uninstall option built in you can use the Windows Me **Add/Remove Programs** facility launched by selecting **Start**, **Settings**, **Control Panel** and clicking the **Add/Remove Programs** icon.

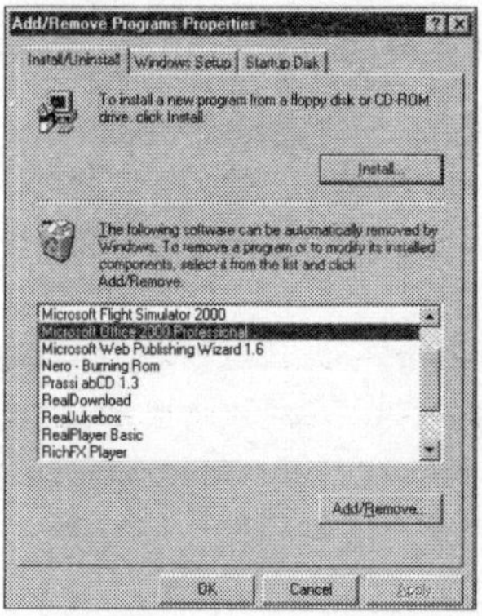

Clicking this icon opens up the **Add/Remove Programs Properties** box. With the **Install/Uninstall** tab selected you highlight the program to be deleted then click **Add/Remove**. You will be given the opportunity to abort the uninstall operation before it is too late. Changing to the **Windows Setup** tab allows you to delete components and accessories of Windows Me which you no longer use.

Summary: Hard Disc Care

- Many maintenance activities are aimed at maximising the free space on your hard disc. This is necessary not only to accommodate new software and data files but also to keep the computer running at its optimum performance.
- The Temporary Swap File (Virtual Memory) uses free disc space to supplement the actual memory which consists of banks of RAM chips.
- The amount of free disc space can be examined in the **Properties** window, accessed by highlighting the drive and selecting **File** and **Properties** in **My Computer**. The **Tools** tab reports on the need or otherwise to use various maintenance tools such as ScanDisk and Disk Defragmenter.
- After a time files can become fragmented on the hard disc and cause the system to slow down. Windows Me Disk Defragmenter re-organises files and compacts the disc free space.
- ScanDisk is a utility which corrects errors in files and on the disc surfaces. Errors may typically be caused when there is a break in the power supply, or a system crash due to a fault in a program.
- Redundant programs, temporary files and unwanted Windows Me components should be deleted regularly to maximise free disc space. This can be done manually or with the help of Disk Cleanup.
- The Maintenance Wizard can be used to schedule ScanDisk, Disk Defragmenter and Disk Cleanup at regular times on certain days of the week.
- Some packages contain their own uninstall facility in their list of components in the **Programs** menu. This should enable all files related to a package to be removed without leaving debris behind.

- Deleted files are automatically sent to the Recycle Bin, which is itself a folder on the hard disc. Therefore to increase free disc space, the Recycle Bin must be emptied.
- Windows Me includes the feature Registry Checker to keep important operating system files free from errors.
- Windows Update is a Windows Me utility which uses an Internet site to carry out an audit of your hard disc. If appropriate, newer versions of programs and device drivers can be downloaded to your hard disc. Technical support is also available from the Internet site.
- System Restore saves regular snapshots of the critical settings and systems files in your computer. If faults develop you can retrieve and install a previous configuration which was saved when the system was working properly.

Please Note:

In order to keep your hard disc and its valuable contents safe the maintenance tasks described in this chapter should be combined with a strategy for regular backing up and virus testing of all discs and files as described elsewhere in this book. If your hard disc is used for serious work, the data files on your hard disc are probably worth far more than the entire hardware system.

3

Backup Activities

Introduction

If you use your computer for any sort of serious work, then backing up is one of the most important (but frequently neglected) tasks to be performed. Imagine working on a project for several weeks or months then suddenly losing all of the files. The result is exactly the same as someone breaking into a filing cabinet and stealing important documents or a fire which sweeps through a building. The difference is that it's very easy to lose a file or folder saved on a hard disc. A moment's carelessness when copying or deleting files or a system crash can easily destroy hours of work. As a teacher, I frequently heard remarks like "The stupid computer has wiped my work...".

Of course, small files like a letter or simple spreadsheet can be created again very easily; this is not the case with a student dissertation, a design project or a set of accounts accumulated over a long period. In many cases the value of the data files stored on the hard disc will be far in excess of the computer hardware.

So it makes sense to devise a strategy for making regular backup or duplicate copies of your work. Several methods are discussed later in this chapter and these are inexpensive in relation to the cost and inconvenience caused by serious data loss.

Apart from the data files representing hours of toil, your hard disc contains all of the systems software such as the Windows Me operating system and applications like Microsoft Office. If necessary, software can be restored from the original CDs and floppy discs. It's essential therefore that all of your software packages (including CDs, discs and documentation) are carefully stored in a safe place.

What is Memory?

The Hard Disc Drive is the main medium for keeping *permanent* copies of your work; it corresponds to the filing cabinet in the traditional office. In order to put the hard disc in context we must first be clear about its role in the operation of the computer.

Many new computer users are confused by the term "memory". When the computer gives an "out of memory..." error, for example, some users mistakenly believe their hard disc is full. In fact, this error refers to the capacity of the chips which form the computer's memory.

Types of Storage

There are two main ways of storing data:

- Temporary storage in the computer's memory.
- Permanent storage by recording on a magnetic medium such as the hard disc (and also floppy discs, tape, ZIP discs and writeable CD-ROM).

The Memory

The memory (also known as RAM - Random Access Memory) consists of several banks of microchips, known as SIMMs. The memory is a temporary store for the programs and data which are currently being used. Any data which is typed in the computer will sit in the memory until:

- You switch the computer off, or
- The data is overwritten by new data which you have typed in or loaded from disc.

Saving Your Work

The memory is said to be volatile i.e. its contents are lost when the power is removed. In order to keep a permanent copy of the data it should be saved on a hard disc or 3.5 inch diskette. Some software has

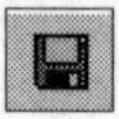

an option to perform a background save at regular intervals (set by the user). Alternatively, it's a simple matter to click the save icon from time to time, for example every 15 minutes.

The Hard Disc Drive

The hard disc (drive) is a sealed unit built inside of the computer and physically inaccessible unless you remove the computer's metal casing. The magnetic disc surfaces (platters) on which programs and data are recorded are an integral part of the drive unit which also contains the moving heads used for reading and writing data.

The hard disc is usually designated as the **C:** drive, and consists of a set of metal discs coated in a magnetic material and rotating about a central spindle. The hard disc unit is housed in a metal case and is sealed to prevent particles of dust from entering and damaging the disc surfaces, which are machined to very fine tolerances.

In normal use the hard disc rotates at several thousand revolutions per minute, making it a very high performance device but also vulnerable to catastrophic failures. If the moving head which "reads" the data from the disc touches one of the disc surfaces (resulting in a "head crash"), the disc surface will be scratched and some, if not all, of the data will be lost. (A head crash might, for example, be caused by moving or bumping the computer while the hard disc is running.)

The Contents of the Hard Disc Drive

Permanently saved on the magnetic surfaces of the hard disc are the programs and data files essential for the running of your computer. The hard disc is not to be confused with the memory or RAM of the computer, which is the temporary store used to hold programs and data while they are in current use. When you switch the computer off the contents of the RAM are cleared, but the contents of the hard disc remain in place. The hard disc normally contains:

- The *systems* software such as the Windows Me operating system needed to start and run the computer.
- The *applications* software such as your word-processor, database, DTP, graphics or games.
- The work you have produced and saved as files - the word processing documents, spreadsheets, graphics files, music, etc.

The hard disc is generally a robust component which can perform reliably for many thousands of hours over several years. However, due to possible accidents and natural disasters, it is by no means uncommon for individuals and even companies to "lose" the entire contents of a hard disc.

In some cases the files of data may still reside on the disc after a disaster, but the user loses the ability to retrieve them by normal methods. (There are companies who specialise in the recovery of data from damaged hard discs but this can be an expensive process).

With a hard disc drive you really have got "all of your eggs in one basket" - if it fails without adequate backup arrangements, your computer will be useless. This could spell disaster for a small business.

Although head crashes are fairly unusual, there are many other ways in which the contents of the hard disc may be lost or damaged.

Ways to Lose Your Data

- The computer or some of its internal components such as the hard disc drive may be stolen.
- You may accidentally delete important files by giving the wrong command.
- Someone may deliberately wipe or format the entire disc.
- The data on the hard disc may be corrupted by a software error or a failure in the power supply.
- The data may be damaged by one of the many computer viruses which can attack your system from various sources, such as a malicious e-mail.
- The hard disc may be damaged by the spilling of drinks or the data corrupted by exposure to a magnetic field by placing it near to another electrical device such as a stereo speaker.
- The computer itself may be totally destroyed by events such as fire, flood, earthquake or explosion.
- After several years' faithful service, the hard disc may reach the end of its useful life.

Your Exposure to Risk

You can assess your exposure to risk by considering the following factors:

- How long would it take to completely restore your system in the event of a total hard disc failure? Consider the time needed for retyping documents and data entry.
- Could you re-install all of the essential software? Do you have the technical expertise? Can you quickly find all of the installation discs and CDs? (Driver software which enables hardware devices such as CD drives to function can be particularly elusive in times of crisis).
- Does the hard disc hold essential business files - customer records, accounts or CAD files, etc? If working in a business, how long could you continue if a major failure occurred.
- Have you spent months typing in your magnum opus, perhaps a dissertation or a new novel? If disaster struck, you wouldn't be the first author to lose the only copy of a 300 page tome.
- What about your Curriculum Vitae, which has been polished and updated over time, into the masterpiece it is today? The day your CV gets wiped is likely to be the time when you want to apply for a new job, and time may be critical.
- Who else uses the computer - might they damage files accidentally or deliberately? Does the business computer on which your livelihood depends also double up as the family games machine? Some children are notorious for experimenting with settings and installing troublesome software.
- Does anyone import dubious files from floppy disc or the Internet which might spread viruses and wipe the hard disc?

The Backup Process

The only way to reduce the risk of a computing catastrophe is to make duplicate or backup copies of all important files (both software and data files). A backup is a copy of some or all of the files from a hard disc drive onto another "non-volatile" storage medium, such as a floppy disc, ZIP disc, CD or tape. (Non-volatile means the data is permanently saved after the computer is switched off - unlike data in the memory, which is cleared when the power is removed.)

The purpose of a *full* backup is to allow a computer system and particularly its software and data files, to be completely restored in the event of a total disaster, including the loss of the computer itself.

For important files, the backup discs or other storage media such as writeable CD and tape cartridges should be kept in a safe and secure place, away from heat and magnetic fields and preferably in a separate geographical location away from the computer. This also applies to the original installation discs and CD-ROMs from which software may need to be re-installed.

Although it is convenient to make backup copies onto another part of the same hard disc, these are of little use if the hard disc is damaged or the computer is stolen. Making backups on the same hard disc only gives protection against the deletion of some of the files.

For important work, a planned backup strategy is essential, with a system of several discs or tapes used in rotation. For a small backup consisting of a few important files, one or more floppy discs may be adequate to store the data. Alternatively, a full backup will copy the entire contents of the hard disc onto a writeable CD or special high capacity magnetic tape cartridge.

Capacities of Magnetic Storage Media

In order to appreciate the type of backup storage medium required for a particular task, it is necessary to be familiar with some of the jargon relating to the representation of data and the units used to measure storage capacities. Then you can estimate the amount of space required to back up a particular set of files.

The basic unit of computer storage is the *byte*. This is the amount of space taken up by one character when it is temporarily stored in the computer's memory or permanently saved on a disc. A character is typically a letter of the alphabet (both upper and lower case), a punctuation mark or keyboard symbol, or a digit in the range 0-9.

Every character is represented in the computer by a code made up of eight binary digits. The binary code employs only the digits 0 and 1 and is used because it is relatively simple for an electronic device like a computer to represent two states.

Examples of character codes used are as follows:

Character	**Binary Code**
A	0 1 0 0 0 0 0 1
a	0 1 1 0 0 0 0 1
9	0 0 1 1 1 0 0 1

The fact that computers perform their internal work using the binary system based on the number 2, rather than our normal decimal system based on 10, gives rise to some rather strange units for large numbers of bytes. The most common units used for describing computer capacities are the kilobyte, the megabyte and the gigabyte.

1 kilobyte (K) is approximately 1000 bytes (1024 to be exact)

1 megabyte (MB) is approximately 1000K or about a million bytes (1,048,576 to be exact)

1 gigabyte (GB) is approximately 1000 megabytes.

A kilobyte represents about a third of a page of text on A4 paper. One megabyte is very roughly the text in a novel of about 300 pages. If you include pictures and scanned images amongst the text, the amount of storage space required increases rapidly. At the time of writing, files saved on disc are usually stated in kilobytes or megabytes and the memory or RAM is given in Megabytes. The capacities of older hard disc drives are generally quoted in megabytes while the size of newer drives is stated in gigabytes.

Comparing Storage Capacities

The table below shows some typical values for the size of current storage devices.

Medium	ypical Storage Capacity
3.5 inch Floppy Diskette	1.44MB (uncompressed)
Hard Disc Drive	500 - 40000MB (40GB)
Tape Cartridge	4 - 70GB
CD-ROM	660MB
ZIP/Jaz Drive Discs	100MB, 250MB, 2GB

Choosing a Backup Medium

The 3.5 inch Floppy Diskette

Some people mistakenly think that the 3.5 inch disc, because of its rigid plastic case, is actually a "hard" disc. In fact, the magnetic disc material (known as the "cookie") inside the plastic case of the 3.5 inch disc, is really quite flexible and "floppy".

The 3.5 inch diskette is portable and very easily inserted into or removed from the floppy disc drive (normally drive **A:**). In the past, most new software packages were supplied on floppy disc. Now, with the increased size of new packages, this role has been taken over by the CD-ROM. Transferring data from a single CD is much faster and less prone to errors than from a large number of 3.5 inch diskettes.

However, the 3.5 inch disc is still a very cheap and convenient way of transferring a few files or a small piece of software from one computer to another. For example, if you want to save a piece of work then take it home and carry on working on it. It's also a quick way to make a backup copy for security purposes of an important file.

Using WinZip to Store Large Files on a Floppy Disc

The main problem with the floppy disc as a backup medium is its limited capacity. Graphics, photographs, video and music files occupy huge amounts of disc space and are often far too big to fit on a floppy disc. Even documents consisting of text and graphics can be very bulky. One way to increase the capacity of a floppy disc is to use a file compression program such as WinZip. The same program is used to compress files in order to speed their transmission across the Internet. A trial version of WinZip can be downloaded from the Internet. WinZip is discussed in detail later in this book, but the basic method is to create a ZIP file, which acts as a container for the files you wish to compress.

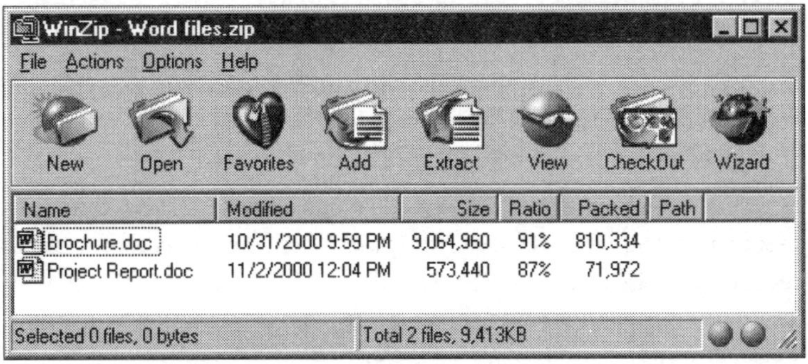

In the above example, the **ZIP** file (which acts more like a folder) contains two Word files. The first, **Brochure.doc**, contains a lot of graphics and occupies a bulky 9,064,960 bytes - far too big for one floppy disc. After compression, the file only takes up 810,334 bytes (shown in the **Packed** column in the above graphic). The compressed files can easily be copied to a floppy disc, which has a capacity of 1,457,664 bytes.

As an alternative to programs like WinZip, Windows Me introduces its own **Compressed Folders** feature (described later in the chapter on compression). This can reduce the above file of about 9MB to a more manageable 796 KB - again well within the capacity of a floppy disc.

Removable Hard Discs - ZIP Drives

These have the capacity of a small hard disc drive combined with the portability of a floppy disc. Two of the most popular systems are the Iomega ZIP and Jaz drives. The smaller ZIP drive takes removable discs of 100MB capacity and there is also a 250MB version. The Jaz drive is the ZIP drive's bigger relative, with a capacity of 2GB.

I have been using an Iomega ZIP drive for about 3 years and have found it to be extremely reliable and useful. While not having the capacity to replace the tape cartridge for a full system backup of a large hard disc, the ZIP drive nevertheless has many valuable functions. It is many times faster than a tape drive and is therefore ideal for quick backups of software and data files which are too large for floppy discs.

The text and screenshots for a substantial book can fit comfortably on one ZIP disc without compression. To achieve the same security with floppy discs would require several hundred "floppies" and an impossible amount of time spent swapping discs in the floppy disc drive.

However, with your important data files copied onto ZIP discs and the essential software safe on its original CDs, you should be able to recover from a hard disc disaster.

After you install a ZIP drive for the first time, an icon for the drive appears in My Computer alongside of the other disc drives.

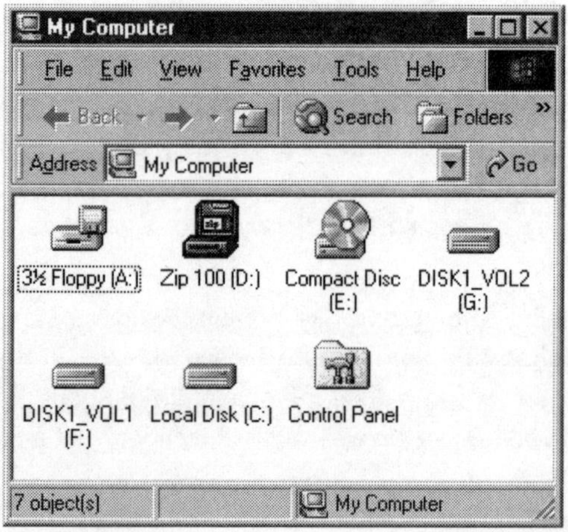

The ZIP drive can be treated like any of the other disc drives. This means it can be opened up in its own folder by double clicking. All the usual Windows Me operations, like copying and moving files by dragging and dropping in the Windows Explorer, can be performed. This enables files to be copied between the ZIP disc and any of the other disc drives.

However, there is also a set of Iomega ZIP Tools providing additional features. These include options to **Format...** the ZIP disc and to **Protect...** the disc with a password.

To save your work on the ZIP drive in applications like Word, you simply click **File** and **Save As...** then select the drive letter which the ZIP drive installation software has allocated. This could be either D:, E:, or F:, for example, depending on what hard drives and CD-ROM drives your machine contains.

The external version of the Iomega ZIP drive is particularly handy for transferring large files and software to other computers. You just plug the ZIP drive's cable into the printer port on the other machine and install the driver. A version of the ZIP drive is available which plugs into the USB port.

Compact Disc as a Backup Medium

Although CDs have been around for a long time, only recently has it been possible to write and rewrite your own CDs at an affordable price. The CD-RW drive is similar in appearance to the earlier "read only" CD-ROM drives and is available in internal and external versions.

There are two main types of writeable CD media:

The **CD-R** disc can be written to only once, after which it can only be used for reading operations. CD-R discs cost less than a £ each.

The **CD-RW** disc can be used repeatedly for writing and rewriting. First it must be formatted to prepare it for the recording process, known as "Packet Writing". This allows the CD-RW disc to be used like a floppy or hard disc, with drag and drop copying operations, etc. CD-RW discs are currently priced at around £2 each. If you buy a CD-RW drive, it can be used to read normal data and audio CD-ROMs, to "burn" CD-R discs in a once only operation, and to format, write and rewrite CD-RWs. Advertisements for CD-RW drives normally state performance in terms of reading, writing and rewriting speeds. For example, **32/12/10** means:

Reads at 32 speed (4800KB/s)

Writes at 12 speed (1800KB/s)

Rewrites at 10 speed (1500KB/s)

Some CD-RW drives are claimed to write to a CD-RW up to a 1000 times. CD-RW drives have their own memory buffer to keep a constant flow of data to the disc during writing operations. Buffer sizes of 2 or 4MB are typical. Some CD-RW drives have a technology known as Burn-Proof to prevent breaks in the recording process, which can ruin CDs.

Installing an Internal CD-RW Drive

If you decide to replace a standard read only CD-ROM drive with a CD-RW drive, it's a simple job if you feel happy removing the casing of your computer. It involves little more than unscrewing the old drive and sliding in the new one. Before removing the old drive, note the position of the coloured edge on the IDE data cable (the wide ribbon cable at the back of the drive). Before sliding in the new drive note the position of the jumper at the back of the old drive, setting the slave or master configuration. Use a jumper to set the new drive to the required slave or master configuration as appropriate.

Now slide the new CD-RW drive into position and connect the power and IDE data cable, ensuring that the coloured edge of the data cable is correctly positioned. Connect the audio cable from the CD-RW drive to the sound card. Secure the drive with the mounting screws and replace the computer casing.

When you restart the computer the CD-RW drive should be detected and the required software drivers loaded. Latest drivers can usually be downloaded from the Web site of the CD-RW manufacturer.

The CD-RW drive I use is the Creative Blaster CD-RW. This comes with the Prassi abCD software which can format a CD-RW disc for packet switching. Then the CD-RW can be used like a floppy or hard disc for drag and drop copying of files and normal saving operations.

The Prassi program is accessed by right clicking over a CD icon on the Windows Me Taskbar. This brings up the menu shown below which

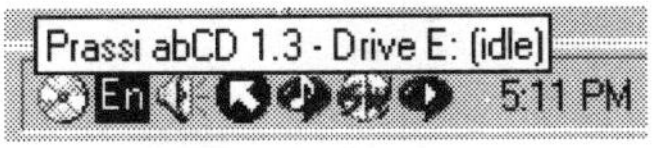

includes the option to format the CD-RW disc for packet writing. The formatting may take about 35 minutes, during which time the computer can be used for other operations.

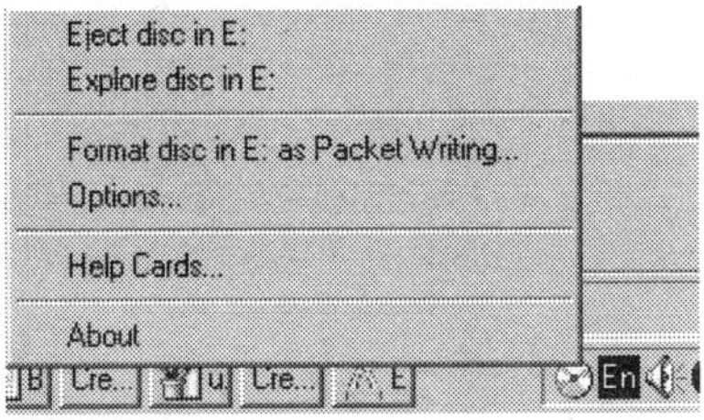

Burning a CD-R

This is a once only write operation, producing a CD-R which cannot be overwritten by dragging and dropping files or normal saving operations.

The Creative Blaster CD-RW drive uses the well-known Nero software for the task of burning a CD-R. Selecting **Nero-Burning ROM** from the **Start** and **Programs** menu leads to the **Nero Wizard**. This holds your hand as you supply Nero with your requirements such as **Data CD** or **Audio CD** or other formats.

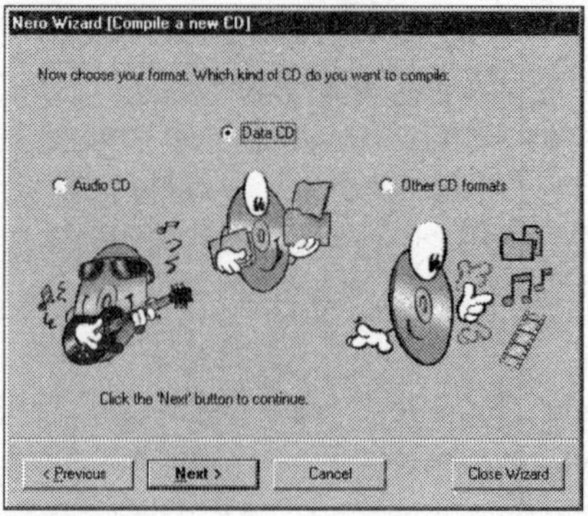

Then you select the files and folders you wish to copy to the CD-R using the windows of Nero's Explorer-like interface. The required folders are then dragged and dropped onto the CD named **NEW** as shown below.

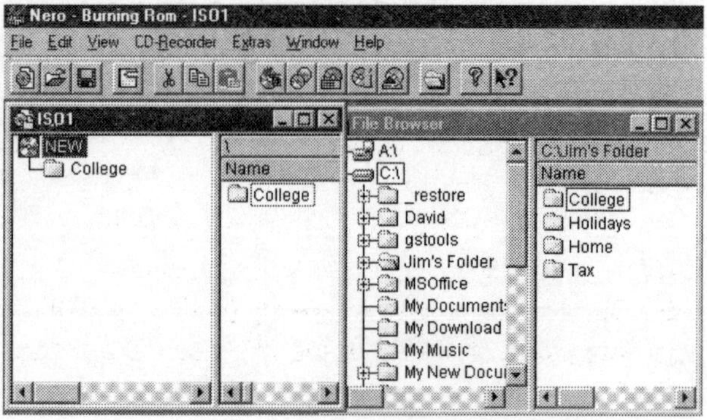

Finally the Nero Wizard gives you the chance to either **Test**, **Test and burn** or **Burn** the CD.

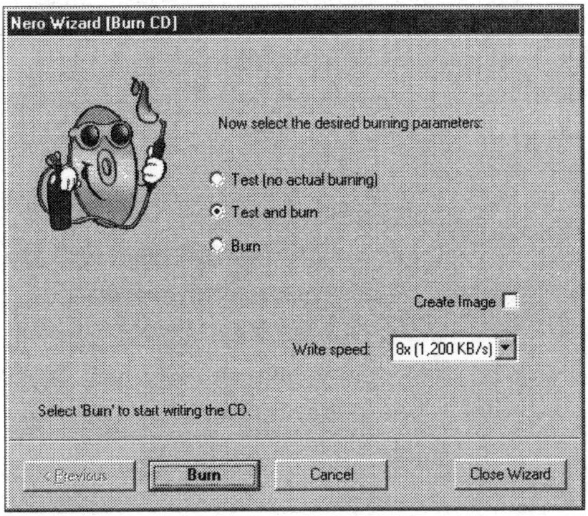

You are informed of progress while the CD is burned and when it has been successfully completed.

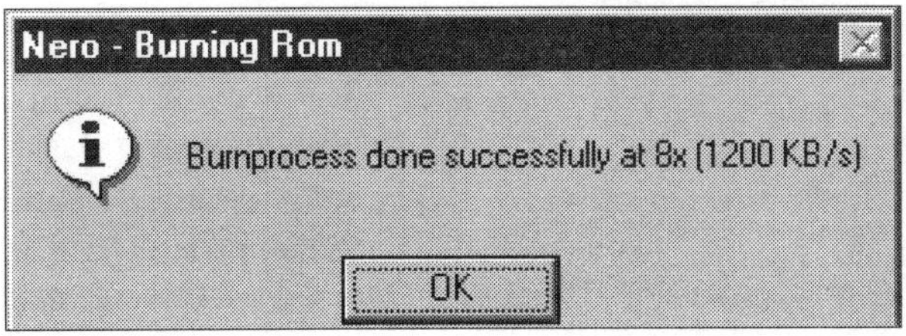

Both CD-R and CD-RW are very suitable as backup media. One of their main advantages is the low price of the media. In particular the CD-R discs are now so cheap that you can afford to treat them as disposables for distributing files to colleagues or for backing up important files. The writeable CD also has a greater capacity (nominally 660MB) compared with the floppy disc (1.44MB) or the ZIP disc (100 or 250MB). Using writeable CDs for backup and emergency recovery is discussed in more detail later in this book.

Backing Up to a Second Hard Disc Drive

If your computer has a second hard disc drive with plenty of free space, it makes sense to use it to make quick backup copies of important work. This is not a very secure backup system as it does not give protection against some of the major causes of data loss. For example, if the computer is stolen or damaged in a fire or flood, you will still lose the data and programs.

However, if you have already fitted a new hard disc drive (discussed later in this book) it may be that your second drive has enough free space to use for backup copies. This is very convenient for making quick backup copies, which will at least give protection against accidental deletion of files or damage to your main hard disc. In addition, you still need to make regular secure backups on a separate medium such as a ZIP disc, CD or tape cartridge.

A system which has served me well in producing numerous books over recent years is as follows: Save the work on the main hard disc (the **C:**

drive) every few minutes by clicking on the disc icon, shown left, on the Toolbar. Backups to the second hard drive (drive **F:**) are made less frequently, perhaps every hour. Secure backups are made to ZIP drive and writeable CD every day.

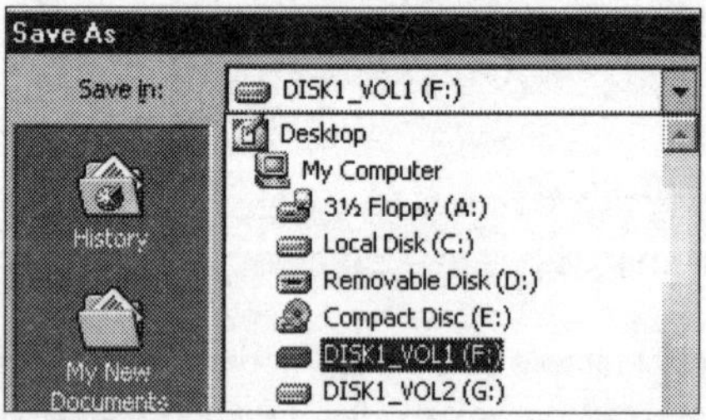

While you are working on a word processing task, for example, simply select **File** and **Save As....** Then select the second drive (the **F:** drive in my example) and make an extra copy. Before saving on the **C:** drive again it will need to be reselected using **Save As...**, as shown above.

Alternatively you can use the Windows Explorer to drag and drop a file onto the second hard disc. To use drag and drop, you must make sure the file is not open in its associated program. For example, to copy a Word file, the file to be copied must not be open in the Word program.

Tape Backup Systems

The previous notes described the copying of files and folders using "drag and drop" in the Windows Explorer. This is quite efficient for copying relatively small sets of files and folders. However, in a business or professional situation it is prudent to make regular backups of the entire hard disc contents. With modern PCs having hard discs of 10, 20 or 40GB capacity, the floppy disc, ZIP disc and CD just do not have the necessary capacity. Even a second high capacity hard disc is not a secure solution since this is vulnerable to fire, theft, etc.

In a business or college with a network, for example, the work of many different people may be stored on the hard disc of one central computer, known as the *file server.* A single backup operation is needed which can save everyone's work and all of the system software on one high capacity storage medium.

For the systematic, regular backups of the entire hard disc, a tape backup system is a popular solution. Systems like the HP Colorado tape drive, using *tape cartridges* of typically 14GB or 20GB, enable all of the system software and applications (programs) and all of the data files (your work) to be backed up. Then the tapes should be stored in a secure location some distance from the computer.

The complete package includes the tape drive and the backup software. A full backup including both programs and data is essential to restore the system if the entire hard disc fails, or is severely damaged or stolen.

There is usually a choice of internal or external tape drives. The internal drive obviously provides a neater and more compact solution; the external drive is portable, enabling you to transfer a backup to another computer, if necessary.

Making a full tape backup is a lengthy process, taking a few hours to copy a large hard disc. It is important to check before buying any tape backup system that it can accommodate a full backup of your entire hard disc on a single cartridge. If a single tape cannot accommodate the full backup, the process will be halted and the computer will "sit" waiting, usually overnight, for another tape to be inserted.

This defeats the object of the automated backup, which should proceed unattended, at a time when the computer is not being used. The software includes many special features such as the ability to schedule unattended backups. In a business situation this is essential, since tape backups are relatively slow, taking hours rather than minutes. It's therefore common to schedule an unattended backup to take place in the middle of the night, when the computer would not normally be used.

Functions of Backup Software

All backup software must be capable of 3 main functions in order to provide a recovery from disaster:

- *Back up* or copy the required files to the backup tape or other medium.
- *Compare* the backup files with the original files on the hard disc - to verify that the backup was accurate.
- *Restore* the backup files by copying them back to the hard disc. The destination may be the original folder on the hard disc or a new location specified by the user.

Some of the features of dedicated backup software are:

- Full backups of an entire drive.
- Selection sets of files which are backed up on a regular basis.
- Scheduling of backups at specified times.
- Back up to various media such as disc or tape cartridge.
- Error checking (verification) to ensure the backup is accurate.
- File compression to maximise storage space.
- Incremental backups which only back up files that have changed (since the last backup).
- *Restoration* to the original location or a specified location on the hard disc.

Fitting an Internal Tape Drive

You don't need any special tools to fit a tape drive - just a small screwdriver. This is a task which anyone can do - you don't need any technical or electronic expertise. A brief outline of the installation process is as follows:

- Make sure the computer is switched off before touching or working on any components.
- Rid yourself of static electricity by frequently touching the metal case of the computer. Alternatively use a special earthing strap obtainable from any electrical components shop.
- Take the cover off the computer and remove one of the blanking plates covering a vacant "bay" at the front of the machine.
- Slide the tape drive into the vacant bay in the casing and secure at the sides with the small screws which should be provided with the tape drive.
- Connect the tape drive to the floppy drive controller (a slot on the computer "motherboard") using a data cable. (This is a wide, flat, ribbon cable with a coloured stripe down one edge). You can either use the existing floppy drive data cable or use the new ribbon cable normally provided with the tape drive. Refer to the tape drive installation guide - the position of the coloured stripe is critical.
- There should be at least one spare set of brightly coloured power leads terminating in a white connecting plug. Carefully plug a set of power leads into the back of the tape drive.
- Replace the computer casing and switch on.
- After fitting a tape unit, your computer should automatically detect the new tape drive on startup and find and install the necessary software from the Windows Me CD, or from the discs provided in the drive package.

Some packages include a diagnostic program which performs a large number of write operations to test that the system can record properly. Then a corresponding number of read operations check that the data can be retrieved from the tape.

Systems like HP Colorado include a *tape retensioning* feature. This only takes a few minutes and should be performed before each major backup.

The Full Backup

The full backup (of an entire hard disc) is essential if you are to recover from a major disaster. This backup includes not only your important data files representing hours of toil, but also the program files like the Windows Me operating system and applications like Microsoft Office.

Also included in the backup are an important set of files known as the **system registry**. The registry files are an essential part of the Windows Me operating system and include numerous settings for the various devices and software you have installed. In order to recover from a complete hard disc failure it is necessary to save a copy of the Windows Me **Registry**.

Restoring Files from Tape to Hard Disc

Tape drives are relatively slow devices, so restoration of a large backup from tape can take several hours. The destination of the restored files may be their original location on the hard disc, i.e. the files are restored to the same folder in which they were originally created. Alternatively it's possible to restore files to an entirely new folder, perhaps on a different hard disc drive.

Developing a Backup Strategy

If you regularly back up all of the files in a particular backup job (either a full backup or selected files backup), you will be repeatedly copying and overwriting files which haven't changed. To avoid this, first make a full backup of all of the files. Subsequently you back up only those files which have recently changed. Then if you need to restore your hard disc you use the full backup together with the backup(s) of the changed files.

The Archive Bit

This is a property or attribute of all files and acts like a flag. When a file is created or modified, the archive bit is switched on. This indicates that a file needs to be backed up. The archive bit can be viewed by selecting the file in Windows Explorer then clicking **File** and **Properties**. It's possible to set the backup software so that when a file is backed up, the archive bit is switched off. This indicates that the file has been backed up and so does not need to be included in future backups. However, if the file is subsequently modified (for example, when a Word document is edited) the archive attribute will be switched on again.

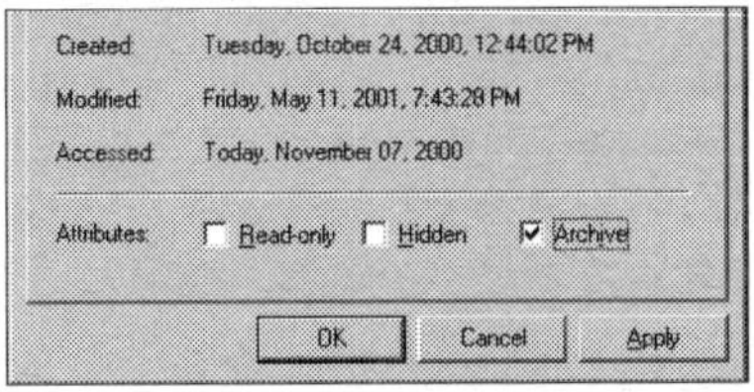

Differential and Incremental Backups

These two options in backup programs examine the archive attribute and back up only files which have changed. They produce different backup sets because of the way they handle the archive bit.

Differential Backup

This backs up all files that have changed at any time since the last full backup. After a differential backup the archive bit remains on. To restore a backup you only need the full backup plus the latest differential backup.

Incremental Backup

This backs up all the files that have changed since the last incremental backup. After an incremental backup of a file the archive attribute is switched off.

The incremental backup should therefore be quicker than the differential backup but is more complicated to restore. Restoring an incremental backup requires the last full backup plus all of the subsequent incremental backups.

The purpose of using the differential and incremental backups is to save time spent unnecessarily copying files when perfectly good backup copies already exist on tape. The cost of managing a backup system should be appropriate to the value of the data. However, an organization with a cavalier attitude to backup systems may find its very survival is threatened in the case of a hard disc failure.

How Many Backup Tapes?

Even with a tape backup system capable of copying the entire contents of the hard disc, it's still possible for disaster to strike unless a reliable backup strategy is devised. Below are some possible scenarios which could lead to a crisis; they can be avoided with a little planning.

- You only have a single tape and you overwrite it with each new backup. There is a problem during the backup, causing the data on both the hard disc and the tape to be corrupted.

  Your data is lost for ever and the data files must be re-created from scratch, by retyping all of the data.

- You only back up once a week and the hard disc fails just before the backup is due.

  The best part of a week's work could be lost.

- You do a daily full backup with a separate tape for each day, but there is a serious problem (possibly caused by a virus) which goes undetected for over a week.

  All of the backup tapes would be damaged.

The safest solution is to have a lot of backup tapes covering as long a time span as possible. However, backup tapes are expensive and the time to manage the backup process must also be considered.

A simple but expensive solution would be to have a separate backup tape for each day of the week and to make a daily full backup. Then to have two or three similar weekly sets of tapes, to be used in rotation. This would help to overcome most of the problems listed above.

You could use fewer tapes by making incremental backups on certain days, including only *modified* files. The incremental backups could be made with the *append* option set so that they all fit on one tape. A possible backup strategy would then be:

1. Dedicate one tape to a weekly full backup. Use another tape for the remaining days of the week to hold all of the daily incremental backups.
2. Repeat the process the following week, but using a different set of tapes.
3. Complete a three week cycle with a third set of tapes.
4. In the fourth week, return to the first set of tapes and overwrite them. Continue to rotate the tapes in a three week cycle.

Summary: Backup Activities

- The contents of your hard disc, including both software and data files, represents a huge investment of time and money, often exceeding the value of the computer itself.
- The main reason for backing up files is to enable a recovery of the contents of your hard disc, which are vulnerable to damage or loss.
- Without an adequate backup system, loss of the hard disc contents can be a catastrophe, because of the time and costs involved in restoring the software and data files.
- A secondary reason for backups is to transfer files between computers; for example, between work and home.
- Archiving is the copying of files which are seldom used, onto a disc or tape, in order to save hard disc space. The archived files can be retrieved later, if necessary.
- Full system backups copy the entire contents of the hard disc onto a tape cartridge. The tape has a storage capacity equivalent to several thousand floppy discs.

- In a partial backup, small selections of files can be backed up onto floppy discs, ZIP discs, writeable CD or tape. Programs like WinZip allow files to be compressed, effectively increasing the capacity of the backup medium.
- Backup discs and tapes should be stored in a secure place well away from the room where the computer is located.
- Removable Hard Discs, such as the ZIP and Jaz discs, can perform a valuable role as a fast backup medium for large groups of data files and software. The Iomega ZIP drive has its own powerful tools to facilitate the copying of files and discs.
- The external ZIP drive is portable and can easily be connected to other computers for the transfer of data files and software. The system is much faster and has far greater capacity than the floppy disc.
- A second hard disc drive is not a complete backup solution, but provides a fast method of duplicating files, giving protection against some eventualities.
- The writeable Compact Disc (CD-R and CD-RW) is a very cheap, fast and reliable backup medium capable of storing substantial amounts of data. CD-R discs can only be written to once. CD-RW discs can be written to many times and can be used for drag and drop copying like a floppy or ZIP disc.
- Files can be restored to the original folder or to a specified folder, perhaps on a different hard disc.
- You can restore all of the files from a backup or just a small selection of files from within the backup.
- It's a good idea, after a backup, to do a test restoration of a few sample files, to check that the backup and restoration are working correctly.

4

Backup Software

Introduction

The copying of files and directories can be carried out using "drag and drop" in the Windows Explorer or My Computer, etc., as described previously. This is quite efficient for copying small sets of files and directories onto removable media on an occasional basis. However, for the systematic, regular backups of larger files or for backing up the entire hard disc, dedicated backup software is necessary which automates the process and provides a lot of additional facilities.

Windows 98, the predecessor to Windows Me, included a dedicated backup program, Microsoft Backup, with the ability to work with a range of backup devices as discussed in the previous chapter. This program does not appear in Windows Me. However, this chapter is based on the dedicated backup program VERITAS Backup Exec Desktop. This is one of a range of VERITAS Backup programs intended for home and business users. On using the program it is clear that the software is very closely related to the program known as Microsoft Backup and included in Windows 98.

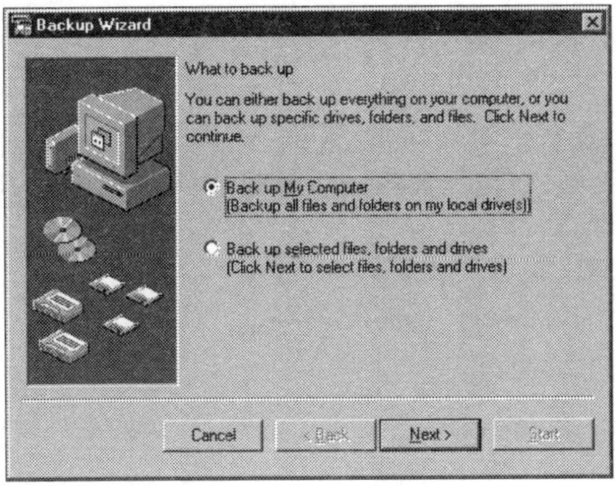

VERITAS Backup Exec Desktop is a comprehensive backup program, easy to use and with many powerful features.

Some of the features of dedicated backup software such as Veritas Backup are:

- Full backups of an entire drive.
- Selection sets of files which are backed up on a regular basis.
- Scheduling of backups at specified times.
- Back up to various media such as floppy disc, ZIP/JAZ discs, CD-R, CD-RW and tape. Disc spanning if necessary.
- Error checking (verification) to ensure the backup is accurate.
- File compression to maximise storage space.
- Differential and Incremental backups which only back up files that have changed (since the last backup).
- Restoration to the original location or a specified location on the hard disc.

Using VERITAS Backup Exec Desktop

Installing VERITAS BACKUP Exec Desktop is really just a case of inserting the CD. Once installed the program can be launched by double clicking its icon on the Windows Me Desktop or by selecting **Start**, **Programs** and **Backup Exec Desktop**.

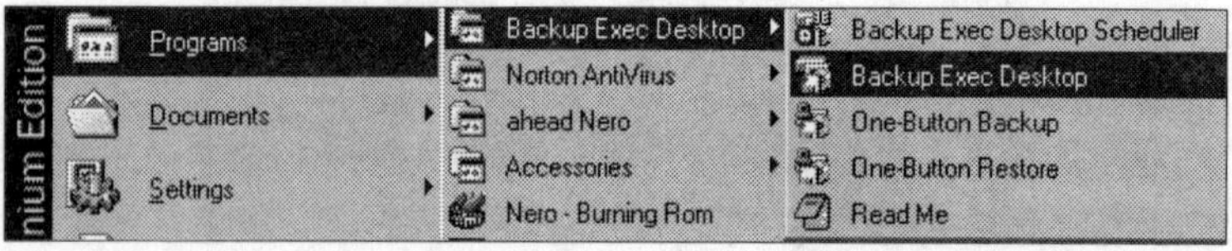

The program opens with a dialogue box showing some of the main phases of the overall backup process, i.e. backup, open existing backup, scheduling and restoration.

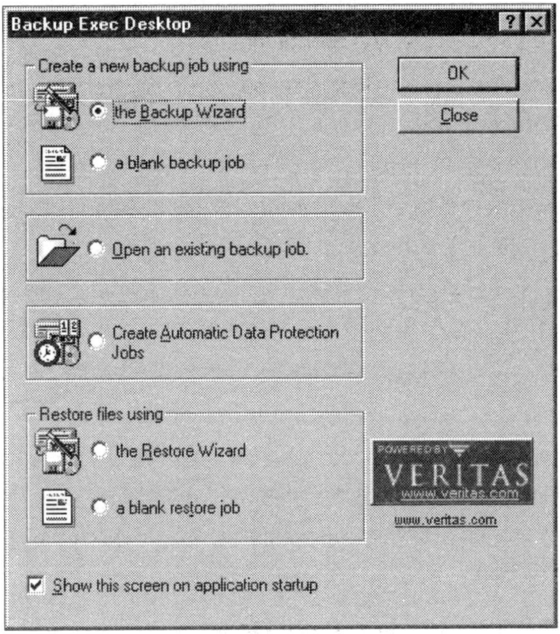

When you set up a backup, you must select what files/folders and discs are to be included and where it is to be copied to i.e. the destination medium such as floppy disc, ZIP/JAZ disc, CD-R or tape, etc. You may also schedule the backup to take place automatically and regularly at a certain time and day of the week. There are options such as *file compression* to save space and *verification* to compare the backup file with the original files. To save time and space, you may choose to back up only files that have changed since the last backup. When all of this information has been entered, the complete specification is saved as a *backup job*.

As shown in the above window, there are Backup and Restore Wizards which guide you step-by-step through the processes by offering you choices. Or you can control the software yourself from the main program window, as shown later.

One way to learn the software is to use the Backup Wizard to make a simple backup of a few files or a folder, onto a floppy disc or CD-RW, say. Each of the windows in the Wizard includes explanatory notes which may be helpful to the user.

First you are asked to choose whether to back up the whole computer and all of its local drives or to make selections from the drives, folders and files. If you chose to select the files and folders, etc., you are presented with an Explorer-like window, shown below. You can open up the disc drives and folders and tick the items you wish to be included in the backup.

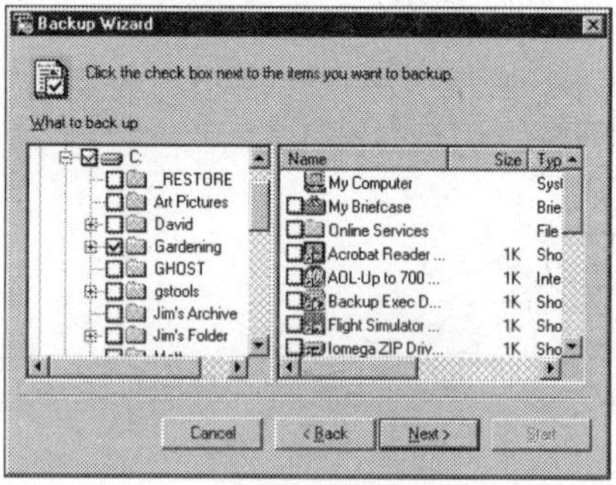

Next there is a choice between backing up all of the selected files or only those that have changed since the last backup. This is discussed later, but basically it means that if a file has not changed since the last backup, it need not be backed up again. This saves time during the backup process and uses less space on the backup medium.

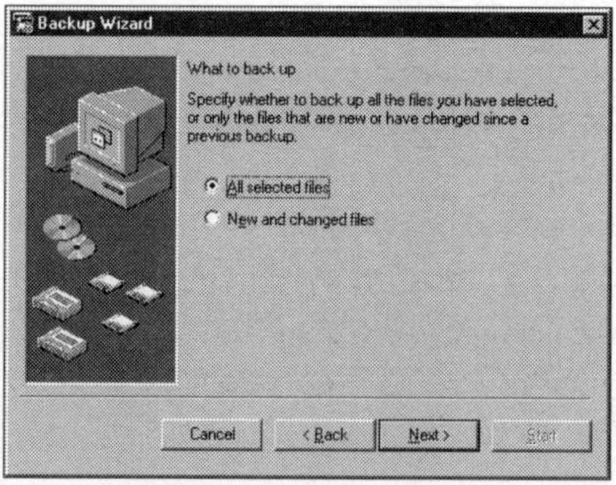

The medium on which the backup is stored must now be selected. For a very small backup this could be a floppy disc, but for medium sized backups is more likely to be a ZIP disc (100 or 200MB), CD-R or CD-RW (650MB) or JAZ disc (2GB). Larger backups require tape cartridges of 20GB or more. The destination of the backup is selected by clicking on the icon in the **Where to back up** bar shown below.

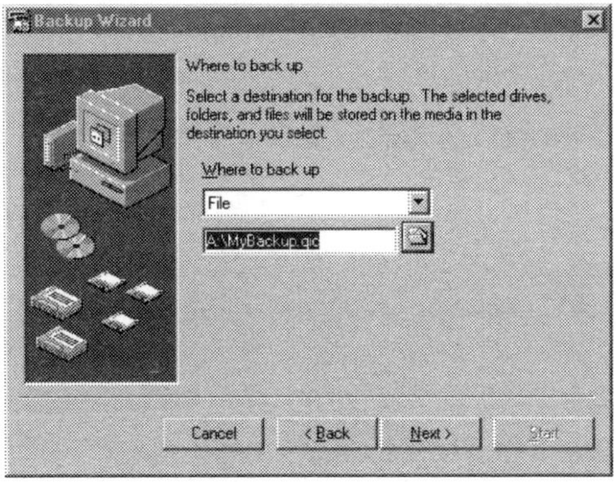

This opens up a choice of backup destinations:

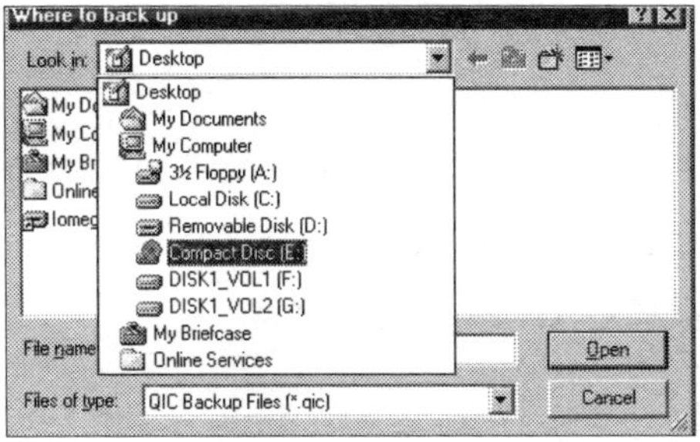

After you have selected the medium for the backup, click **Open** and **Next** and move on through the Wizard. You are given the chance to turn options like *verification* and *compression* on or off. Then you can decide to run the backup **Now** or **Later**.

Opting to start the backup **Now** requires you to enter a name for this particular backup job. Choosing later enables you to schedule regular backups at specified times on certain days of the week.

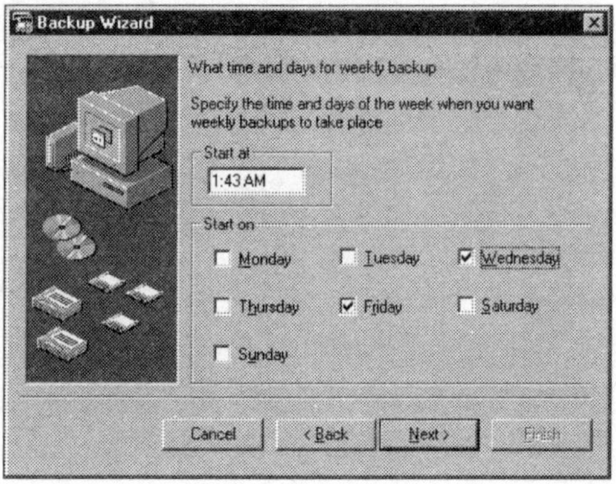

Having set up the backup job and given it a name, the backup process is started. The **Backup Progress** window appears, as shown below.

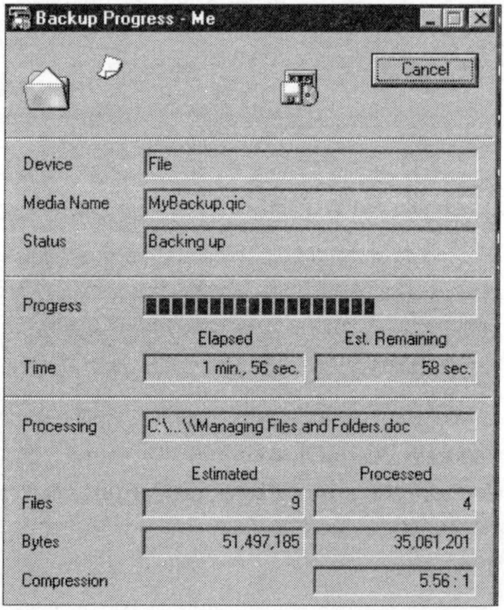

All being well you will be informed that the backup was completed without errors and you leave the Backup Wizard to enter the main VERITAS Backup Exec Desktop window. This can also be entered on startup by selecting **a blank backup job**.

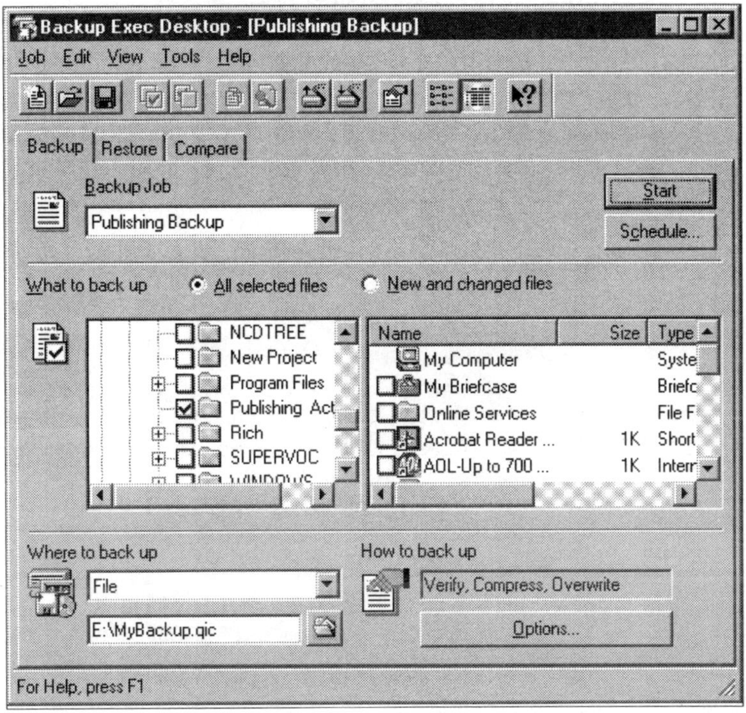

The main backup window above contains all of the features mentioned previously in the Backup Wizard. Clicking the arrow to the right of the Backup Job bar lists all of your previous backups, which can be called up and modified or deleted, if necessary.

A new backup can be set up by clicking the icon on the Toolbar or selecting **Job** and **New** from the menu. The items to be backed up are selected by ticking the boxes for the required discs, folders and files.

If you click **Options...** from the button on the right of the main window (or from the **Job** menu) you can switch on or off the options to:

- Compare the original and backup files to *verify* that the data was successfully backed up.
- Select from three levels of *compression* to save disc space.
- Select to append this backup to media or overwrite media with this backup.

If you select the **Type** tab from the **Backup Job Options** the window shows two main choices. You can either back up **All selected files** or you can back up **New and changed files only**.

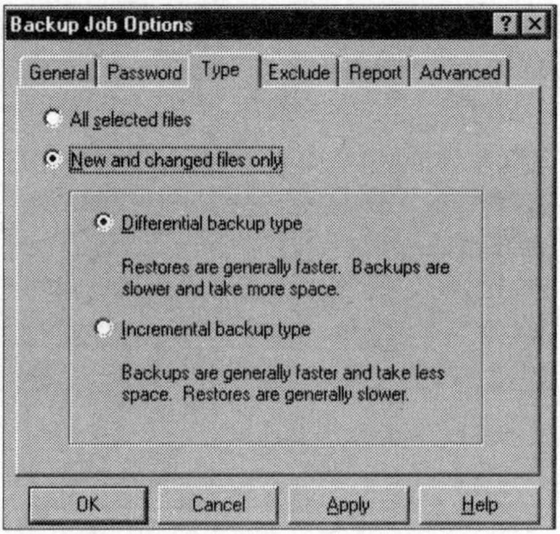

If you select **New and changed files only** two alternatives appear, having been previously greyed out. These are two special types of changed file backups, namely **Differential** and **Incremental**. The purpose of only backing up changed files is to save time and disc space. Clearly, if a file or folder has already been backed up, there is no point in replacing it with an identical copy of itself.

The archive bit, discussed elsewhere in this book, is used to "flag" the fact that a file needs to be backed up.

Differential Backup

This backs up all the files that have changed since the last **All selected files** backup.

Incremental Backup

This backs up only the files that have changed since the last incremental backup.

The Differential and Incremental backups are obviously faster and use less space than the full backup, but they are also more complex to manage and restore. Differential or Incremental Backups must be used together with a full backup. Restoration involves a full backup followed by either a differential backup or a set of incremental backups.

Selecting **Options...** and **Advanced** enables you to switch on or off the backing up of the **Windows Me Registry**. The Registry contains many of the important settings peculiar to your own computer.

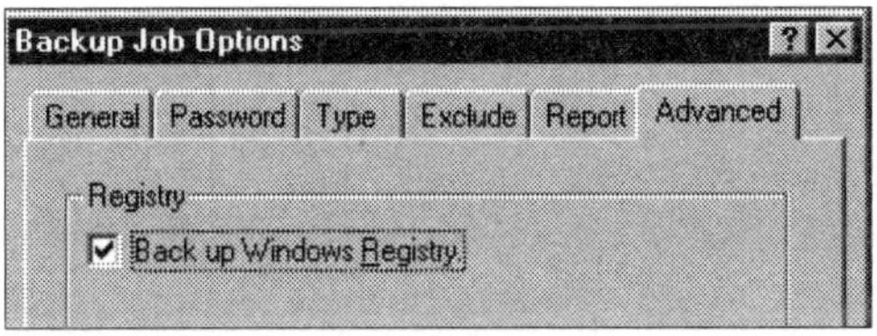

At the end of the backup there is chance to look at a report, which gives details of the various operations in the backup process i.e. **Backup**, **Compression** and **Compare** (or **Verification**).

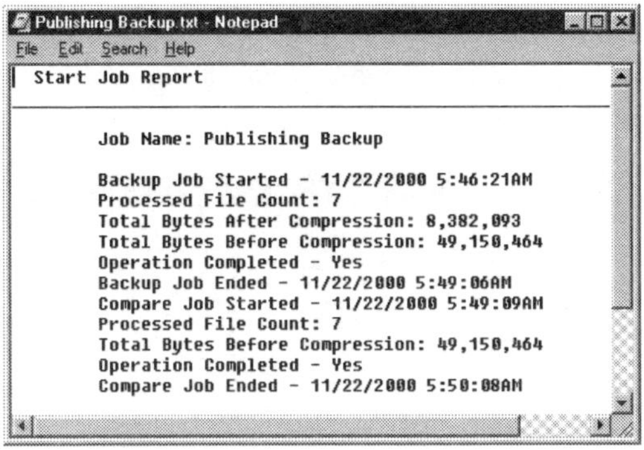

Keeping the Backups Safe

At this point, your backup should now be safely stored on one or more removable backup discs or tapes. The backup can *span* several media if necessary. These should be clearly labelled and locked away in a different physical location from your computer, to guard against the risk of a disaster such as fire, theft or flooding.

The Restoration Process

Restoration is the process of copying files from the backup disc or tape, back onto the original hard disc or onto a different hard disc. The entire backup set of files may be restored or, alternatively, it's possible to restore just a small selection of files. Although we hope backups will never need to be restored in a crisis, it makes sense to find out how to do the job beforehand. As a practice exercise, you don't need to restore the entire backup, just select one or two files to make sure everything is working correctly.

VERITAS Exec Backup Desktop has a set of **Restore** options to control the restoration process. There are three **General** options relating to the possible replacement of existing files on a hard disc. Obviously if the hard disc already contains the latest copy of a file then there is no point in replacing it. However, you may have generated a later version of a file on another machine and are using **Backup** for file transfer. In this case you would switch the **Replace the file...** radio button on in the above dialogue box.

You can display a report on the restore process and the **Report** option allows you to specify what information (errors, warnings, etc.) is to appear in the report. The **Advanced** tab gives you the opportunity to restore the Windows Registry.

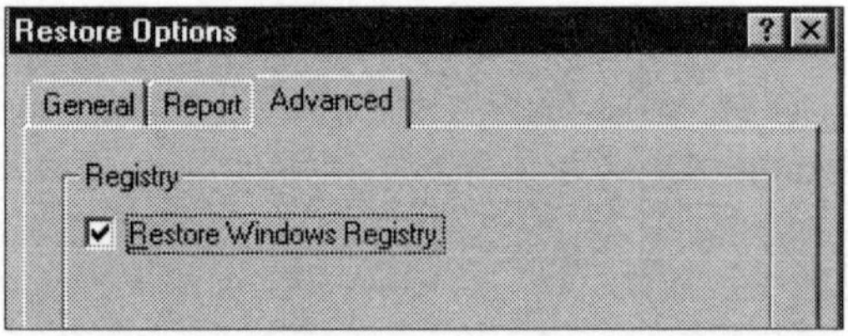

Restoring a Backup

You will need your backup media (floppy discs, ZIP discs, CD-RWs or tapes, etc.) at hand.

There are several ways to launch the **Restore** process. If you prefer to work from the main window just click the **Restore** tab. Or you can select the **One-Button Restore** from the Start, Programs and Backup Exec Desktop menu.

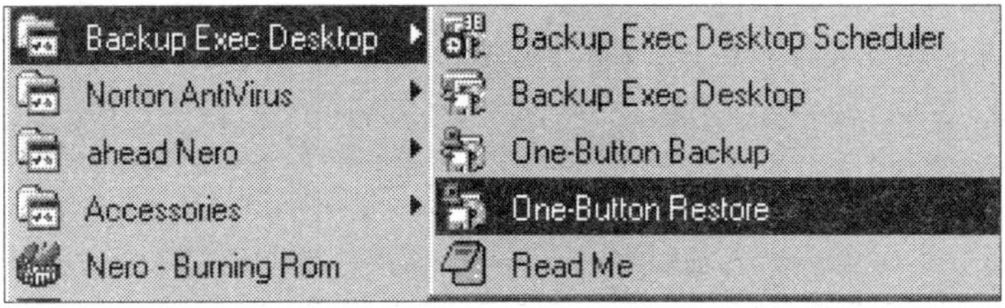

The opening window in Backup Exec allows you to select either the **Restore Wizard** or a **blank restore** job.

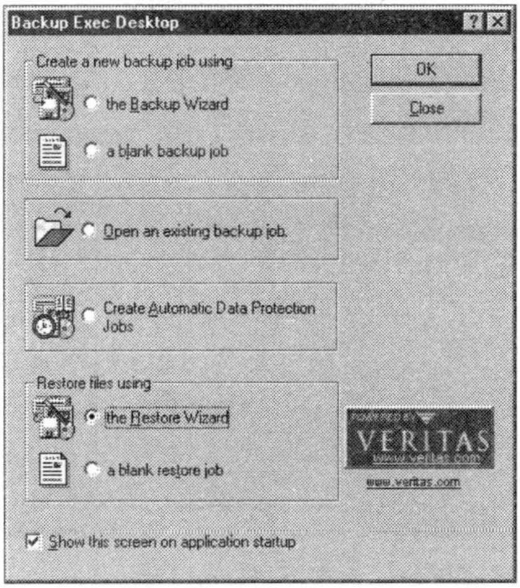

This section will use the Restore Wizard as it gives a simple guided tour through the whole restore process.

The Restore Wizard (and the Backup Wizard) can also be started from icons in the main Backup Exec window.

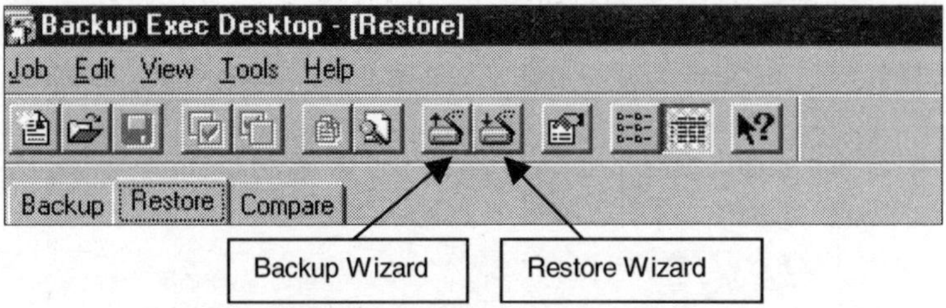

The first step in the Restore Wizard is to select the location to restore from.

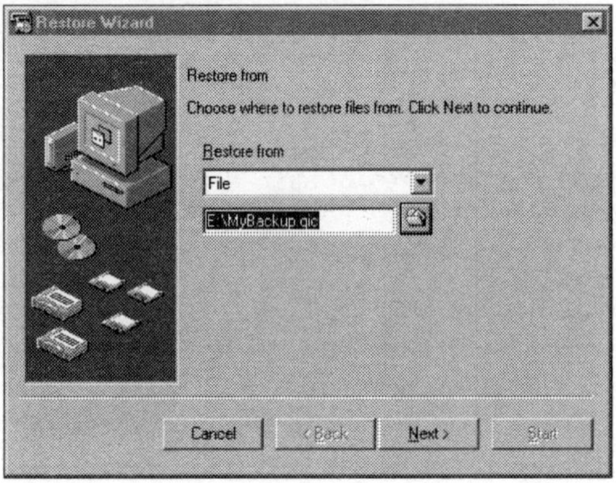

If you double click the folder icon in the bar below **File (**shown on the left), you can select the location i.e. ZIP drive, CD-RW drive, tape drive, etc., from where the files are to be restored. In the example above, the **CD-RW** drive (**E:**) has been selected.

Next you must decide what is to be restored. You can either restore the entire backup or simply pick out individual files from an Explorer-like window as shown on the next page.

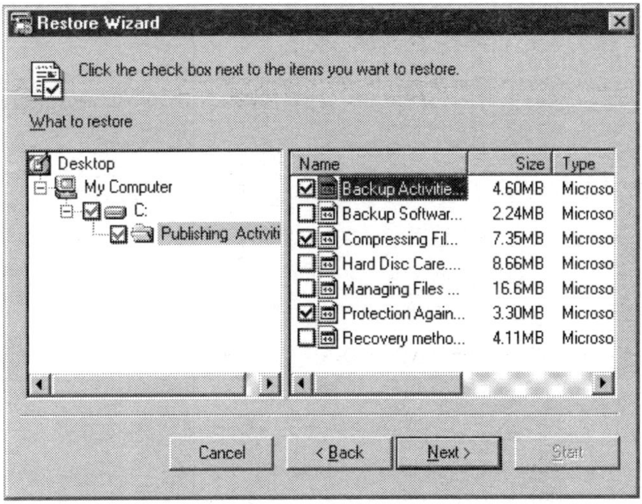

In the above window, click on a + sign to open up a disc and double click the folder icon to open up a folder. Click to place a tick in the boxes of any disc, folder or file to be restored.

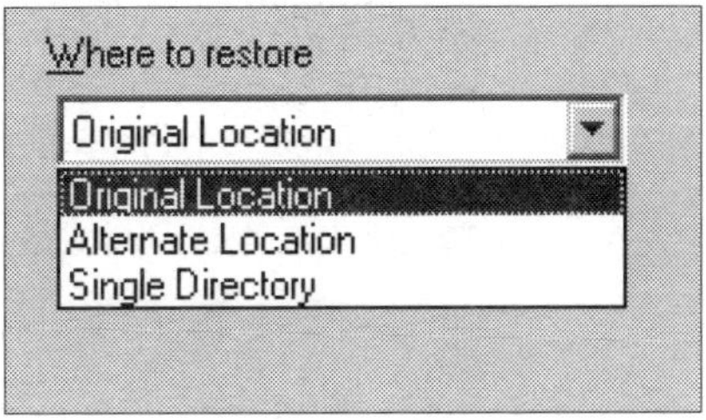

Before starting to copy the files you are asked about the location on the hard disc into which the files are to be copied from the backup medium. If the files are being restored to their original location, there may be existing copies of the same files. You must therefore decide if the existing files on the hard disc are to be replaced by the copies from the backup.

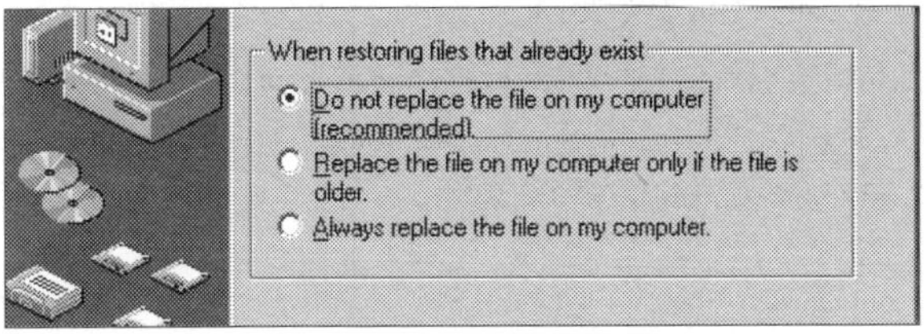

After clicking **Next** you are told that the backup media is required and when this is in place you should then see the **Restore Progress** window, as shown below.

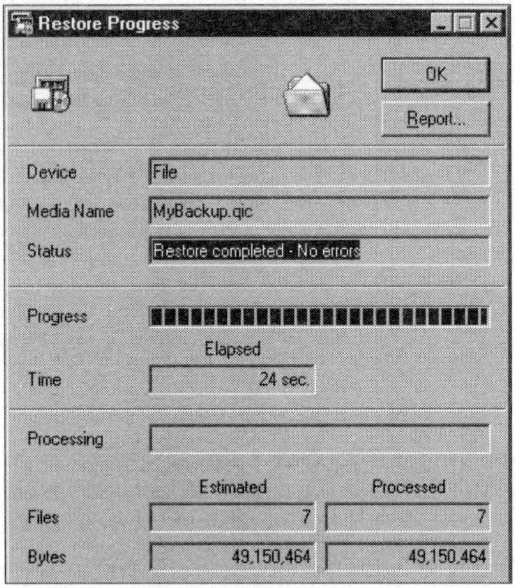

All being well the restore process will be completed with no errors and you can see more details by clicking the **Report** button.

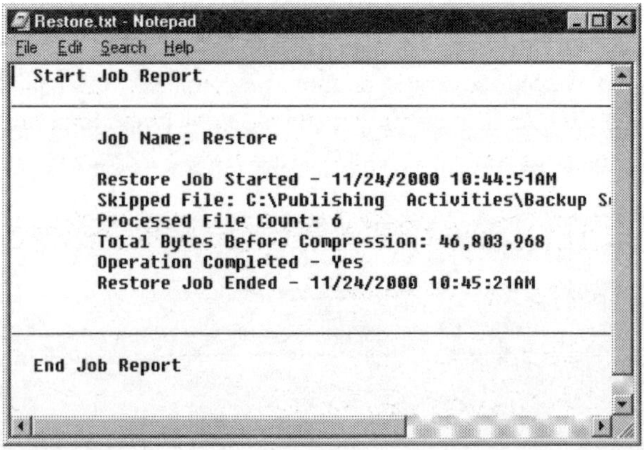

In the previous restore, one file was skipped because it already existed on the hard disc. At the end of the restore process you are returned to the main Backup Exec Desktop window. This gives direct access to all of the features mentioned in the previous description of the Restore Wizard.

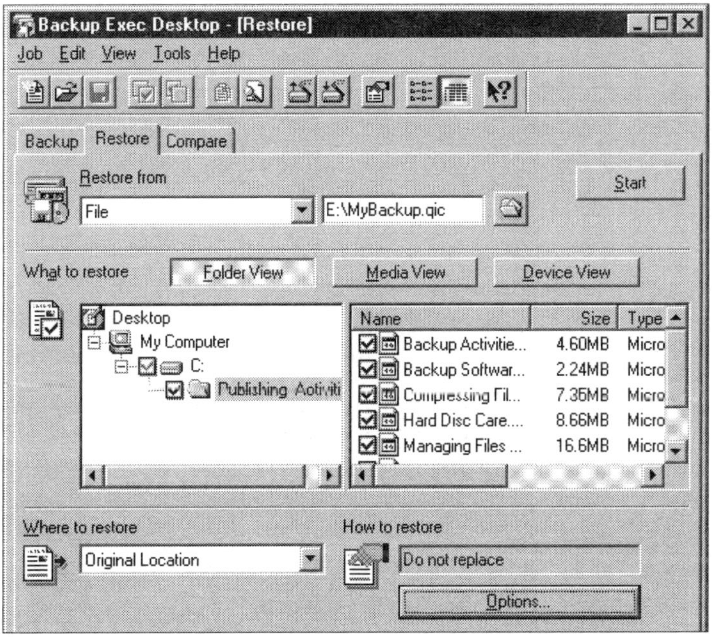

By selecting **Options...**, and the **Advanced** tab, you can request that the Windows Me registry is restored, assuming it was included in the previous back up. The registry contains many of the important settings for the computer and you should always have a registry backup.

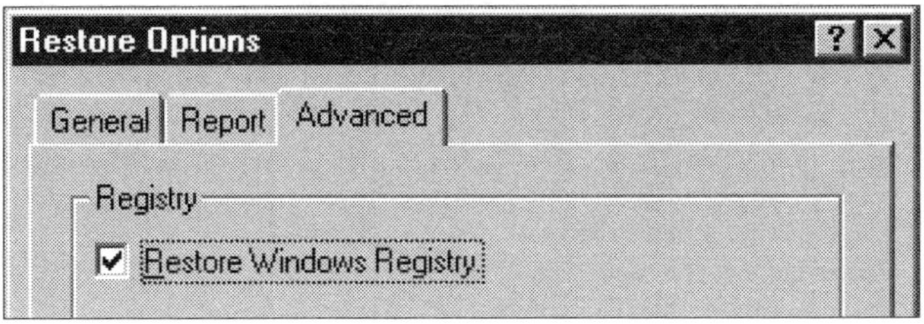

Summary: Backup Software

- Veritas Backup Exec Desktop is a fully-featured backup program. Facilities include verification, compression and full system backups, including the Windows Me Registry.
- Backup Exec Desktop can be operated using Backup and Restore Wizards or from a main window giving direct access to all of the features and options.
- Windows Me does not include its own backup software. However, VERITAS Backup Exec Desktop is almost identical to Microsoft Backup, which is a component of Windows 95 and Windows 98.
- Backup software allows you to copy to floppy disc, ZIP/JAZ disc, CD-R and CD-RW and tape cartridge. (Backups to another hard disc within the computer are not secure backups since they do not give protection against theft or fire, etc.)
- A backup can include all selected files or only those files that have changed since the last backup.
- Backup software includes the option to compress the files onto the backup storage medium, increasing the effective capacity of the medium.
- Windows Me allows long filenames; backups can be given meaningful names which help in the identification and efficient management of backups.
- The *compare* or *verify* option checks that the files on the backup medium are an exact copy of the original files on the hard disc.
- Files can be restored to the original folder or to a specified folder, perhaps on a different hard disc.
- It's a good idea, after a backup, to do a test restoration of a few sample files, to check that the backup and restoration are working correctly and that you are familiar with the process.

5

Recovery Methods

Introduction

This chapter deals with some of the ways of restoring your computer to working order after a major failure, in situations where you are unable to start the computer as normal and access the hard disc. This may be because essential files have been deleted or because you have decided to wipe the hard disc and start afresh. A similar situation arises when you fit a new hard disc drive to your computer. This may be necessary because the old drive is faulty or you need more storage capacity. For example, you may wish to install a 10GB or 20GB drive because your existing 3GB drive is unable to hold all of your programs and data files. Installing a second hard drive is covered later in this chapter.

The Windows Startup Disc

A startup disc is just an ordinary floppy disc, onto which you copy essential files needed to rescue your computer in times of crisis or major modifications. A Windows Me startup disc may have been created during the installation process when Windows Me was first set up on your computer. Alternatively you can create a startup disc at a later date. Creating a startup disc is a quick and simple task. Even if you don't feel confident to carry out major repairs or upgrades yourself, you should still create a startup disc. This will be invaluable to anyone else who has to bring your machine back to life.

Sometimes a situation arises where you are unable to "boot up" or start your computer in the normal way from the hard disc. This can happen when problems arise during hardware or software modifications. If you create a startup disc you can get the computer up and running again.

A major problem in this situation can be the inability to access the CD-drive. This is because the "driver" programs (which enable the CD drive to work with your computer) are no longer present. The Windows Me startup disc should contain the necessary software to get your CD drive working again. Then you can use the original Windows Me CD to restore the Windows Me operating system. Next you need to restore any other software and data files which you have backed up onto CD, ZIP disc or tape cartridge.

Creating a Startup Disc

During the installation of Windows Me you are prompted to create a startup disc. If this was done, the startup disc should have been clearly labelled and kept in a safe place. However, if this disc is not available you can create a startup disc at any time using an option within the **Control Panel** accessed from **Start**, **Settings** and **Add/Remove Programs**.

Place a new disc in the floppy disc drive. If it has not been formatted, start **My Computer** by clicking its desktop icon. Right click over the icon for the floppy disc drive in My Computer and select **Format...** from the menu which appears.

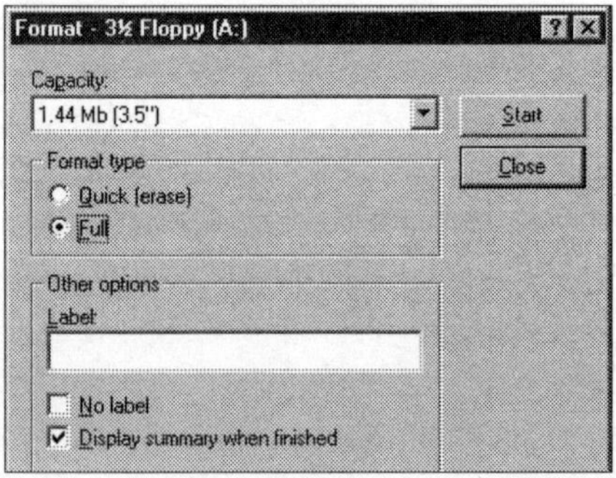

As this is a vitally important floppy disc, take the extra time to carry out a **Full** format, selected from the **Format** dialogue box shown above. Unlike the **Quick** format option, the **Full** option will scan the disc to check for any damage to the disc surface.

Now select **Start**, **Settings**, **Control Panel** and click the **Add/Remove Programs** icon. Select the **Startup Disk** tab as shown below:

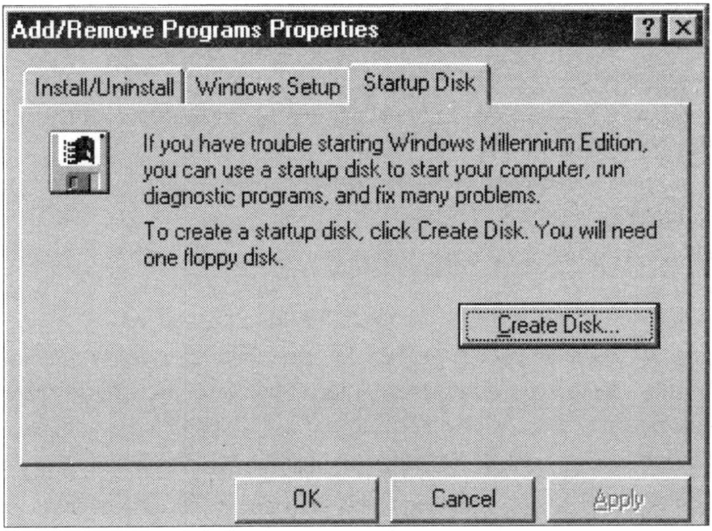

Click **Create Disk...** to start copying the essential files to the startup disc.

Booting from a Floppy Disc

When the copying process is finished you can use the floppy disc to boot up your computer, should the normal method of starting from the hard disc fail. First you need to check that your computer will start from the floppy disc. Computers are normally set to start up from the hard disc, without looking at the floppy disc drive. Some people and organizations prefer to set their computer so that they cannot boot up from a floppy disc. This is because floppy discs are a common source of viruses. Leaving an infected floppy disc in a computer is a dangerous practice. When the computer is next switched on, if it is able to boot from an infected floppy disc, the virus will spread to the hard disc. (Please also see the chapter on protection against viruses.)

To enable your computer to boot up from a floppy disc you may need to change the startup options in a special section of memory known as the CMOS RAM. The CMOS memory is powered by a battery so that the settings are not lost when the computer is switched off.

To change the CMOS settings, you need to enter the **SETUP** program of your computer. Soon after switching the computer on, watch for a message such as:

"Press del if you want to run SETUP"

On entering the setup program, look for a line like:

BOOT SEQUENCE : A,C

Or **Ist Boot Device : FLOPPY**

Both of the above settings will cause the computer to try to boot from the startup floppy disc first, before trying the hard disc. If you need to change the setting, a common method is to highlight the setting and then press **Page Up** or **Page Down** to cycle through the alternatives. Follow the instructions on the screen to save the new settings and then leave the CMOS setup program.

The computer should now boot up from the startup disc. The screen will now display the text-only format of the DOS operating system, which preceded Windows. You can choose from a menu offering options to start the computer with or without CD-ROM support. Choose the CD-ROM support option and you will be informed that the CD-ROM drive is drive **D:** or **E:**, etc. The contents of my startup disc are shown below:

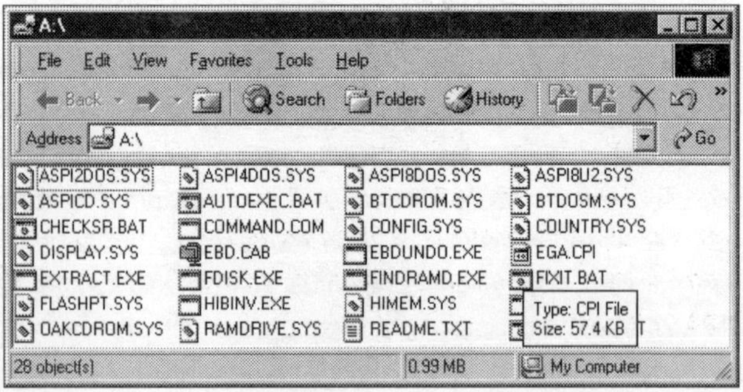

The startup disc shown on the previous page contains not only the files to start the computer with CD support, but also a number of utility programs. **OAKCDROM.SYS** is the CD-ROM support, while **FDISK.EXE** is used for *partitioning* a hard disc drive, discussed later in this chapter.

Reinstalling Windows Me

To reinstall Windows Me, boot the computer from the startup disc as previously described. When startup is complete, type the drive letter (**D:** or **E:**, etc.) for the CD-ROM drive and press **Enter**. Now place the Windows Me CD in the drive, type **setup** and press **Enter**. Follow the instructions on the screen to complete the installation of Windows Me. If your Windows CD is an *upgrade* rather than a *full* version, you will be asked to temporarily insert the CD from an earlier *full* version of Windows 95 or Windows 98. This is to verify that you are entitled to use the upgrade edition of Windows Me, which is cheaper than the full version.

Although your *data* files should be unaffected after reinstalling Windows, you will probably need to reinstall your applications software such as Microsoft Word, Access or Excel.

Please note that although the previous procedure to reinstall Windows Me is not difficult and doesn't take long, it should only be used when all else fails. In particular, before reinstalling Windows Me you should try System Restore as described elsewhere in this book. This allows you to return to a previous configuration of Windows Me, recorded at a time when the computer was working well.

The next section looks at the creation of complete hard disc images, rather than backups of selected files, as discussed in the previous chapter. These enable *everything* on a hard disc to be backed up, including all of the configuration and startup files, all of the applications software and all of the data files. Once the disc image is restored to a new or newly-formatted hard disc, there is no need to reinstall individual programs or files.

Disc Images

The previous chapter discussed the making of regular backup copies of important files. It is also possible to copy an entire hard disc onto backup media such as CD-R, CD-RW, ZIP or JAZ discs, etc. If more than one disc is needed for a single backup, the software normally announces this at the outset. During the backup process the user is prompted to insert additional discs as required.

Disc imaging software can also copy individual *partitions* on a hard disc drive. As discussed later, a single physical hard disc can be divided into a number of partitions, or "logical" drives. These can be accessed like separate physical drives. For example, on the computer shown below, the second hard drive is divided into partitions or logical drives **F:** and **G:**.

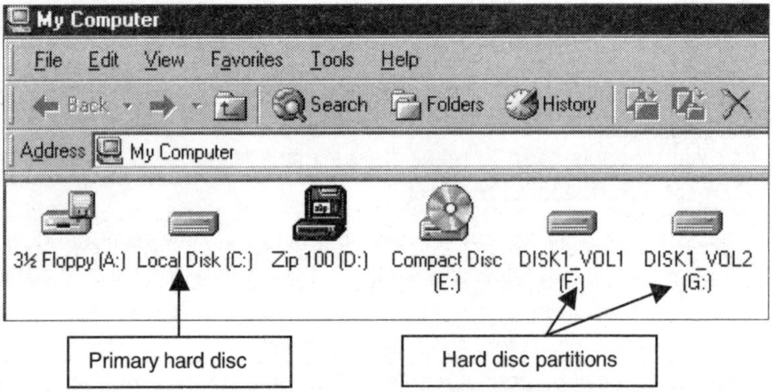

If you have a CD-RW recorder capable of recording your own CDs then you may already have the software necessary to make a disc or partition image. The Creative CD-RW drive in my machine came equipped with the well-known Nero software from Ahead Software GMBH.

There are some limitations to the method of disc imaging. For example, there may be problems if you try to make an image of a disc drive or partition which contains files which are currently in use. This means that you may not get a safe backup of a hard drive or partition if it is currently running the Windows Me operating system. Therefore, before making a disc image, as far as possible, you should close all files and programs that are running. However, there should be no problem backing up any other partitions on the hard disc. In the case of a machine with two physical hard drives, each with their own operating system (such as Windows Me on one and Windows 98 on the other), you can run Nero from one hard drive and make a disc image of the other.

Some disc imaging software, such as Norton Ghost discussed shortly, overcomes this problem by booting from a special floppy disc, similar to the Windows Me Startup Disc. This contains the DOS operating system and the imaging program, which are very compact and don't need to be run from the hard disc. Therefore the Windows Me operating system on the hard disc is not opened and can be backed up safely during the disc imaging process.

Another consideration is that if you back up an entire hard disc or partition using Nero, then the image must be restored to a hard disc as a single entity - it is not possible to restore individual files. Please note however, that the Nero Wizard, discussed in the previous chapter, allows selections of individual files to be "burned" to a CD. These may be selectively restored to a hard disc using normal drag and drop methods in the Windows Explorer.

Creating a Disc Image

From **Start** and **Programs** select **Nero-Burning Rom**.

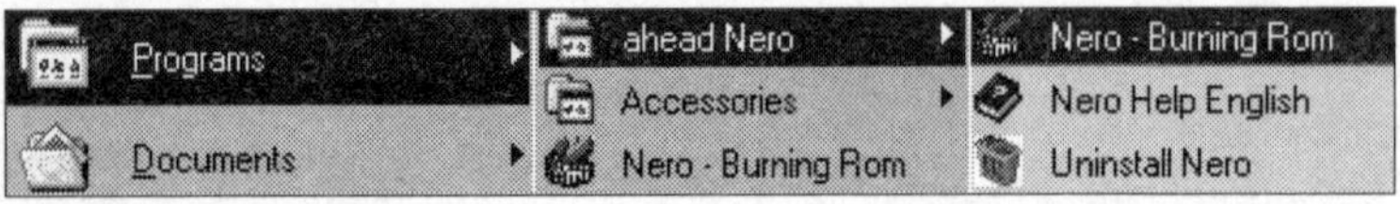

The **Nero Wizard** opens, but as this is not used for burning disc images, click **Cancel**. This opens the main Nero window shown below.

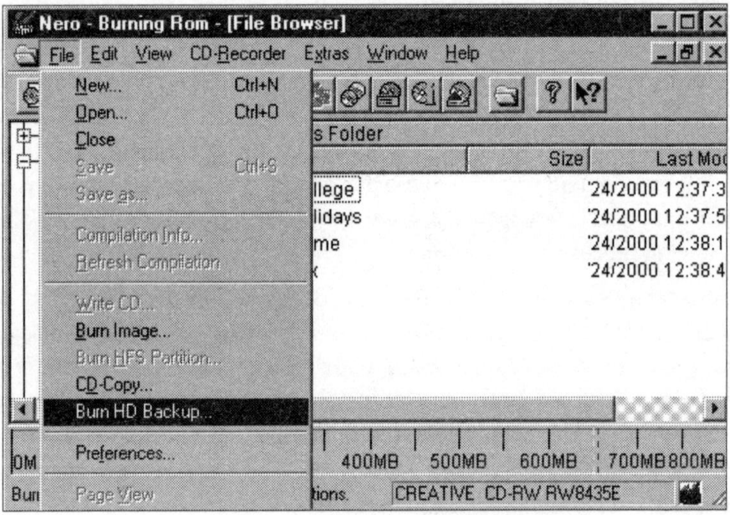

From the **File** menu shown above, select **Burn HD Backup...** and you are presented with a screen listing the limitations of disc image backup as discussed earlier. Click **Proceed** and a window opens allowing you to choose which hard disc or partition is to be backed up, shown on the next page. If any disc or partition contains an operating system which is currently running, it is marked with a red triangle containing an exclamation mark. This signifies that there may be problems if you back up this particular hard disc or partition.

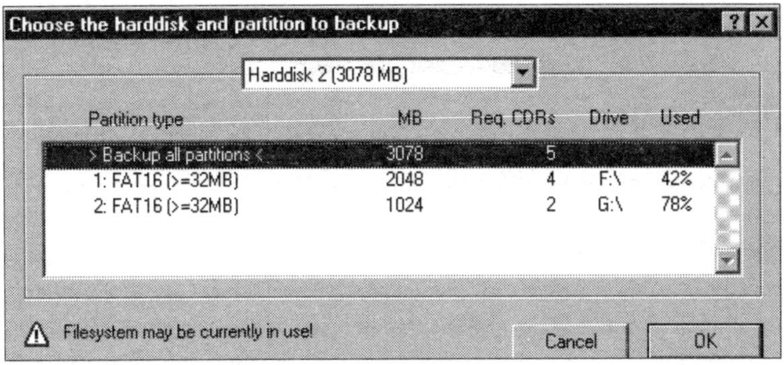

Also shown is the number of CD-Rs required to back up the entire hard disc or partition. To proceed with the backup, click **OK** and you will be asked to insert a blank CD-R. Click **OK** to start the burn and the following window appears, indicating the progress of the **HD-Backup**.

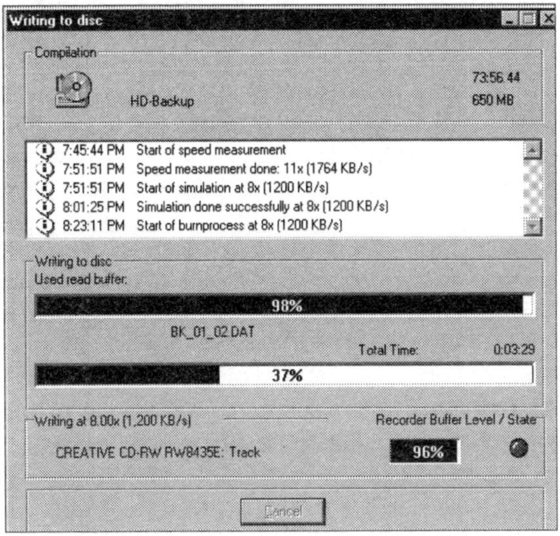

If the backup cannot be accommodated on a single CD-R, you will be prompted:

Please insert an empty CD to write to

If all goes well, you will eventually see the message:

Burn process done successfully

In this example, a hard disc partition (logical drive **G:**) was copied to CD-R in about 30 minutes. It had a used capacity of 1024MB (or 1GB) and spanned 2 CDs. (1 CD has a *nominal* capacity of about 650MB).

Restoring a Nero Hard Disc Backup

After the previous exercise, the end result would be a copy of an entire hard disc or partition on a CD. This is no use if it can't be restored to the original hard disc or a new hard disc, in a time of crisis. If you tried to restore a disc image containing the Windows Me operating system, from a CD to a hard disc with Windows Me currently running, the files in the operating system would be overwritten and damaged and the computer would then be useless. Nero avoids this problem by using a restore program, **NRESTORE.EXE**, which runs in the old text-based DOS operating system. This can be run from a floppy disc without the need to start the Windows Me operating system from the hard disc.

First you boot the computer from the Windows Me Startup Disc, as described at the beginning of this chapter. You must select the option to enable CD support, from the menu which appears after booting from the floppy. Otherwise you will not be able to access the backup image stored on the CD-R.

A copy of the program file **NRESTORE.EXE** is stored on the Nero CD and can be copied to your floppy boot disc in Windows Explorer. Use **Start**, **Search**, **For Files and Folders...** to find a copy of **NRESTORE.EXE**. To run the program, type **nrestore.exe** (or **NRESTORE.EXE** if you prefer) at the **A:\>** prompt and press the **Enter** key. You are asked to select the drive letter for your CD drive e.g. **E:**. Then you are asked to place the first (or perhaps only) backup CD in the drive.

Finally select the destination drive or partition for the backup image to be restored to and select **RESTORE** from the menu.

Norton Ghost

This is an efficient way of copying an entire hard disc to a removable medium such as a CD-R or CD-RW, either for regular security backups or before major modifications to the computer. Alternatively the hard disc can be duplicated to another hard disc, either in the same computer or in another computer on a network or linked by a cable.

Norton Ghost is capable of "cloning" an entire hard disc (and all of the necessary startup and configuration files) to a CD-R, for example. It is an excellent way of managing major changes on your computer, such as upgrading to a bigger hard disc drive, as follows:

- The old drive is copied to a CD-R or CD-RW (or other medium) creating a disc image.
- The new drive is fitted to the computer.
- The computer is started from a special Ghost boot disc or CD.
- The hard disc is partitioned and formatted and the disc image is copied from the CD-R to the new hard disc.

A number of variations on the above are possible. For example, if you are keeping both the old and new hard disc drives installed in your computer, Norton Ghost can be used to copy directly between the two.

If copying to a removable backup medium, a number of ZIP or JAZ discs can be used as an alternative to CD-R or CD-RW. Various levels of *compression* are selectable allowing more files to be copied to a given backup disc. Ghost will allow the disc image to *span* several media. You are informed of the number of backup discs required before the copying process begins.

Norton Ghost Components

All of the software for Norton Ghost is supplied on a single CD ROM. There are several components to the Ghost software:

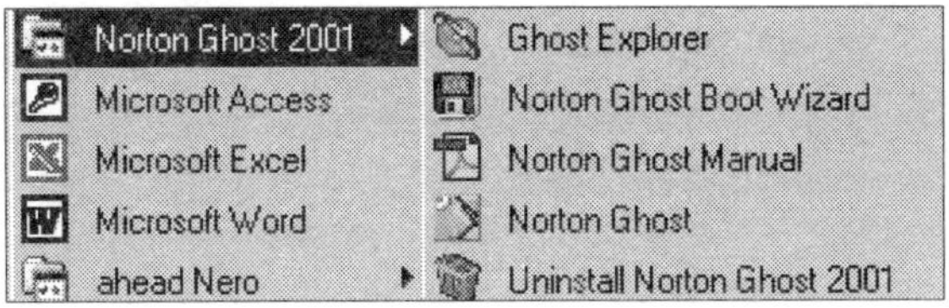

Norton Ghost is the main program which creates a disc image on a backup medium (e.g. CD-R or CD-RW). Ghost also restores the disc image from the backup medium to the new hard disc. This is a DOS program, meaning that it runs under the older MSDOS/PCDOS operating system which preceded Windows. A version of DOS is provided on the Ghost CD. This means Norton Ghost is a relatively small program and can be run from a floppy disc. Alternatively the program can be copied to your hard disc drive.

Please note that although it is technically possible to run Norton Ghost from within Windows Me, it is not advisable. This is because there may be problems if you back up files which are open while Windows Me is running.

To avoid these problems the computer is started from a special Ghost Boot Disc which runs the Ghost program in the DOS operating system.

Ghost Explorer is a Windows program which allows you to manage files within a disc image. Individual files and directories can be added and deleted.

GDisk is a utility which enables you to carry out the preparation of a hard disc for use, namely formatting and creating partitions (discussed later).

Ghost Boot Wizard creates a boot disc (on floppy disc) which can start a computer having an unprepared new hard disc or a faulty hard disc which needs formatting. Then the hard disc can be partitioned and formatted as required before restoring a complete disc image using Norton Ghost. The Boot Wizard itself is a Windows program.

Installing Norton Ghost

Place the Norton Ghost CD in the drive. It should autorun to show the following:

Select **Install Norton Ghost 2001** then follow the instructions on the screen, which mainly involve clicking **Next** and completing a registration on-line to the Internet.

Creating a Ghost Boot Disc

Select the **Norton Ghost Boot Wizard** after clicking **Start**, **Programs** and **Norton Ghost 2001**. The wizard opens allowing you to choose between different types of boot disc.

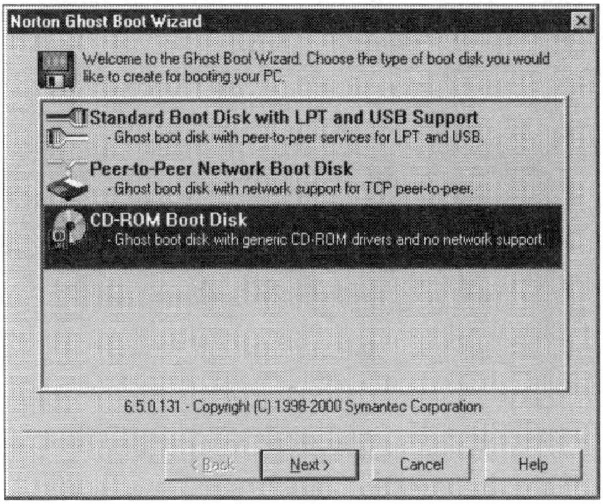

The third option has been selected in this example to enable disc or partition images to be recovered from CD-R or CD-RW.

Place the appropriate disc in its drive and select the required boot disc. In the case of a floppy disc, it will be formatted before the files are copied. An example of a boot disc for using Norton Ghost on a standalone computer is shown below.

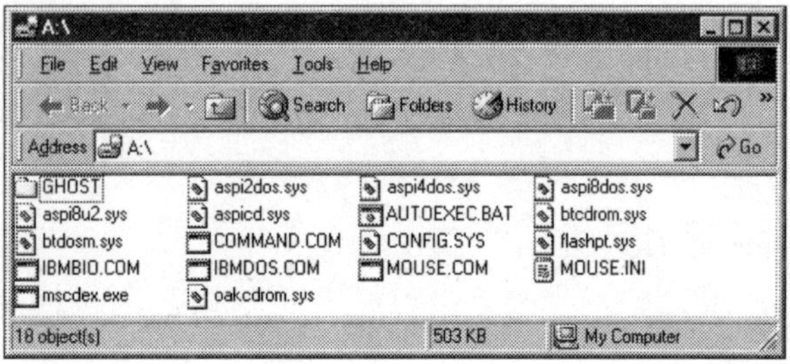

Apart from the actual Ghost folder shown in the above window, there is a driver to enable your mouse to work with the DOS-based Ghost program. Also shown are the files needed to start up your computer and run an IBM version of the DOS operating system and files to enable the CD-ROM drive to be accessed.

Once you have created a boot disc it can be used to start your computer and use the Ghost program to create a disc image on a removable backup medium or another hard disc.

Creating a Disc or Partition Image

Start the computer using the boot disc described previously. The Ghost program will start up with the menus shown below.

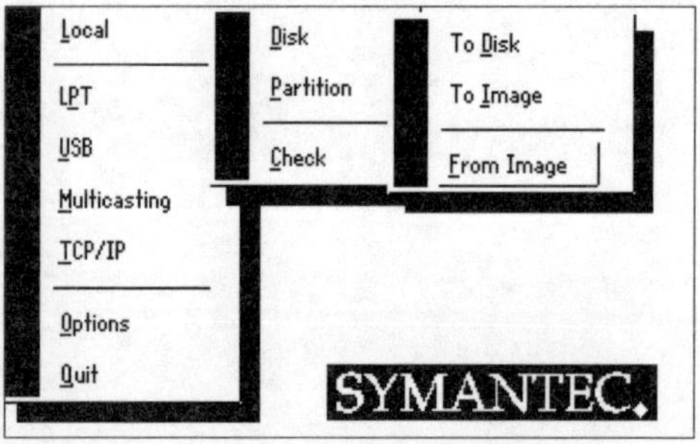

If you are using a standalone computer, select **Local** from the previous menu. (**LPT** and **USB** are for copying between computers connected by cable between either their LPT ports or their USB ports. TCP/IP is for computers connected by a peer-to-peer network using the TCP/IP protocol). **Options**, amongst other things, allows you to switch on **Spanning**. This means a large disc or partition image will continue onto several backup discs if necessary.

Select either **Disk** or **Partition** depending on what you want to back up. Then select **Disk** if you are copying between two discs and **Image** if you are copying onto a backup medium such as CD-R, CD-RW, ZIP or JAZ disc.

If there is more than one hard disc or partition in the computer, you then choose the disc or partition to copy. Click **OK** and you are asked to select the medium (CD, etc.) and give a name to the backup.

Click **Save** and before starting the copy operation you can choose between **No**, **Fast** and **High** Compression. Higher compression causes the copy operation to take longer.

Ghost then informs you how many discs will be needed, if you are copying a large backup which is too big to fit on one disc. Click **Yes** to proceed with the backup.

The backup begins and you are informed of progress by a window showing statistics such as the elapsed time and the number of megabytes copied so far. If disc spanning is required, you are asked to insert another backup CD or ZIP or JAZ disc when necessary.

At the end of the process the backup medium is ejected and a message appears to say that the "dump" has been completed successfully. As an example, a 2GB backup of programs and data took about half an hour to copy.

Restoring a Disk or Partition Image

Place the floppy boot disc in the drive and start up the computer. The Ghost program starts up, from which you select **Local**, **Disk** or **Partition** and **From Image**, as shown below.

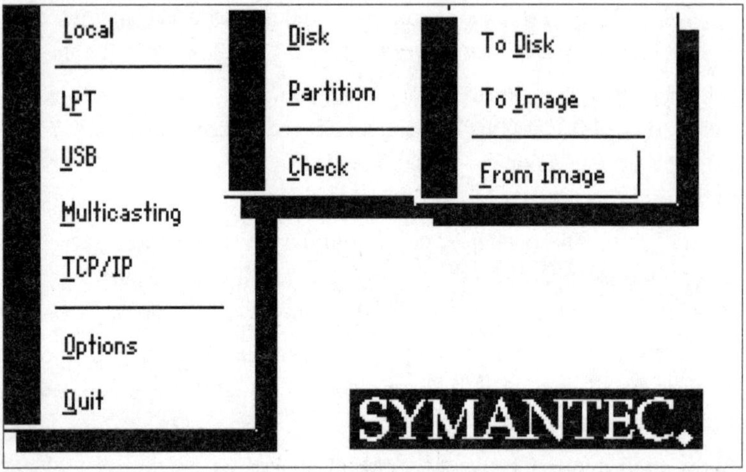

You will be asked to place the appropriate backup medium, i.e. CD or ZIP disc, in its drive. Then you select the location of the image to be restored and a window appears listing the contents of the disc or partition image.

After you click **Open** you are required to select the destination location on the hard disc into which the disc or partition image is to be restored. On my machine, restoring a 900MB partition from CD to hard disc took only a few minutes.

Ghost Explorer

This program is similar to Windows Explorer. It allows you to view the files and folders in the disc image. In the case of writeable media you can drag and drop files and folders from the Windows Explorer and delete files.

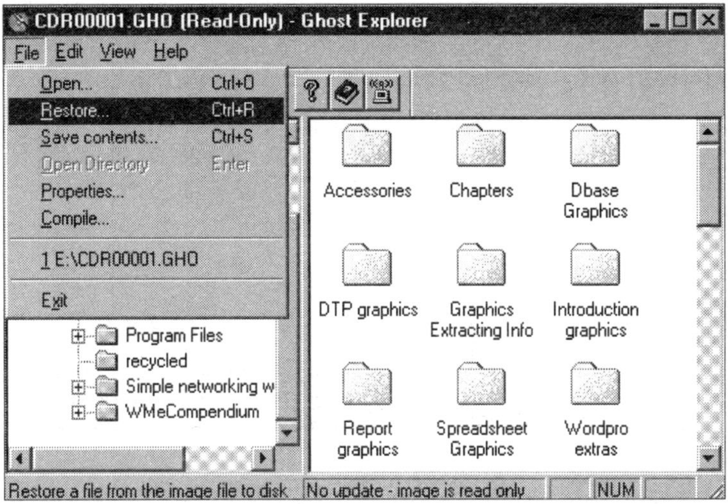

The above is a partition image saved on CD-R. Therefore it is **Read-Only** and it is not possible to add or delete files. To do this you must use a rewriteable medium such as a ZIP disc, a JAZ disc or CD-RW.

The **File** menu allows you to **Restore** a file or folder to any location of your choice. Simply highlight the file or folder, then select the destination location for the restored file or folder.

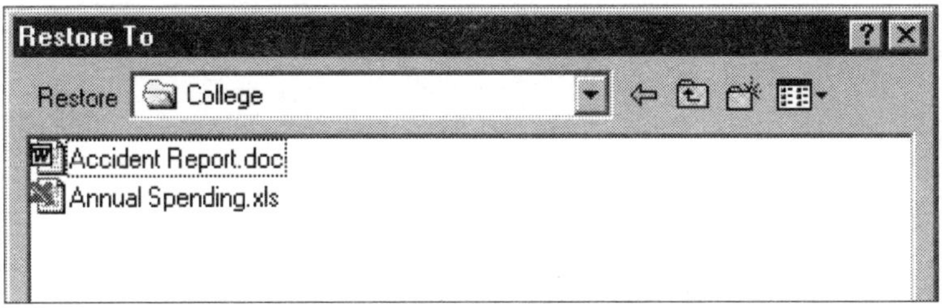

Wiping a Hard Disc

Sometimes it's necessary, perhaps after hours of problems and frustration, to wipe the hard disc completely and start again from scratch. This is probably the most dangerous thing you can do with your computer and must be undertaken with extreme care. The worst case scenario is that you could lose all of your software (programs) and all of your work (data files). However, with a little care and planning, the risks can be minimal. Before attempting this work you should ensure the following:

You have a floppy "boot" disc which will enable your computer to start up the computer, **with access to the CD drive**. Such a disc is the Windows Me Startup Disc, described earlier in this chapter. If you didn't create one during the original installation of Windows Me, then one can be created from **Start**, **Settings**, **Control Panel**, **Add/Remove Programs** and **Startup Disk**. Alternatively, if your machine is too incapacitated to create a startup disc, you will have to gain access to another computer running Windows Me and create a startup disc.

This will enable your machine to be started and the hard disc to be wiped and prepared for use. However, in order to recover all of your programs and data files you must have either:

- A complete backup on tape, CD-R or CD-RW, ZIP or JAZ disc of your entire hard disc, as discussed earlier in the sections on tape backups and disc images.

Or:

- All of the original CDs and discs, (including the Windows Me CD and applications like MS Office on CD) to enable your software to be installed from scratch.

Plus backups of all your data files on disc or tape.

Partitioning and Formatting

A hard disc can consist of one partition which occupies the entire hard disc area, or the disc can be divided into several smaller partitions. Partitions can act as separate drives, with their own drive letter, enabling them to be treated like physical drives. The example below shows a computer containing two physical hard discs. Drive **C:** is the primary hard disc and consists of one partition comprising the whole of the hard disc. The second hard disc has been divided into two partitions, **F:** and **G:**. (Letters **D:** and **E:** having been used for the ZIP drive and the Compact Disc CD-RW drive).

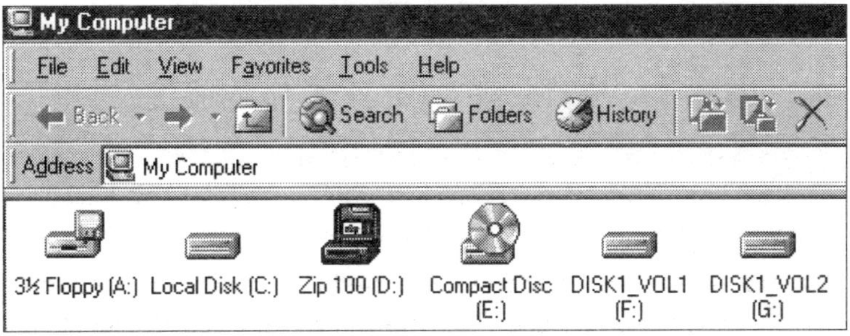

The simplest configuration is to have one primary partition taking up the whole of the **C:** drive. However, it is also possible to have a primary partition taking up say 50% of the **C:** drive. The remaining 50% is created as an *extended partition.* An extended partition can be divided into a number of further *logical drives*, each having their own drive letter, **D:** and **E:** for example. Drive letters are allocated automatically by the computer. (The extended partition doesn't have a drive letter itself.)

So, for example, a 10GB hard disc could have a primary partition of 6GB on which you install the Windows Me operating system and all of your software. The primary partition would be set as *active* during the partition process. This means the computer will start up from this drive. The remaining 4GB would be created as an extended partition, which could then be sub-divided into two logical drives of 2GB each. These would be used for storing data files.

Dividing up a large drive in this way makes for some simplification in managing and backing up the hard disc. For example Nero or Norton Ghost, as discussed earlier, can be used to create a backup image of an entire partition.

If you have more than one hard drive fitted to your machine, the second drive can also be divided into a number of logical drives in an extended partition. It is not necessary to have a primary partition in the second drive.

Creating Partitions

First boot the computer from the Windows Me Startup Disc. (You need to make sure your computer is set up to boot from a floppy disc, as described on page 93.) Then select, from the menu which appears, the option to start with CD-ROM support. The screen will show the **A:\>** prompt.

The program which divides the hard disc into partitions is known as **FDISK** and this is contained on the startup disc in drive **A:**. To start the partitioning process, at the **A:\>** prompt, type **FDISK** and press the **Enter** key.

You will be informed that your computer has a disc larger than 512MB. You will then be asked: **Do you wish to enable large disk support (Y/N)...? [Y]** which you should answer in the affirmative.

The FDISK menu options are presented on the screen in text mode. To select an option, type the number and press **Enter**.

```
                    FDISK Options

Current fixed disk drive: 1

Choose one of the following:

1. Create DOS partition or Logical DOS Drive
2. Set active partition
3. Delete partition or Logical DOS Drive
4. Display partition information
5. Change current fixed disk drive

Enter choice: [1]
```

If the hard disc has been used before, you will need to remove any existing partitions. (Please note, this operation will destroy any existing programs or data, which should have been backed up as mentioned earlier.) Select option **4. Display partition information**.

```
                    Display Partition Information

Current fixed disk drive: 1

Partition  Status  Type    Volume Label  Mbytes  System   Usage
  C: 1       A     PRI DOS                 8032   FAT32    100%


Total disk space is 8033 Mbytes (1 Mbyte = 1048576 bytes)
```

Note the drive letter (such as **C:** or **D:**) and any volume names which may have been given. Now remove the existing partitions using the option:

3. Delete partition or Logical Dos Drive

After removing all of the existing partitions, you can now create the primary partition using:

1. Create DOS partition or Logical DOS Drive

The menu shown below appears:

```
             Create DOS Partition or Logical DOS Drive

      Current fixed disk drive: 1

      Choose one of the following:

      1. Create Primary DOS Partition
      2. Create Extended DOS Partition
      3. Create Logical DOS Drive(s) in the Extended DOS Partition

      Enter  choice: [1]
```

Choose the option:

1. Create Primary DOS Partition

You are then asked:

Do you wish to use the maximum available size for a Primary DOS partition and make the partition active (Y/N)...? [Y]

If you choose **Y**, the whole of the hard disc will be devoted to this one partition. (As mentioned previously, *active* means the computer will start up from this partition/hard disc.)

If you want to set up additional logical drives, choose **N** in reply to the above question. You are given the chance to enter a % or a size in MB for the primary partition to occupy. The remainder of the hard disc will become an extended partition on which the logical drives can be created. This is done using options **2** and **3** off the previous menu. After you have created an extended partition and logical drives, you need to set the primary partition as **Active** using the option off the first menu, shown on page 110:

2. Set active partition

When you have partitioned the hard disc, each partition must be formatted. This wipes clean the partition, destroying any existing programs and data. The format program should be on your boot disc.

Formatting a Drive

This is used to format an entire hard disc or a logical drive. To format the **C:** drive, at the **A:\>** prompt, type **format C:** and press **Enter** i.e.

A:\> format C: <Enter>

You are warned that all data will be lost and asked to choose **Y** or **N** to proceed with the format. Choose **Y** to start the format. You are informed of progress during the format and at the end are given the option of adding a volume label. The formatting process must be repeated for any of the logical drives you may have created, such as **D**, **E**, or **F**.

Care must always be use with the format command, since its effect is to wipe clean the entire hard disc or partition.

Restoring Your Software and Data Files

Software

You are now ready to begin reinstalling your software, starting with the Windows Me operating system. (This step will not be necessary if you have created a disc or partition image containing the Windows Me operating system, using a program like Norton Ghost.) To reinstall Windows Me, place the original CD in the drive. Then select the CD ROM drive by typing the drive letter followed by a colon, **E:** for example, and pressing **Enter**. To start installing Windows Me, at the prompt type **setup** i.e:

E:\> setup <Enter> (if **E:** is the CD-ROM drive)

The installation of Windows Me now proceeds largely unassisted, although you will be asked to enter an alphanumeric product key, a 25 character string on a label on the back of your Windows Me CD case. If you are installing an *upgrade* version of Windows Me, (rather than a standalone *full* version) you will be asked to briefly install the CD containing a previous full version, such as Windows 95 or Windows 98.

You will now need to reinstall all of the applications software such as Microsoft Office, from their original CDs or floppy discs, using the setup procedures given in the documentation.

Data Files

Any data files you have backed up to CD-R, CD-RW, ZIP or JAZ disc can be restored by drag and drop methods in Windows Explorer or My Computer.

If you have used a dedicated backup program then this will need to be reinstalled (after first installing Windows Me from its CD), before restoring the programs and data from the backup media such as tape or disc.

If you have used a disc imaging program like Ahead Nero or Norton Ghost discussed earlier in this chapter, reboot the computer using a special boot disc as described earlier. Then you can restore the entire hard disc drive or partition from the CD-R, CD-RW or other media.

If you created an image of a primary disc partition containing the Windows Me operating system, restoring this should avoid the need for a separate installation of Windows Me from its original CD.

Installing a New Hard Disc Drive

This seems like a major technical operation, but I have found it to be fairly straight forward. The main reasons for fitting a new hard disc would include:

- An old hard disc has failed completely and must be replaced.
- The capacity of the present hard disc is inadequate for your burgeoning collection of software and data files.

The second situation is commonplace, with the ever-increasing bulk of new software. The relatively low price of hard discs of 20GB capacity, and with 70GB drives hard discs also available at a price, make this a cost effective upgrade to a computer. If your machine is a few years old, you need to check with the manufacturer that it can use the full capacity of a new high capacity drive. It may need a software upgrade to its BIOS, an operation which can sometimes be carried out by a download from the Internet.

If you are fitting a new hard disc to increase storage capacity, then you may decide to keep the old hard disc in the computer, in addition to the new one. In this arrangement, the main hard disc drive is known as the **Master** and the old one is labelled the **Slave**.

In this case, the new, high capacity drive would be set up as the active primary partition, as discussed earlier in this chapter. This is the configuration in one of my machines. The new hard disc drive (drive **C:**) has a capacity of 20GB while the older one has two logical drives (normally **D:** and **F:**) of 2GB and 1GB. Using this sort of arrangement you can still access all of your old data files. Alternatively, if you wish to transfer all of your programs and data files to the new hard disc, you can use a disc imaging program like Norton Ghost (described earlier) to "clone" the old hard disc to the new one in the same computer.

The old drive is also very useful as a fast backup system for providing an extra copy of important files, bearing in mind that you still need more secure backups on a removable medium like a CD-R, CD-RW or ZIP disc.

N.B.

Before starting work it is essential that you back up all of your programs and data files as described on the previous pages.

Before starting work with a screwdriver, make sure the computer is switched off and the power lead disconnected. Discharge any static electricity (which can damage components in the computer), by touching a metal object, such as the chassis of the computer. Alternatively wear one of the special anti-static wrist straps available from computer and electronic stores.

Installing the new hard disc involves removing the casing and fitting the new drive, either in the place of the old one or in a vacant bay in the case of a second drive. A hard disc is normally held in place by four small screws. Note the position of the coloured edge on the wide, flat ribbon cable at the back of the drive. This connects the hard disc drive to the EIDE slot on the motherboard (the main circuit board of your computer). If you are removing the old disc drive, disconnect the ribbon cable and the multi-coloured power cable. Now set the jumper on the back of the new hard disc to *master*. A diagram showing the positions for the jumper for the various configurations normally appears on the disc drive itself. If you are keeping the old hard disc drive in the machine, set it as the *slave*. Often the slave configuration is achieved by removing the jumper altogether.

Each hard disc drive should be connected to the original EIDE ribbon cable attached to the primary EIDE connector on the motherboard, with the coloured edge in the correct position, as in the old hard disc configuration. The coloured edge should be nearest the pin marked 1 on the connector at the back of the hard disc and on the motherboard EIDE connector. If in doubt, consult the installation guide for the new hard disc drive or the manufacturer's Web site.

Make sure that the hard disc(s) are securely held in place by the retaining screws and that a multi-coloured power cable is fitted to each hard drive. If you don't have a spare power lead for a second hard drive, it's possible to obtain a y-shaped piece which converts one connector into two. Replace the cover of your machine.

You are almost ready to start your machine from a Windows Me startup disc or perhaps a boot disc created by a program like Norton Ghost.

However, you need to check that your computer is set up to detect all of the hard disc drives. This done by checking the CMOS/BIOS settings as described on page 94 of this book. Switch on the computer and press **Delete** (or whatever) to enter the BIOS. Your computer may have an option called **LBA** (Logical Block Addressing) to support large hard discs. If so, make sure LBA is switched on. Also check that the BIOS is set to **Auto Detect** the hard disc drive(s) when the computer starts up again for the first time after the modifications. Auto Detect picks up all of the hard disc parameters (the technical specifications of the particular hard disc), so they don't need to be entered manually.

After checking the BIOS setup, use the on-screen instructions to save the settings and exit the setup feature. The computer will then resume the floppy disc boot up process which was interrupted by diverting into the CMOS setup. Then you will be able to partition and format your new hard disc as described earlier in this chapter. You may wish to copy your old hard disc to the new, as described earlier, or install Windows and all of your software and data files from scratch. To use your old hard disc as an additional backup storage device, partition and format the drive as described previously. (Please note that a *secure* backup requires copies of important files to be stored onto *removable* media such as CD-R or ZIP disc and kept in a safe place.)

Summary: Recovery Methods

- A Windows Me Startup Disc can be created (with CD-ROM support), to enable your computer to be restored to life after serious problems or major modification. The startup disc can be created during the Windows Me installation process or at any time afterwards.
- Label all of your CDs and removable discs and keep them in a safe place. This includes CDs for Windows Me and Microsoft Office, etc., and backup media containing your data files. Also support software *(drivers)* for devices like CD-RW drives.
- To boot up your computer from a floppy "boot" disc, it may be necessary to alter the CMOS settings. These are entered by pressing the **Delete** key (or similar) soon after the computer is switched on.
- A hard disc consists of one or more *partitions*. The *primary partition* is set as *active* and, in normal operation, is used to boot the computer. The primary partition can take up the whole hard disc or just a portion, the remainder being divided into a number of small partitions. These are known as *logical drives*, each having a drive letter such as **D:** or **E:**. The logical drives can be treated like separate physical drives.
- A disc image is a copy of *everything* on the hard disc. The disc image may be stored on a backup medium such as CD-R, CD-RW, ZIP or JAZ disc. Later the disc image may be used to restore everything to the hard disc, if necessary.
- Disc imaging software may be supplied with your CD-RW drive or bought separately, e.g. Norton Ghost and Ahead Nero.
- There can be problems if you try to copy files which are currently active. Some disc imaging software runs from floppy discs, using the old DOS operating system, instead of running in the Windows Me operating system, from the hard disc. This enables all Windows Me files to be copied successfully.

- Disc imaging software allows large image files to span several backup discs. You are prompted to insert a new CD-R (or whatever medium) during the backup process.
- Various file *compression* options may be available, allowing more files to be copied to a given backup disc. Higher compression results in a slower copying process.
- Norton Ghost Explorer allows individual files to be added to a disc image on a rewriteable media such as CD-RW or ZIP disc, using "drag and drop" from Windows Explorer. Individual files may also be deleted from an image in Ghost Explorer, when using rewriteable media like CD-RW. On a read-only medium like CD-R, Ghost Explorer allows individual files to be copied from CD-R to hard disc.
- Partitioning and formatting a hard disc removes all programs and data. Make sure you are capable of restoring all of your software and data files *before* using these commands. Unless you are restoring a complete disc image containing the Windows Me operating system, you will need to re-install your original Windows Me CD. If this is an *upgrade* version of Windows Me, you will also need to briefly insert a *full* version of Windows 95 or Windows 98, for verification.
- If fitting a new hard disc to increase your computer's storage capacity, you may wish to retain the old hard disc in the computer as an additional backup device. The new drive is set as the *master* while the old one becomes the *slave*. The master or slave configuration is determined by the positioning of a movable jumper on the back of each hard disc drive.
- If necessary, the contents of the old hard disc can be "cloned" across to the new one, using a program like Norton Ghost. The old hard disc can then be partitioned and formatted to create a blank storage area.
- Using a second hard disc for extra storage is fast and convenient, but is not a *secure* backup method compared with removable media like CD-R, CD-RW, ZIP or JAZ disc.

Protection Against Viruses

Introduction - What is a Virus?

A virus is a small computer program written maliciously to cause damage to software and data and to cause maximum inconvenience to the ordinary user. The virus enters a computer system insidiously, often from a floppy disc. If not detected the virus replicates and spreads throughout a hard disc; some viruses may only cause trivial damage - such as displaying a 'humorous' message - while others can destroy files or wipe an entire hard disc.

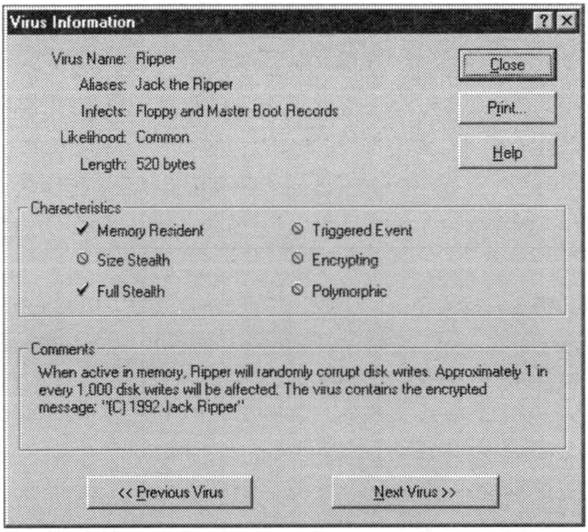

Even when a virus doesn't do any serious damage to files and software, the time spent in eradicating it is likely to be considerable - not to mention the anxiety caused to the user whose work is interrupted, possibly for a long time.

Writing viruses is an act of vandalism and can result in a prison sentence. Virus writers are invariably male, presumably seeing the virus as a demonstration of their misplaced skill.

Viruses can exist on floppy and hard discs. They can also reside temporarily in the computer's memory - but they are removed from the memory when the computer is switched off. Viruses do not permanently damage the physical parts of a computer - hardware components such as the memory or the printer.

Floppy discs are a major source of virus infection, but viruses can also enter your system via a modem from the Internet, perhaps through email *attachments*, the programs or documents "clipped" onto an email.

The Norton AntiVirus 2001 software package has a scanning program which constantly monitors email attachments being downloaded to your computer from an Internet mail server.

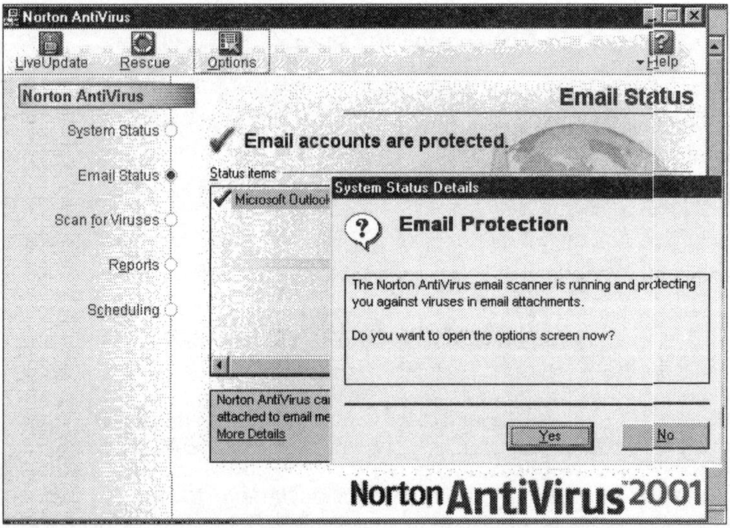

Great care should be taken when opening emails of doubtful origin; if you are suspicious the email should be deleted immediately without opening the attachments.

Types of Virus

The File Virus

These viruses attach themselves to program or executable files. These files (having extensions such as .EXE, .COM, .SYS, etc.) are part of applications software packages like Word 6 or Excel 5. The file virus itself will not infect the documents or spreadsheets produced using the software, although they can be infected by the macro virus discussed next.

The Macro Virus

This type of virus has been developed to infect the *documents* produced using programs such as Word and Excel. These documents have their own inbuilt programming language. This allows the advanced user to write *macros*, or small routines for automating groups of frequently used instructions. Unfortunately the virus writers have found ways of writing viruses in the macro language. Now even Word documents and Excel spreadsheets are vulnerable to virus attack.

So it's possible for your hard disc to be infected with viruses spread in document files received via the Internet or email (as well as files transferred from floppy disc).

Boot Sector Viruses

The boot sector is an area of a floppy or hard disc and contains information needed when the computer is started up or "booted".

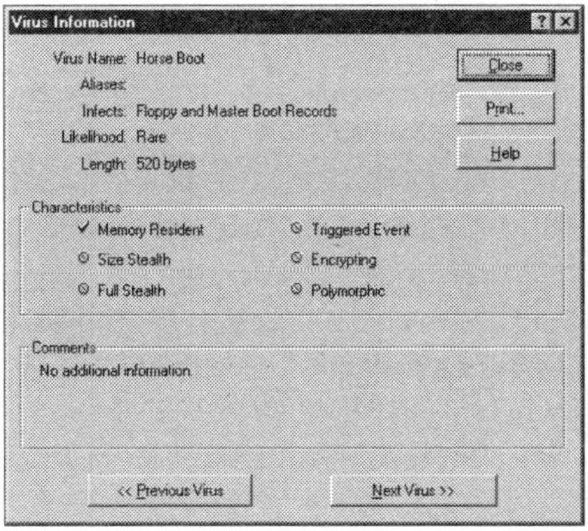

Even a floppy disc containing only data files has a boot sector which can be infected by a virus. If such an infected floppy disc is inadvertently left in a disc drive when the computer is switched off, next time the machine is "booted", the virus can spread via the memory to the hard disc.

Stealth Viruses

There are many ways in which the virus writer tries to cause damage whilst avoiding detection. The stealth virus actively tries to conceal itself by making the computer behave normally until it's ready to strike.

Trojans

The Trojan, as its name implies, is a program with an apparently genuine function, but which is really designed to do damage. It is not a virus since it does not replicate itself.

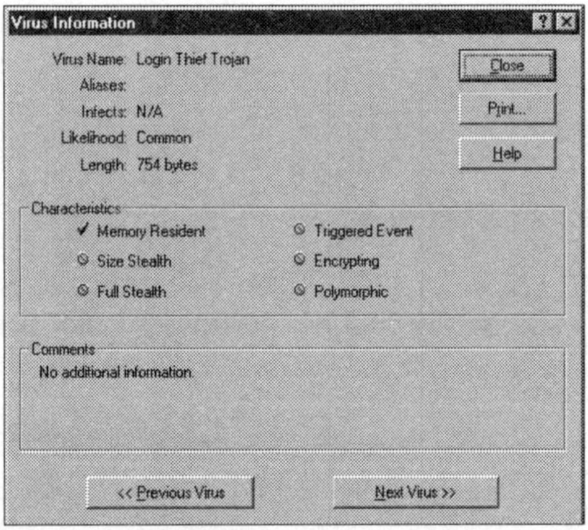

One such Trojan takes over a user's email and uses it to send offensive messages - damaging the reputation of the innocent user. Logic Bombs and Time Bombs are types of Trojan which are triggered when a certain event or date occurs such as Friday 13th. The Michelangelo virus is triggered on the painter's birthday, March 6th.

The Polymorphic Virus

This changes its identity every time it replicates; it does this by repeatedly encrypting or encoding itself.

At the time of writing there are over 48,000 known viruses, with hundreds of new ones discovered every month. The names are assigned by the anti-virus firms or by the virus writers themselves. Each of these known viruses contains a unique piece of programming code which the main anti-virus packages can detect. This code is known as the virus "signature".

An increasing problem at the moment is the hoax email, warning of the dangers of a non-existent virus. Although harmless in that no damage is caused to the computer or its software, the effect is to spread panic and anxiety amongst a large number of people.

Requirements of Anti-Virus Software

The last ten years have seen the evolution of an ever-increasing list of computer viruses. Windows Me does not contain its own anti-virus software. However, several major companies have developed anti-virus software to detect and eradicate virus infection. Three of the leading software packages are Norton AntiVirus 2001, McAfee VirusScan, and Dr. Solomon's Anti-Virus Toolkit. These provide users with regular updates of virus definitions. Then the viruses can be detected and dealt with.

The anti-virus software must find and destroy the existing base of many thousands of known viruses. A small extract from the **Virus List** from Norton AntiVirus 2001 is shown on the right. The anti-virus software must also recognize any 'virus-like activity,' possibly caused by new and unknown viruses.

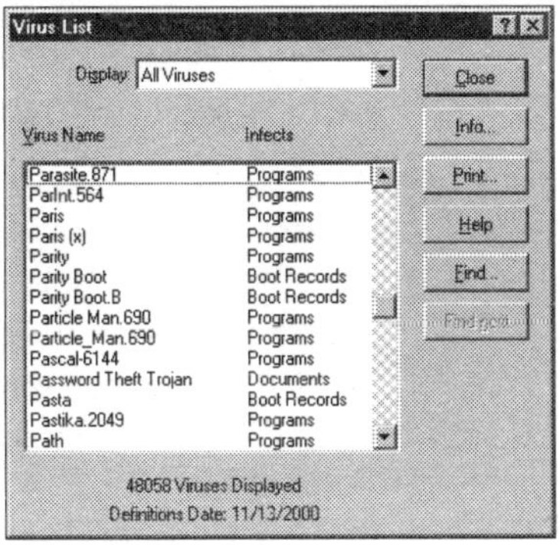

Virus-like activity would include the computer trying to alter program files - this shouldn't happen during the normal operation of the computer.

The main functions of anti-virus software are therefore:

- To continually monitor the memory and vulnerable files, to prevent viruses entering the hard disc and spreading, causing havoc and destruction.
- To allow the user to carry out manual scans to check the memory, floppy and hard discs, whenever it is felt necessary.
- To remove viruses by repairing or deleting infected files.
- To provide a list of definitions of known viruses, which is regularly updated and distributed to the user, perhaps through the Internet.

It is also possible to *schedule* regular scans at certain times on particular days of the week.

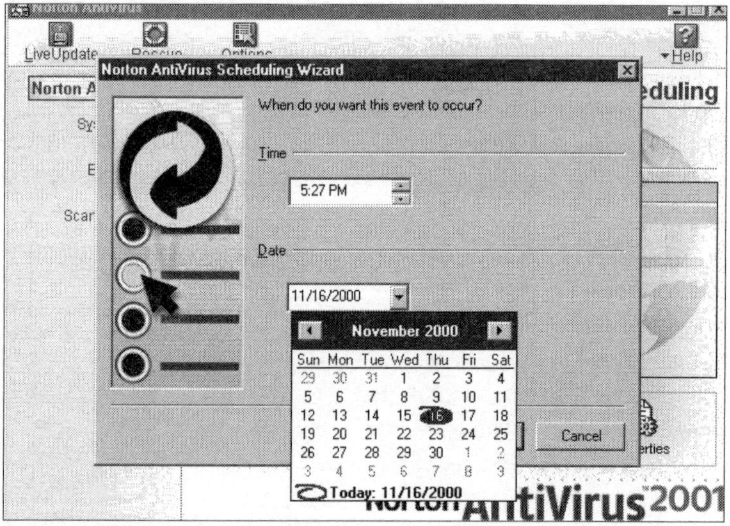

The complete anti-virus software is permanently installed on the hard disc from where a manual scan can be run from the **Programs** menu.

In addition, should the hard disc become severely infected, a "bootable" floppy disc containing the main virus repair program should be available. If a virus strikes, the computer should be shut down to stop the virus spreading. Then the computer can be started from the emergency rescue "disc" and the virus removed from the hard disc.

Features of Anti-Virus Software

When you buy a complete anti-virus package such as Norton AntiVirus 2001, McAfee VirusScan, or Dr. Solomon's Anti-Virus Toolkit, the package will usually comprise a suite of programs providing two different modes of scanning:

First, a scan available "on demand" from the Windows Me menus, like any other piece of software. This will be referred to as a Manual Scan in the following sections.

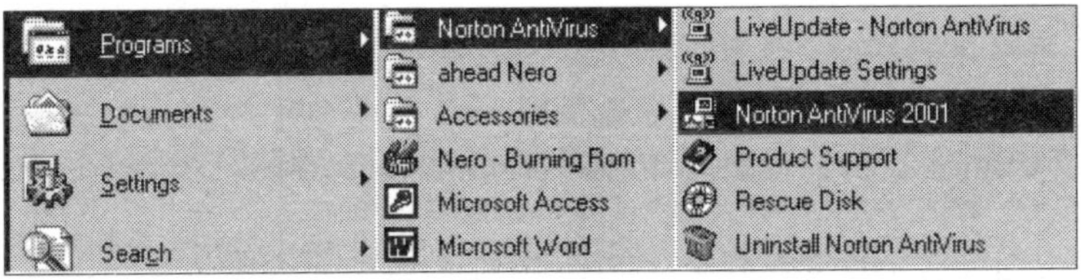

Secondly, a virus scanner which starts up automatically and runs continually in the background, checking files before they are used or as they are received from the email server. Norton AntiVirus 2001 runs the Auto-Protect feature from the time Windows Me starts up.

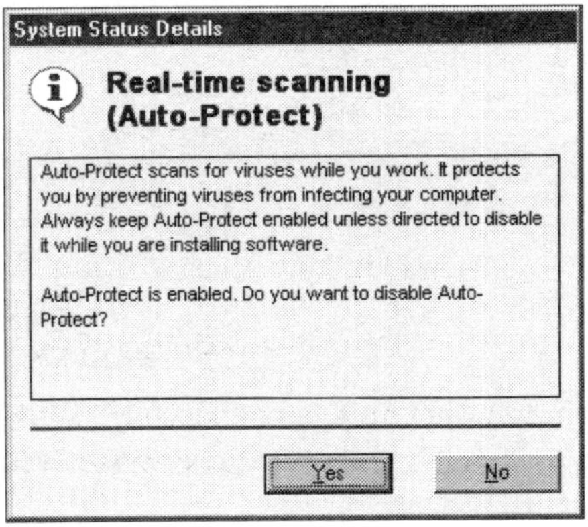

Anti-virus scanners which run continually may need to be temporarily disabled (but not uninstalled) while new software is installed. To temporarily disable the **Auto-Protect** feature in **Norton AntiVirus 2001**, you right click over an icon on the Windows Me taskbar.

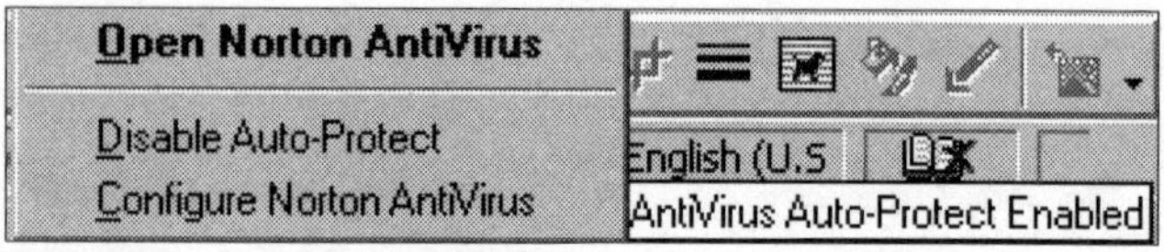

When you are ready to switch the auto scanner back on, invoke the above menu again. This will have changed to display the option **Enable Auto-Protect**.

The Manual Scan

This is the main scanning program launched from the Windows Me program menu. The user can select this scan whenever they wish to check the hard disc or a newly acquired floppy disc. This scanner also carries out the repair of files containing viruses.

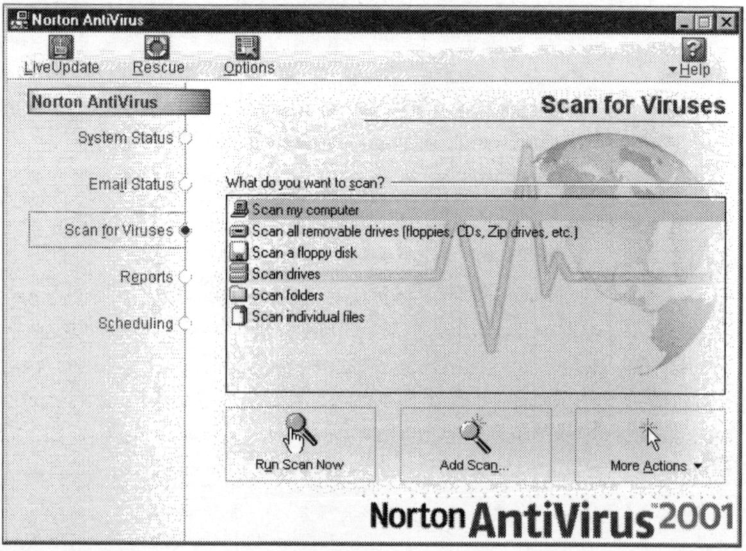

If you select the **Options** button from the previous window, you are presented with the dialogue shown below. You can choose when to start **Auto-Protect** and to switch on or off the scanning of files downloaded from the Internet. The types of file to scan can be selected according to their file extensions such as **.doc**, etc. You may wish to be ultra cautious and scan **All files** or you might just scan those most likely to be infected, i.e. **Program files and documents only....** Norton AntiVirus 2001 examines *compressed files* (discussed later.) Files are not normally infected in their compressed state, but a compressed file might contain a virus which was contracted before it was compressed.

You can also select how the program is to respond if a virus is found.

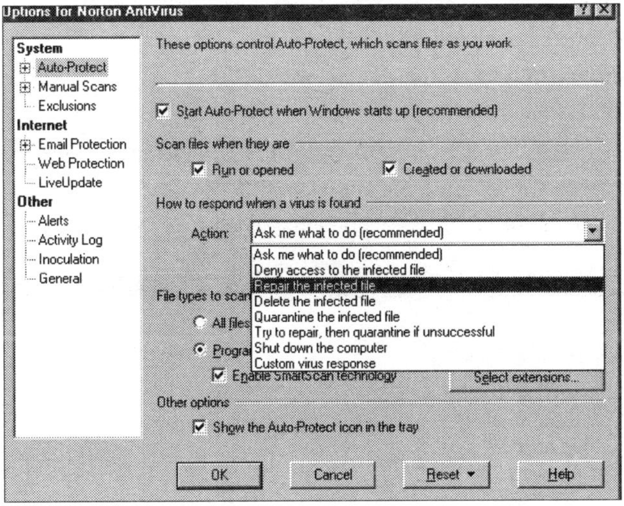

In the above dialogue box, **Quarantine** in Norton AntiVirus 2001 refers to a method of isolating unknown viruses which can't be removed with the existing list of virus definitions. Once in the Quarantine, the virus can't infect the files on the hard disc. Files in the Quarantine area can be sent over the Internet to the Symantec AntiVirus Research Center where they can be examined.

If a new virus is discovered it can be added to the list of virus definitions. This can be downloaded by other Norton AntiVirus 2001 users next time they update their list of virus definitions, then used to detect and eliminate the new virus.

Inoculation in the above window refers to a process where information is recorded about the critical boot records used to start a computer. These are very susceptible to virus attack. The danger is that a brand new, unknown virus could go undetected. Inoculation involves recording exact details of the boot records, like taking a fingerprint. When the boot records are later scanned, any changes to the fingerprint indicate that the boot records may have been infected by an unknown virus. Alternatively, the boot records might have been altered innocently, during the installation of new software.

Once the scan is underway you are informed of progress.

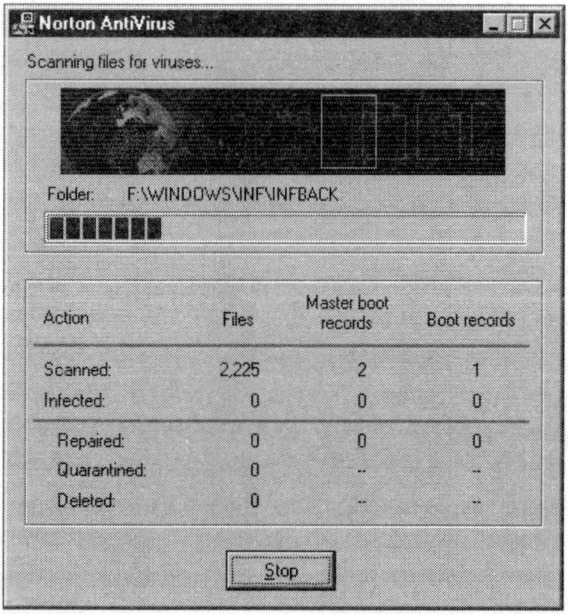

During the scan, viruses which are known can be detected by their "signature" - a unique set of program code or lines of instructions. In the case of new, unknown viruses, the anti-virus software looks for "virus-like activity". For example, if a virus attaches itself to a program, the size of the program file will increase, not something you'd expect in normal usage. However, the stealth virus, for example, tries to avoid detection by falsifying the file size entry, so that the file appears not to have changed.

If a Virus Strikes

If you are unfortunate enough to suffer a virus infection, a warning message will appear on the screen, possibly accompanied by an alarm sound. On finding a virus, the anti-virus programs will prevent access to the infected file.

Normally the software will try to "clean" the infected file by removing the illicit lines of code which constitute the virus. Otherwise the file must be deleted or excluded. Alternatively the program can be set up to take a specific action if a virus is found.

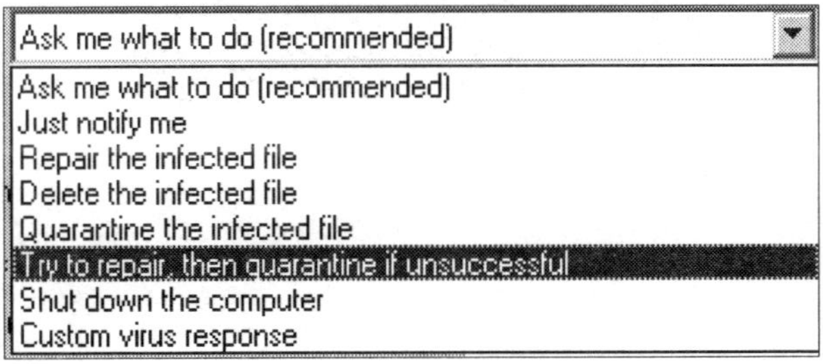

The Virus in Memory

This is an extremely dangerous situation, since the virus is ideally placed to damage any files which are run or accessed from hard or floppy disc.

On finding a virus in memory:

- Shut down the computer immediately, using the correct procedure.
- Switch off the power to the computer. (This will remove the virus from memory).
- Re-start the computer using a write-protected floppy boot disc (which must be known to be free from viruses.)

The main anti-virus packages include a diskette version of the virus detection/repair program. Use this floppy disc version to find and repair any viruses on the hard disc.

Infected Floppy Discs

If it is suspected that a large number of floppy discs may be infected, they must all be checked and repaired using the main scanning program. In a business, this could be a massive task requiring the allocation of considerable time.

If a New Virus is Discovered

If your software has detected a possible virus, but cannot find it within its list of virus definitions, contact the supplier of your anti-virus software for more information and possible help.

Creating a Rescue Disc

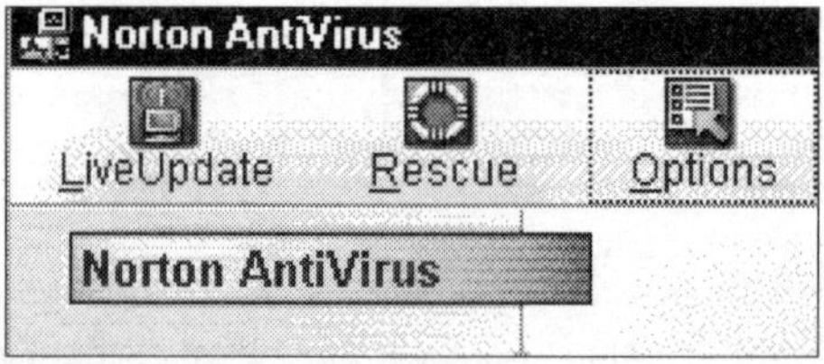

Norton AntiVirus 2001 has a button on the main window, enabling you to create a rescue disc. In fact, what is created is a set of rescue discs.

There are two options for creating sets of Norton rescue discs:

The **Norton Zip Rescue** uses one Zip disc and one floppy disc. The idea is that you shut down and switch off immediately after a virus is discovered. Then you boot up from the rescue discs. In this option, the Zip Rescue, the computer starts in Windows Me, from where you can repair or remove the virus on the hard disc.

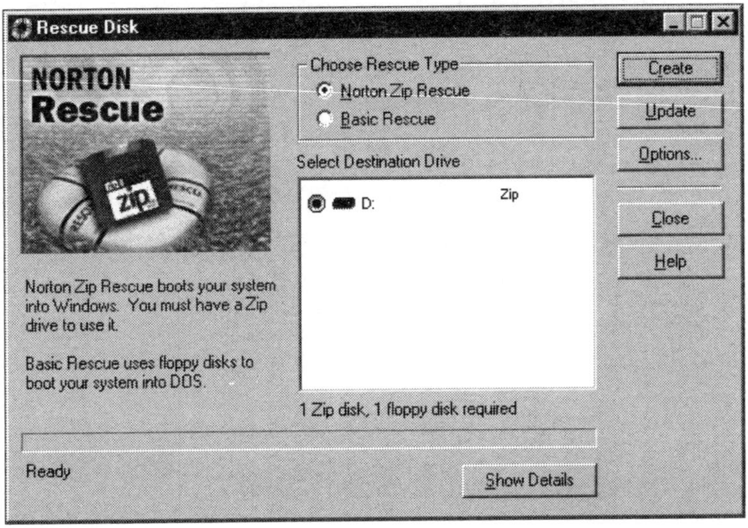

If your machine is not fitted with a ZIP drive, the **Basic Rescue** in Norton AntiVirus 2001 requires a total of five floppy discs. This starts the computer in the old DOS operating system and runs a version of the anti-virus software, allowing viruses to be removed from the hard disc.

In order to boot up from a floppy disc, you may need to alter the CMOS settings in your computer, as discussed earlier in this book.

Updating Your Virus Definitions

Since new viruses are being discovered constantly, you are advised to update your virus definition list at regular intervals, weekly say. If you cannot use the Internet, it should be possible for the supplier of your anti-virus software to send the updates on floppy disc. Norton AntiVirus allows your virus list to be updated automatically when you connect to the Internet or when you select a LiveUpdate from the main window.

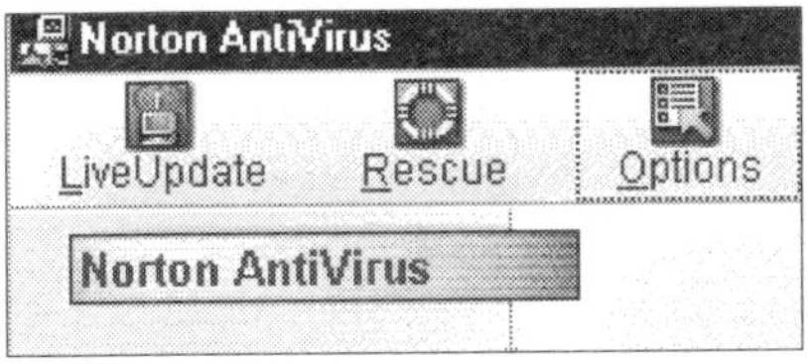

The computer is connected to the Internet and **LiveUpdate** checks to see if you need any downloads to bring your system up to date. At the end of the process you are informed of the components of your system that now contain the latest information.

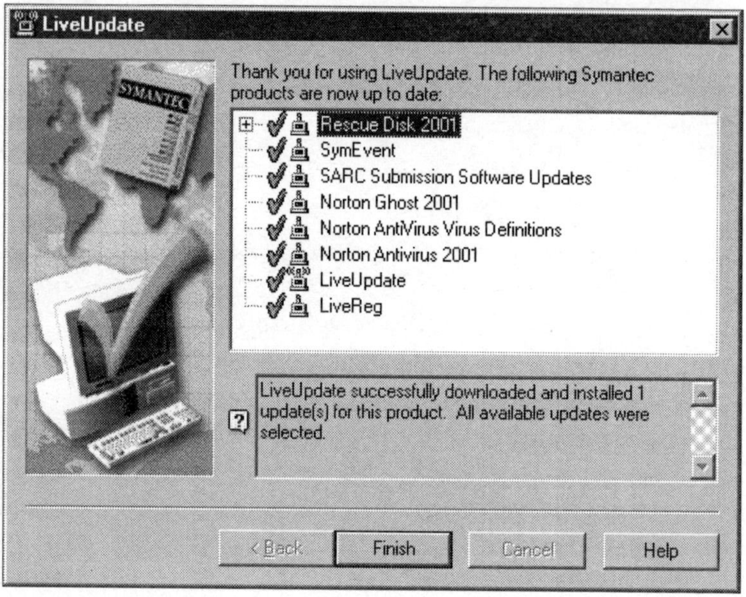

As the list above window shows, other Norton products, apart from AntiVirus 2001, installed on your computer, are also checked and updated if necessary.

Summary: Protection Against Viruses

- Obtain an established anti-virus package such as Norton AntiVirus 2001, McAfee VirusScan, or Dr. Solomon's Anti-Virus Toolkit.
- Install the anti-virus software on your hard disc, configured to provide scans:
    1 automatically on startup and continually in the background while the computer is running
    2 manually i.e. selected from the menus on demand
    3 at regular times, scheduled automatically
- Obtain and install regular software upgrades so that the virus definition list is always up-to-date with the latest known viruses.
- Always run a manual check on all floppy discs acquired from elsewhere. Be extremely sceptical about all discs - even packaged software from reputable companies has been known to be infected.
- If you distribute files yourself, either on floppy disc, ZIP disc, CD or via the Internet, make sure they are scanned and virus free. Although organizations should, in theory, scan all incoming files and discs, it is better to safeguard your own interests by scanning everything before you send it out.
- Carry out regular (weekly, say) manual or scheduled checks on all hard and floppy discs.
- Be vigilant when other people use the computer - insist that any removable discs are scanned before use. Formatting will remove viruses from a floppy disc.
- Make sure you have a clean, i.e. virus free, write-protected boot disc which will allow you to start the computer after a virus attack. A copy of a virus scanner on floppy disc (or ZIP disc or CD) is essential for situations where the hard disc is infected and unfit to use.

- Make backup copies of important files when you know they are clean. An infected file can be repaired by overwriting it with a clean version.
- "Booting up" or starting from an infected floppy disc accidentally left in the drive is a common entry route for viruses. Set your computer to boot up by reading from the hard disc straightaway, without looking at the floppy disc. This is described earlier in this book. This is essential when a large number of people have access to computers.
- Increasing use of the Internet is providing greater opportunities for the virus writers to create havoc. Always carry out a virus check on all files downloaded from the Internet or received as email attachments.
- The compression program WinZip (discussed later) can be set to check downloaded Internet .ZIP files. It does this by extracting the compressed files into a temporary folder before scanning them with your own installed virus scanner. Then the temporary folder is deleted and (assuming they are virus free) the downloaded files are extracted and installed onto your hard disc.
- If you install a program like Norton AntiVirus 2001, which has a virus scanner running permanently in the background, whenever the computer is in use, this will probably need to be briefly *disabled* (not uninstalled) whenever any new software is installed.

7

Compressing Files

Introduction

The process of compressing files has been around for some years. It was pioneered by software such as PKZIP and in recent years, WinZip from Nico Mak Computing, Inc. The compressed files are generally known as .ZIP files. The purpose of compression is to reduce the size of files, thereby increasing the effective capacity of storage media such as hard discs, floppy discs and CDs. While the arrival of hard discs of gigantic size has lessened the pressure for ultra compact storage, there are still advantages to be gained by compressing files:

1 Compressed files can be transmitted much more quickly across the Internet and as email attachments.

2 When transporting files between computers or making security backups on removable media such as floppy disc, ZIP disc or writeable CD, many fewer discs are required.

3 Files which are not used frequently but which may be needed in future can be *archived* effectively by saving them as compressed files.

Compression is achieved by storing the data in the files more efficiently. Some files compress more than others. This is because compression works by picking out common patterns in a file (words like "to" or "the" and spaces, for example) and representing them in a shorter code than normal. So file compression might allow you, for example, to store data on one floppy disc which would otherwise require several.

Previous versions of Microsoft Windows did not contain file compression software. Instead the user had to rely on third party products such as WinZip, mentioned previously. However, Windows Me has introduced a feature which provides a very simple means of creating .ZIP files,

involving little more than dragging and dropping files into special **Compressed Folders**. Compressed Folders can work with .ZIP files created by other file compression software such as WinZip. This chapter describes the features of Compressed Folders and also discusses WinZip, which contains many useful features for creating and managing .ZIP files, including virus checking using your own anti-virus software (if installed).

Before compressed files can be used again they must be expanded to restore them to their original size. This process is known as *unzipping* or *extraction*. Normally, to extract a .ZIP file you must have a copy of the extraction program installed on your hard disc. However, it is possible to produce a special type of compressed file which can extract itself. When the new compressed file is created, instead of being saved as a .ZIP file, it is saved as an .EXE file. This includes, within the compressed file itself, the program which does the "unzipping".

This self-extracting file may therefore be used on computers without a separate installation of the compression/extraction software. As it is an .EXE file, it can be invoked like any other application, i.e. by clicking on the filename in Explorer. Existing .ZIP files can usually be converted to self-extracting .EXE files in software like Winzip, using a menu option.

Although Windows Me now provides the Compressed Folders feature, programs like WinZip contain many features which may justify their purchase. A full evaluation copy of WinZip is available over the Internet. (Downloading software is discussed elsewhere in this book). After an initial evaluation period, a registered version can be purchased, on-line if required. Alternatively, you can buy the boxed package from mail order suppliers like Atlantic Coast Software of Colyton, Devon. Several other file compression packages are available from different companies.

Compressed Folders

The Compressed Folders feature is a component of Windows Me but you may need to make sure it is installed on your hard disc. Select **Start**, **Settings**, **Control Panel** and double click the **Add/Remove Programs** icon.

Now select the **Windows Setup** tab and scroll down and highlight **System Tools**, then click the **Details...** button. Make sure that **Compressed Folders** is ticked, as shown below.

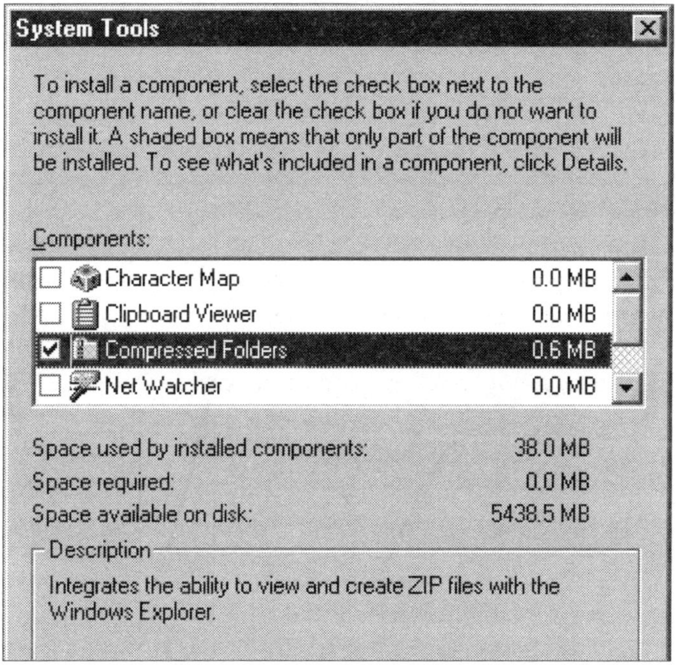

If **Compressed Folders** was not previously ticked, on clicking **OK** you will be asked to insert the Windows Me CD so that installation of the **Compressed Folders** component can take place.

Creating a Compressed Folder

The basic method is to create a Compressed Folder in the location of your choice - perhaps within another folder or on the Windows Me Desktop. Any files you wish to compress are then dragged and dropped into the Compressed Folder. To extract (or decompress) the files they are either dragged to a new location and dropped or you can use the Extraction Wizard.

To create a new Compressed Folder within another folder, open up the folder in **My Computer**. Then select **File** and **New** from the menu. One of the options is to create a **Compressed Folder**:

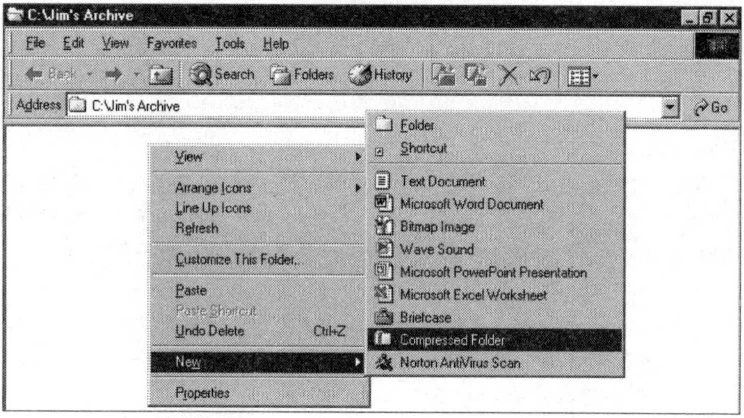

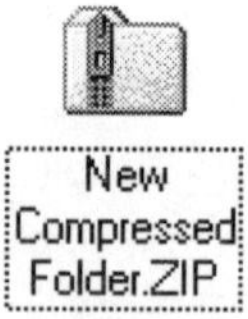

If you select **Compressed Folder** an icon for the Compressed Folder appears and you can replace the name **New Compressed Folder.ZIP** with a name of your choice, such as **Squashed Files.ZIP**, not forgetting to include the **.ZIP** extension. A Compressed Folder can be created on the Windows Desktop by right clicking over an empty spot then selecting **New** and **Compressed Folder**.

Once you have created a Compressed Folder, you can drag files into it in **My Computer** as shown in the example on the next page.

The two windows below have been *tiled vertically* to display the folders on the screen simultaneously. Tiling (discussed earlier in this book) is achieved by selecting from a menu which appears after right clicking on an empty part of the Windows Me TaskBar at the bottom of the screen.

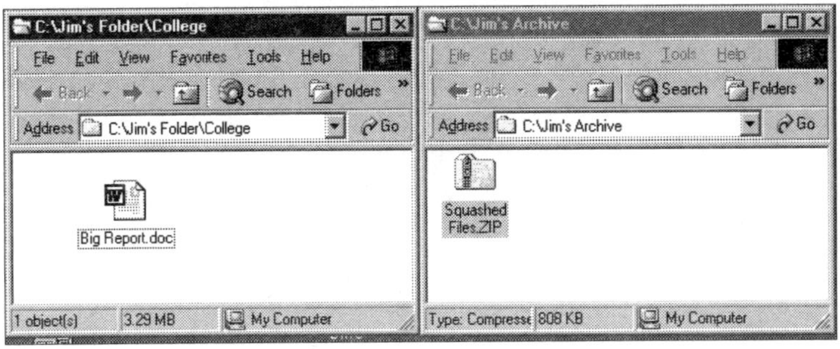

The tiled windows above show the situation after a copy of the file **Big Report.doc** has been dragged and dropped into the Compressed Folder **Squashed Files.ZIP**. The figures at the bottom of the window show that the original file of 3.29MB has been reduced to 808KB - approximately a quarter of the original size. Considerably greater compression ratios than this are possible.

A very quick way to create a Compressed Folder is to right click over a file or folder in My Computer. A menu appears including the options **Send To** and **Compressed Folder**.

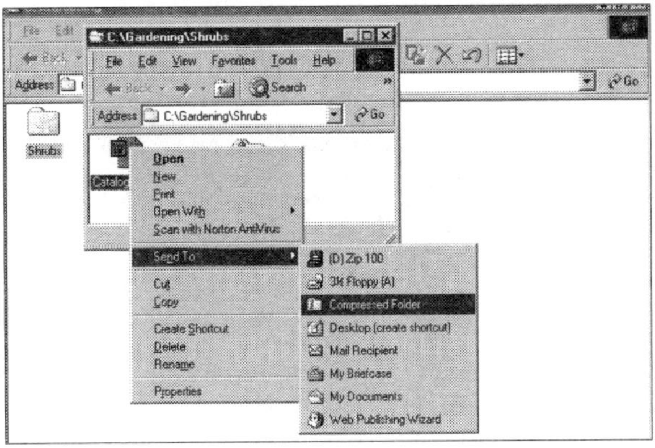

If you choose the **Send To/Compressed Folder** option, a new Compressed Folder is created alongside of the original file or folder and bearing the same name, apart from the .zip extension.

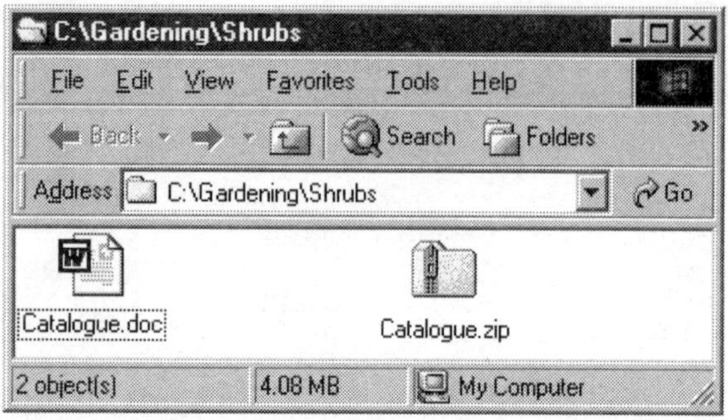

You can **Copy** (or **Move**) a Compressed Folder to another destination by dragging and dropping using the *right* mouse button. (The right button gives a menu allowing you to choose either **Copy** or **Move**.) This includes copying to a floppy disc. Using the above example, a Word file of 3,375KB was compressed to 809KB. This enabled it to be copied to a floppy disc of only 1440KB capacity.

The statistics of a Compressed Folder can be examined by selecting **View** and **Details** from the menu in My Computer.

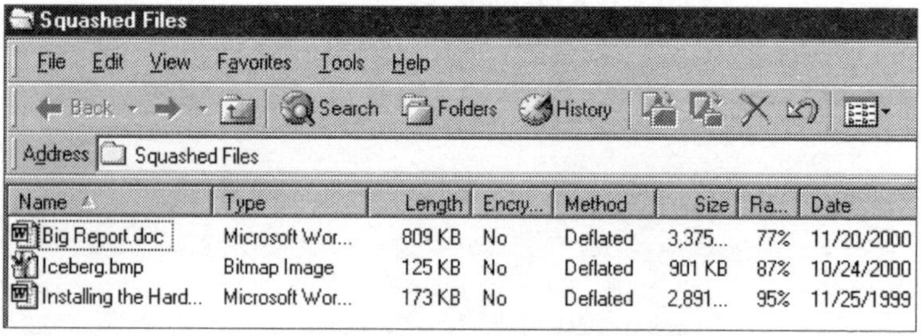

In the above example, **Length** refers to the compressed file and **Size** refers to the uncompressed file size. You can see that the compression ratio **Ra...** varies from 77% to 95% for different documents.

If you double click one of the files shown in the previous Compressed Folder, it will be opened in its associated program, such as Microsoft Word.

Files can be added to an existing Compressed Folder by dragging and dropping. Files can also be deleted by highlighting the file in the Compressed Folder in My Computer and either pressing the **Delete** key or selecting **File** and **Delete** from the menus.

Encrypting a Compressed Folder

This allows you to protect a Compressed Folder with a password and to encrypt the files within it. Right click over the Compressed Folder and select **Encrypt...**. You will be required to enter a password, after which the files in the folder are encrypted.

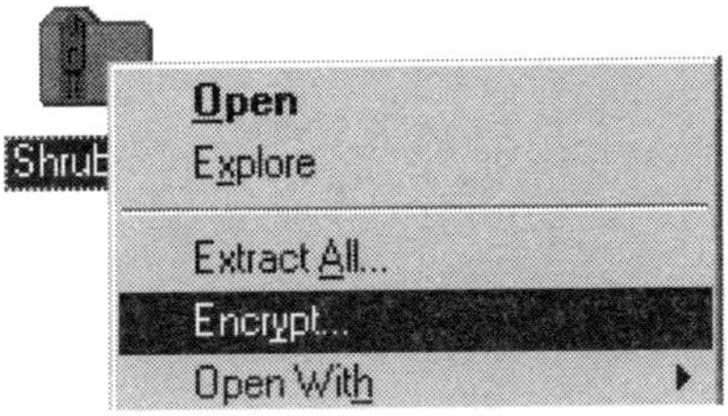

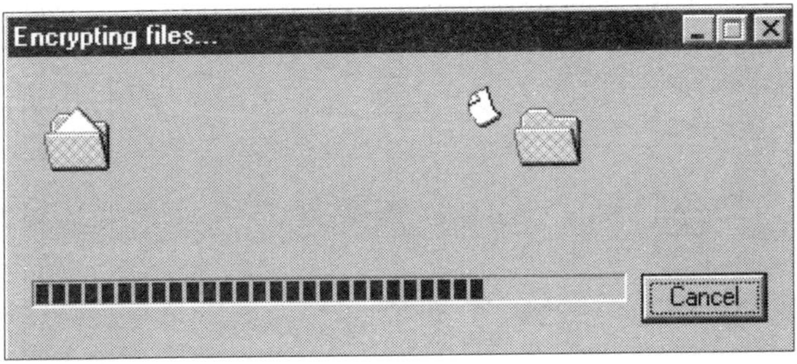

This would be useful, for example, if you sent some files as an email attachment. You could limit access to the folder to those people knowing the password. There is an option to **Decrypt** the Compressed Folder, accessed by right clicking over the icon for the folder.

Extracting Files from a Compressed Folder

Individual files can be extracted i.e. decompressed, by dragging and dropping into their new location. This could be another folder on a hard disc or a removable medium like a floppy or ZIP disc.

When you extract a file from a Compressed Folder, the compressed version of the file remains behind. If this is a very bulky file, you may wish to delete it from the Compressed Folder.

There is an option to extract all of the files from a Compressed Folder. With the Compressed Folder open in My Computer, select **File** and **Extract All...**. After entering the path of the folder (or directory) in which the extracted files are to be placed, the **Extraction Wizard** decompresses the files. The destination for the extracted files could be a removable medium such as a floppy disc, ZIP disc or CD-RW.

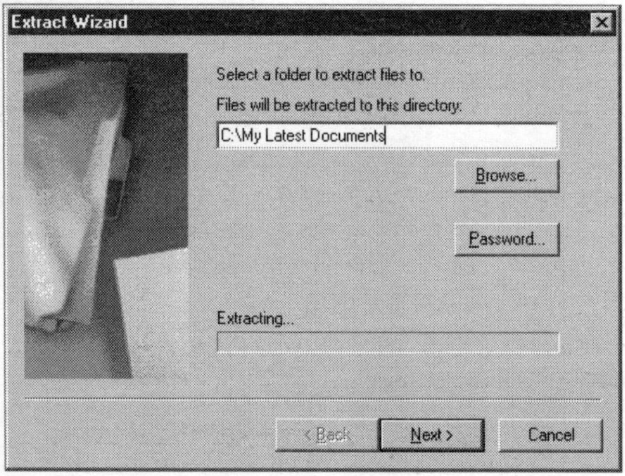

Suppose you transfer a Compressed Folder to another computer, either via a removable medium such as a floppy disc or by sending over the Internet. If the machine is running Windows Me with the Compressed Folders component installed you can extract the files as described in this chapter. Otherwise the files can be extracted using a file compression program like WinZip, described on the following pages. The Compressed Folder behaves like a normal .ZIP file.

WinZip

This is a well-established file compression program from Niko Mak Computing, Inc. and contains many useful features. The program is easy to use yet fast and powerful. You can download a trial version from the Internet from **http://www.winzip.com/** or purchase through the normal mail order suppliers.

WinZip can be launched from its icon on the Windows Me Desktop or from the **Start** menu or the **Programs** menu.

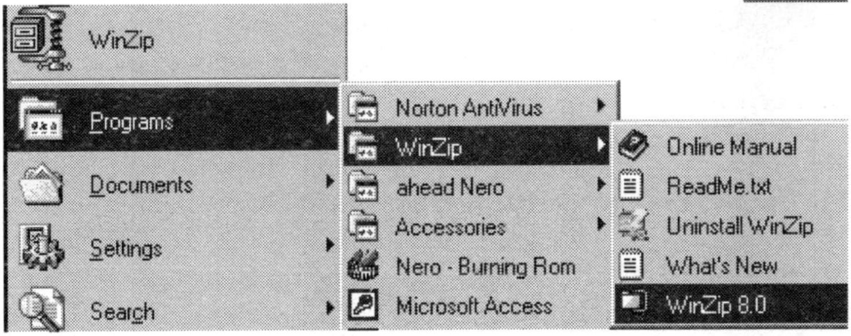

There are two basic modes of operation. In WinZip Classic the user is presented with a Windows style interface with drop down menus. In WinZip Wizard you are guided through the various steps after answering questions about what you want to do, then clicking **Next**.

The WinZip Wizard is particularly useful for searching the hard disc for .ZIP files and adding to the sorted list of **Favorite Zip Folders**.

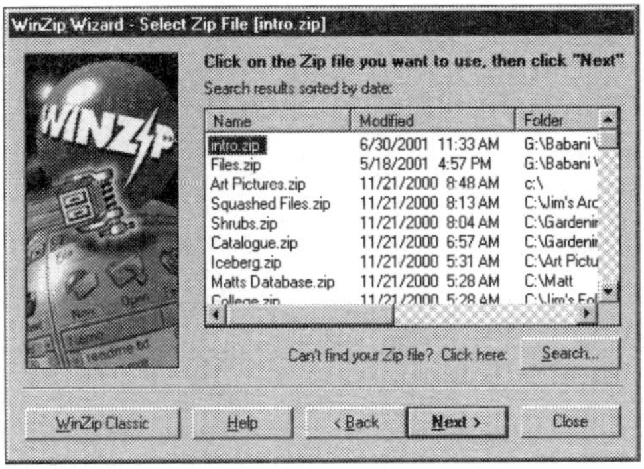

Single buttons allow you to easily switch between the WinZip Wizard and the WinZip Classic interfaces. If you have downloaded a .ZIP compressed file from the Internet, the WinZip Wizard will take over the extraction of the file and its installation into a directory of your choice.

For creating a new .ZIP file or archive, the WinZip Classic interface below is fast and easy to use.

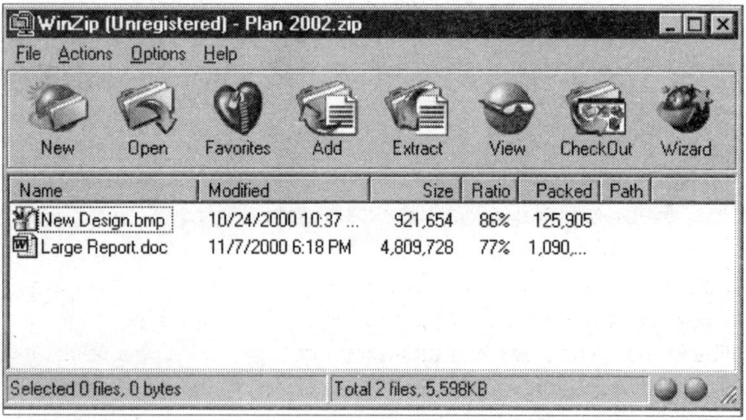

Reading from left to right, the WinZip Classic options shown on the above toolbar are:

Create a **New** .ZIP archive. This is a single file, in this case **Plan2002.zip** as shown in the title bar. The above .ZIP file contains two compressed files.

Open a previously created .ZIP archive. Individual compressed files may be unzipped and there are various file operations such as copying, moving, deleting and renaming.

Clicking the **Favorites** icon opens up the list of .ZIP files on your hard disc. From this you can choose a particular archive to work on.

The **Add** option allows you to browse through your hard disc and add any files to the archive (i.e. .ZIP file) which is currently open in WinZip.

Clicking **Extract** expands a compressed file and allows the user to select a destination folder for the extracted file.

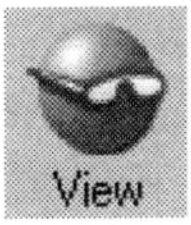

The **View** option allows you to see a selected file running in its associated program. For example, a compressed Word document could be examined running in the Word application. You can also view a file by double clicking on the file name in the .ZIP archive. In fact, this extracts the folder into a temporary folder. Later, after viewing in its associated program, the temporary file is deleted from the hard disc.

The **CheckOut** feature is used to examine files and programs you have received as .ZIP files. WinZip creates a program group in the main Windows Me menu system accessed from **Start** and **Programs**. Each of the individual files in the archive appears as a menu item. If the file is a document, clicking its name causes the file to be viewed running in its associated program. The CheckOut feature can also include a virus scan (discussed later).

The last icon on the WinZip Classic menu bar switches control of the program to the WinZip Wizard.

Creating a .ZIP file in WinZip

The .ZIP file is like a folder in that it contains a set of compressed files. These may be documents produced in programs like Word, Excel or Paint, etc. Once the archive is created, files may be added or deleted. In this example, a new .ZIP file will be created from the following folder, called Future Plans, containing documents created in Word and Paint and shown below in the Windows Explorer.

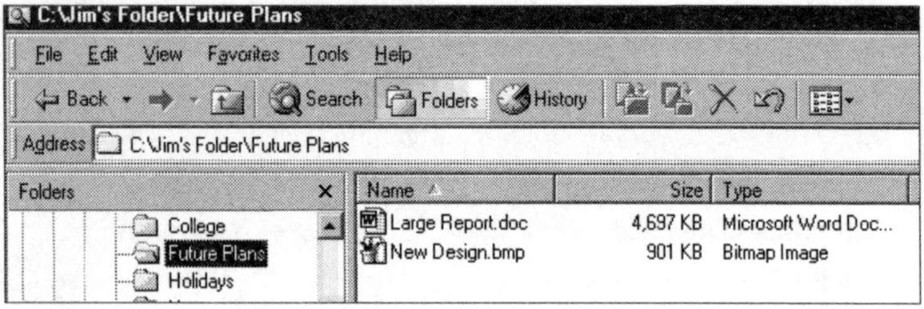

After selecting the **New** icon from the WinZip toolbar, we are asked to give a name to the .ZIP file, **Plan 2002** in this case and select a location for the new archive.

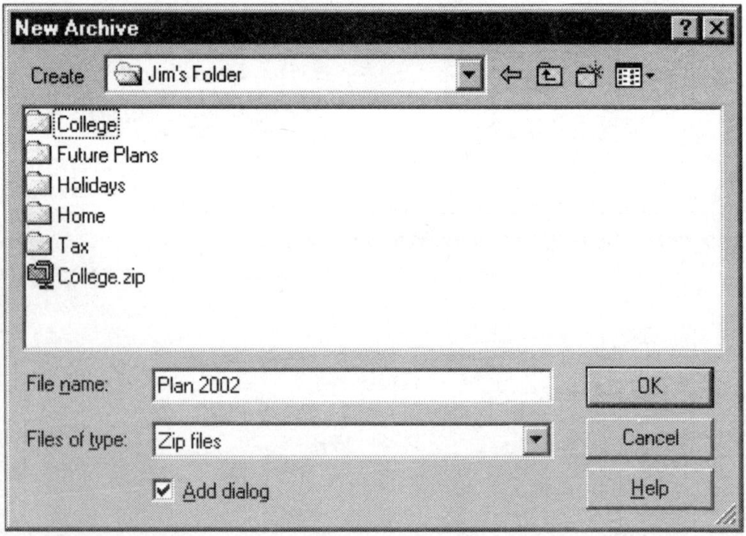

Then we are required to select from our hard disc the files which are to be added to the new archive.

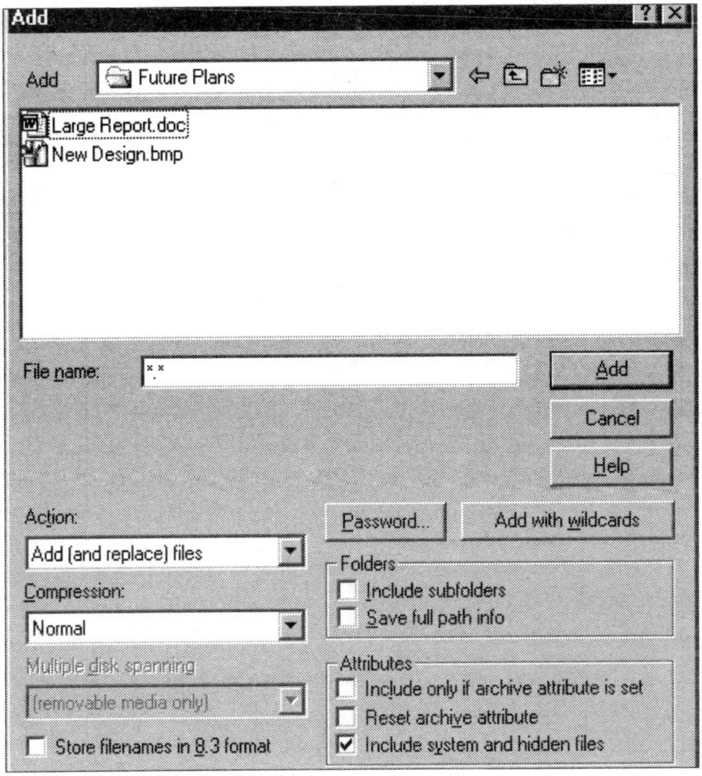

You can highlight an individual file to be added or leave the wildcard *.* to add all files in a folder. Entering *.EXE for example would add all files with the .EXE extension to the new .ZIP file.

Note in the above window, WinZip can be used to compress programs according to the state of their *archive bit*. As discussed elsewhere in this book, the archive bit is used to signify if a file needs to be backed up. You could use WinZip to make regular backups and only record files if they had changed since the last backup.

Once we have clicked on **Add**, the WinZip Classic window appears showing the archive containing, in this example, 2 compressed files. It can be seen that the Word document has been compressed to less than a quarter of its original size whereas the bitmap graphic file has shrunk to a mere seventh of the uncompressed file.

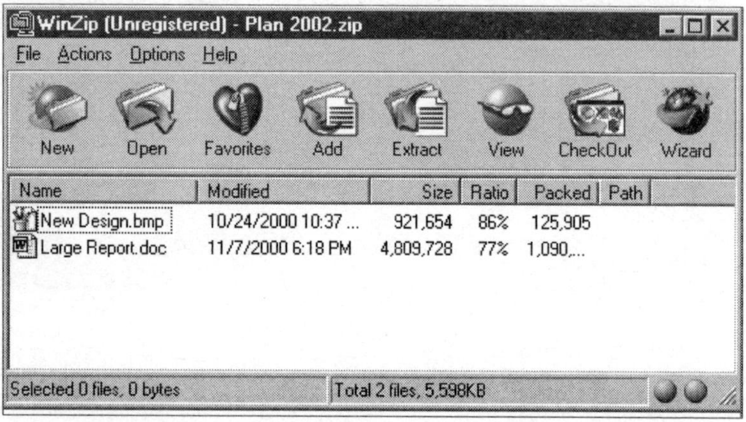

From this archive, you can extract files into a chosen directory, delete them or add new files. Double clicking on a file starts the associated program allowing you to examine a fully working copy of the file.

You can also add files to an existing archive using the Windows Explorer. With the archive open in its window, a file is dragged from the Explorer and dropped over the list of files in the archive. Alternatively, you can select the file in Explorer, then use **File** and **Add to Zip** off the Explorer menu bar. (Or press the right mouse button over the file name then use **Add to Zip**).

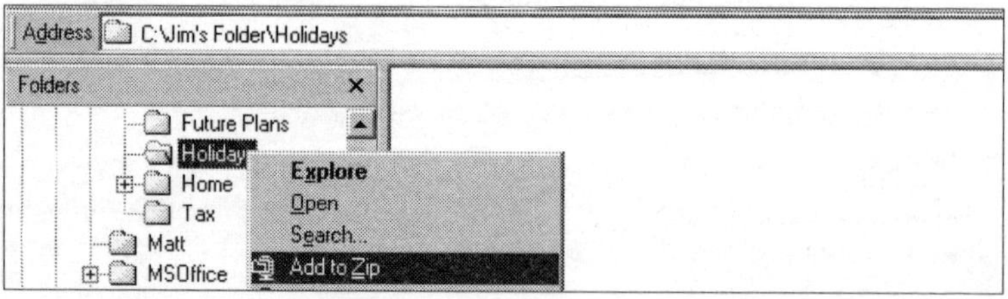

Extracting Files Using WinZip

This is very easy using either WinZip Wizard or Classic. First you open the required .ZIP archive. Then you select the files you want to extract and the directory into which the extracted files are to be placed.

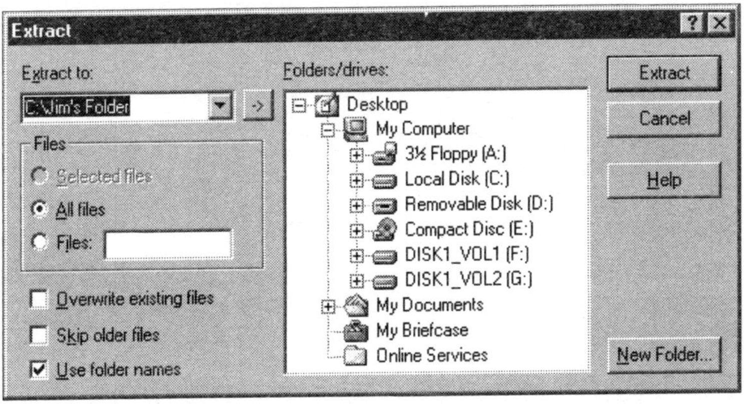

Clicking the **Extract** button will expand the files and place fully working copies of the files in the selected directory on your hard disc.

Self-Extracting Archives

Suppose you want to take some compressed files and use them on a machine which isn't equipped with a program to extract the files, like WinZip or PKUNZIP or Windows Me with the Compressed Folders feature set up. The solution is to create a self-extracting archive. This is a compressed file which has an unzip program built into it. The self-extractor has the .EXE extension. This is the format for many of the files downloaded from the Internet. The file is copied into a folder on the hard disc and to unzip or extract the file you simply double click on its filename in the Windows Explorer or My Computer. You can choose the folder into which the unzipped file is to be placed.

To convert a .ZIP file into a self-extracting .EXE file, click the drop down **Actions** menu in WinZip and select **Make.Exe File**.

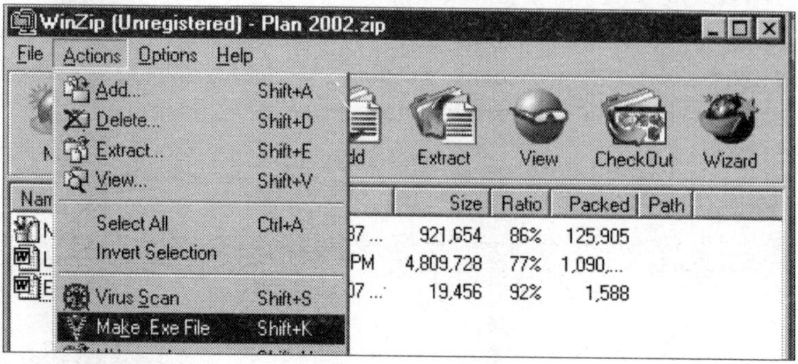

You can specify the directory into which the self-extractor will unzip itself. This may be on another person's computer, if you are using WinZip as a vehicle for transferring files. By default WinZip self-extractors unzip themselves into the user's TEMP= folder.

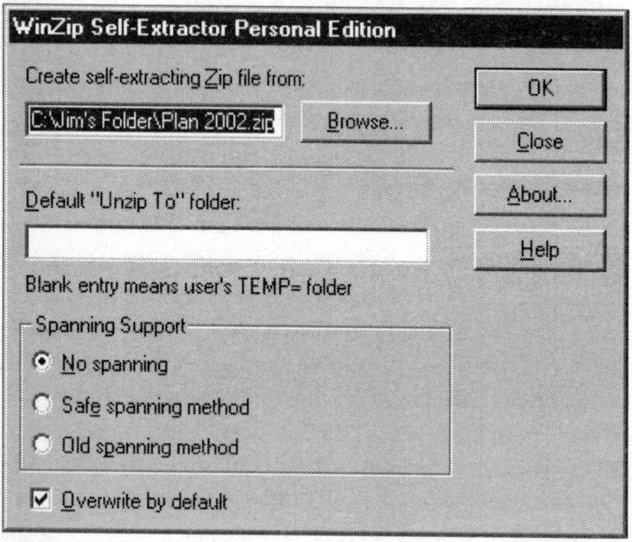

The term **spanning** in the above dialogue box refers to the continuation of a .ZIP file over several floppy discs or other removable media.

Checking .ZIP Files for Viruses with WinZip

There are dangers of viruses when downloading .ZIP files from the Internet or from floppy discs of uncertain origin. When WinZip is first set up it can detect if your computer has a virus scanner installed.

To carry out a virus scan, click the option on the WinZip Actions menu shown below.

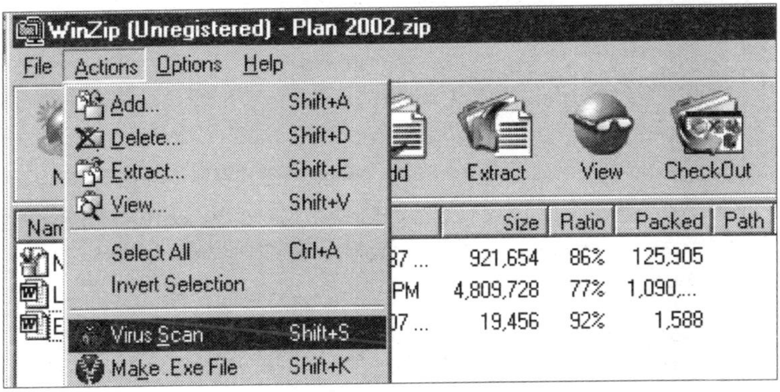

First the .ZIP file is extracted, then the files are virus checked using your own installed scanner. If no virus warnings are given, you know the file is virus-free when you see the message:

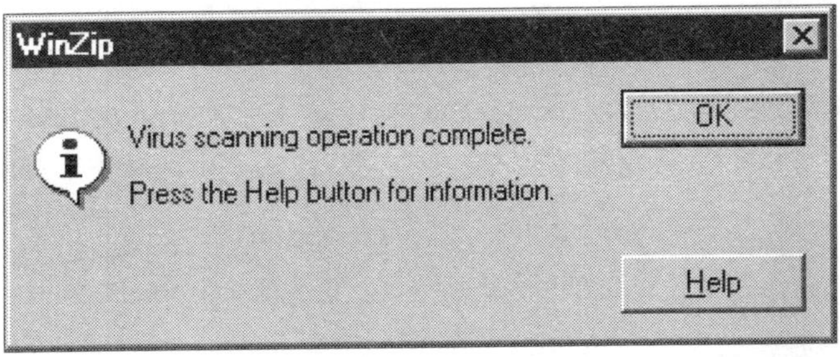

You can also include a virus scan by ticking **Run Virus Scanner** in the **CheckOut** feature of WinZip, as discussed earlier in this chapter.

Summary: Compressing Files

- Files may be compressed to a fraction of their original size, depending on the type of data. File compression converts common words and shapes into a shorter than normal code.
- File compression allows more files to be stored on a given storage medium such as floppy disc and gives increased speed when files are transferred around a network, including the Internet.
- Files which are not used very often may be archived by compressing and storing in another folder. If necessary, the original uncompressed files can be deleted to save space.
- Windows Me introduces Compressed Folders, which are compatible with .ZIP files created in programs like WinZip.
- Compressed Folders are easy to create and enable files to be compressed and extracted by simple drag and drop methods.
- Compressed Folders in Windows Me can be *encrypted* and provided with a password.
- In programs like WinZip, a .ZIP archive file is created which acts as a folder for compressed files. Files can be compressed by dragging and dropping them onto the .ZIP file.
- Files must be uncompressed or extracted before they can be used as normal files in applications.
- Special self-extracting files can be created in programs like WinZip. These have the .EXE file name extension and "unzip" themselves when you double-click on their file name. Self-extracting .EXE files are useful for sending compressed files to people who don't have an "unzip" program on their computer.
- The WinZip Wizard simplifies the extraction of software downloaded from the Internet, as well as installing the software on your hard disc, ready to run.
- WinZip can run a virus scan on downloaded compressed files, after first unzipping them into a temporary folder.

8

Simple Cable Connections

Introduction

The simplest and cheapest of networks is formed when two computers are connected by a single short cable costing only a few pounds. A typical use for this rudimentary network is to copy files from a laptop to a desktop computer or from an old machine to its new replacement. Or to make backup copies of important files onto another machine; or to share one printer between two computers.

This simple network will lack the speed and sophistication of a more expensive arrangement such as the peer-to-peer and client/server networks discussed in the next chapter. However, since it requires none of the network hardware such as network interface cards and hubs, it is an extremely cheap method of connecting two machines, in order to share resources. Windows Me contains all of the software to operate this simple network, so the system can be up and running for the cost of the cable and a few minutes work.

The Windows Me software provided for this task is the Direct Cable Connection and this chapter describes how to install the program from your Windows Me CD and then how to set up and use the connection. Third party software packages such as Traveling LapLink can also be used for this purpose. Against the cost of buying third party packages must be considered their enhanced facilities for copying files and additional features for use with local and wide area networks. The third party packages usually include a suitable data transfer cable.

The Cable

It's essential to obtain the correct cable when setting up the **Direct Cable Connection.** Third party packages like Traveling LapLink usually include a cable in the box but with Direct Cable Connection you'll need to buy one from a local dealer or by mail order.

Direct Cable Connection can use either a cable connecting the *serial ports* on the two computers or one connecting the *parallel ports.* The serial ports are the 9 or 25-way connectors on the back of the computer into which you normally plug a mouse or modem. The parallel port (often referred to as LPT1) is the connector normally used for the printer and other devices. The speed of data transfers over a parallel cable is several times faster than over a serial cable.

When buying a cable you must specify that a *data transfer* cable is required. In the case of a serial cable it must be a *null-modem* i.e. non-modem cable, also known as a *cross-over* cable. The parallel cable must be either a *parallel link* or *LapLink* cable. An ordinary printer cable will not work with two-way data transfer programs like Direct Cable Connection or Traveling LapLink.

The Maplin Electronics catalogue, **http://www.maplin.co.uk/**, contains a range of serial and parallel cables, some of which are listed as being suitable for data transfer.

Extra Ports

As mentioned earlier, the serial ports (COM1, COM2, etc.) are often used for mice and modems. It's possible to buy serial data cables with both 9-way and 25-way connectors at each end so that you can utilise both types of port on each of the computers to be connected. The parallel port (LPT1) is normally used for a printer and may also be used for a Zip drive or scanner. In many cases there is a socket for the printer on the back of the scanner or Zip drive but these sharing arrangements can cause problems. If you want to use the parallel port connection regularly for data transfer work, you will have the inconvenience of having to unplug devices such as printers, scanners and Zip drives.

The answer is to fit an expansion card containing extra parallel ports. These can be bought for under £20 and plug in to a vacant slot in your computer's motherboard. If you don't wish to fit the card yourself, a local computer shop should be able to undertake the work. Expansion cards containing one or two parallel ports or a mixture of serial and parallel ports are available. For more information, please see **Appendix B: Fitting a Parallel Pot Expansion Card**.

USB

USB (Universal Serial Bus) is a relatively new system which makes the connection of devices much simpler, with genuine "plug and play" capability. You can attach a 4-port hub to the USB port on the back of your computer. Then further hubs can be connected to the first and subsequent hubs so that, in theory, by stacking the hubs, up to 127 peripheral devices can be connected. USB also provides "hot swapping" - the installation of new devices while the computer is running - there's no need to switch off or experiment with complex settings.

In the context of this chapter, however, USB technology can be used to provide extremely fast data transfers (several times faster than a parallel connection) over a short USB cable linking two adjacent computers. Traveling LapLink supports USB and requires a special LapLink USB data transfer cable.

If you have a newish computer, it will probably already be fitted with USB ports. Older machines can be modified fairly cheaply but if you are not happy to remove the cover of the computer and "tinker" with your machine, it should be possible to have the work done locally by a computer repair shop.

For more information, please see **Appendix A: The Universal Serial Bus**. This describes how to check your computer for USB support and the fitting of various components to provide one or more USB ports. For modern computers this may involve, at most, the fitting of a cheap back plate or a card containing the USB connectors.

The Direct Cable Connection

Windows Me provides its own program, known as the **Direct Cable Connection**, to enable two computers to communicate via a short cable. At the time of writing, the Direct Cable Connection supports serial and parallel cables and the infra-red connection provided on some laptop computers. The parallel data cable is currently the best option for the DCC but as discussed in the previous section, it's essential to get a cable of the correct specification. Letters in the computer press frequently refer to the complexity of setting up the DCC. You must install a number of Windows Me networking components (discussed shortly) before it will work. The Direct Cable Connection does, however, lack some of the ease of use and additional features of third party data transfer packages such as Traveling LapLink (discussed shortly).

Although DCC is provided free on the Windows Me CD, it may not be installed on your computer. You can check by selecting **Start**, **Programs**, **Accessories** and **Communications**.

If the **Direct Cable Connection** doesn't appear on the list then the program will have to be installed from your Windows Me CD. First select **Start**, **Settings**, **Control Panel**, and **Add/Remove Programs**. Then choose the **Windows Setup** tab and **Communications**.

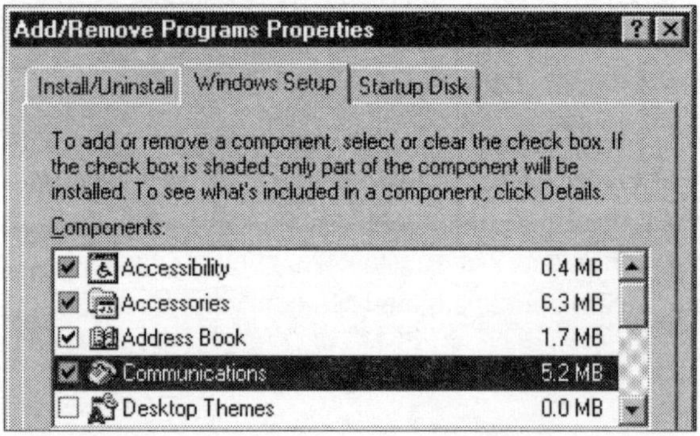

Now click **Details...** and make sure there's a tick on the box next to the entry for **Direct Cable Connection**, as shown below.

Click **OK** and if **Direct Cable Connection** was not previously ticked as shown above, you will be asked to insert the Windows Me CD to complete the installation.

Essential Windows Me Components

Before you attempt to run the Direct Cable Connection you need to ensure that a number of Windows Me networking components are installed on each of the computers. Examine these in the **Network Configuration** tab (**Start**, **Settings**, **Control Panel**, **Network**) shown on the next page.

The components which must be present for DCC to work are:

- **IPX/SPX** - A network protocol or language
- **Client for Microsoft Networks**
- **File and Printer Sharing for Microsoft Networks**

Any missing components can be installed after clicking the **Add...** button shown below. You will need to have your Windows Me CD to hand.

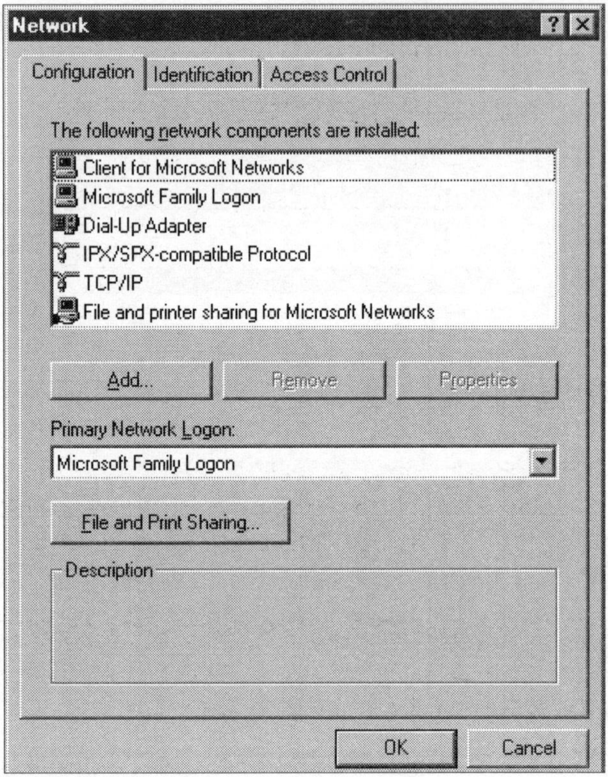

Client for Microsoft Networks is obtained by clicking **Add...** then **Client** then **Add...** and then selecting **Microsoft**. If you now select **Client for Microsoft Networks** and **OK** you will be asked for the Windows Me CD so that the component can be installed.

IPX/SPX is installed in a similar manner. Select **Add...** then **Protocol** then **Add...** then **Microsoft** then **IPX/SPX-compatible Protocol**.

File and printer sharing for Microsoft Networks is installed after selecting **Add...** and **Service**.

While the main **Network Configuration** window is displayed you can give permission for other people to share your files and printer. This is done by clicking the **File and Print Sharing...** button in the **Network** window, open at the **Configuration** tab as shown on the previous page.

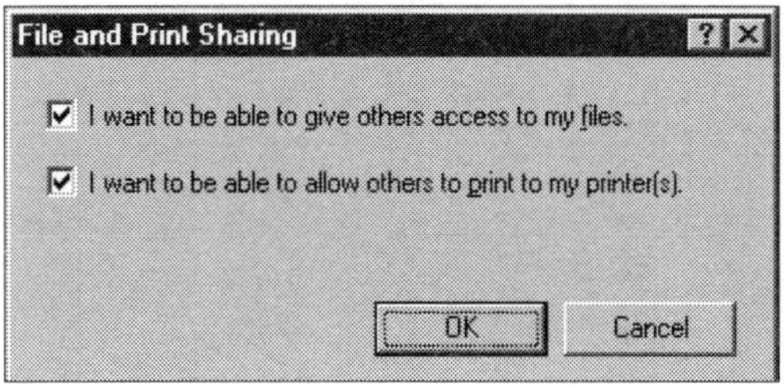

Enabling Sharing

Ticking the above boxes does not allow specific hard discs, folders and printers to be shared. *Sharing* is a property of each folder, disc drive or printer which must be set in My Computer or the Windows Explorer on *both machines*. Right click over the disc drive or folder and select **Sharing....**

The **Properties** window opens, as shown on the next page. In this case, the primary hard disc drive (**C:**) is being made shareable, but the same method can also be applied, in the above example, to the floppy disc drive (**A:**), the ZIP disc drive (D:), the CD drive (**E:**) and the two secondary hard disc drive partitions (**F:**) and (**G:**).

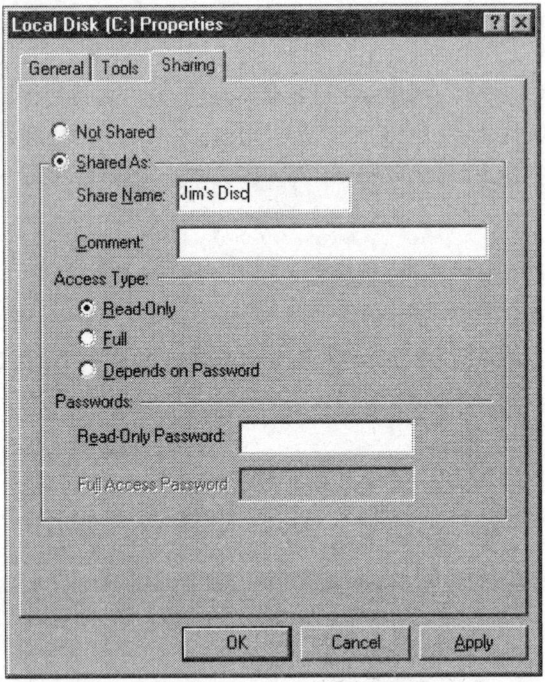

Now click the radio button to switch on **Shared As:** and if you prefer, change the **Share Name:** which has been provided automatically.

At this stage you can set the access to **Read-Only** or **Full** and set passwords for each type of access.

After you click **Apply** and **OK** a small hand appears under the icon for the device or folder in My Computer, to indicate that sharing has been enabled.

Sharing Printers

The Direct Cable Connection is a cost effective way to share a printer between two computers and neater than using a physical switch and cabling. Once the printer has been made shareable in My Computer, the Direct Cable Connection will do the rest. To make a printer shareable, a similar procedure is used to that for sharing disc drives and folders. First select the printer to be shared, by locating it in the **Printers** folder (**Start**, **Settings**, **Printers**), while working on the machine to which the printer is attached.

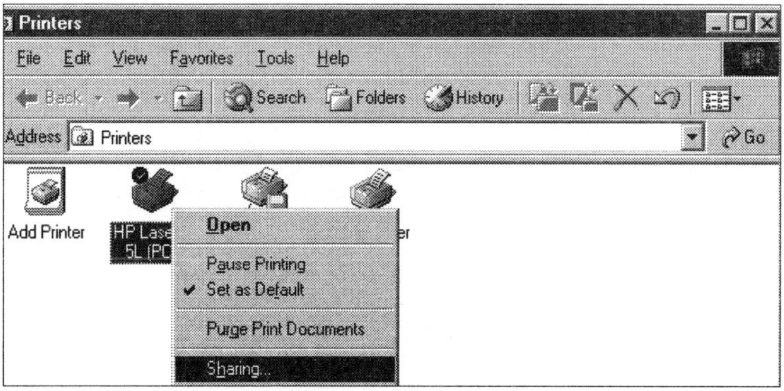

Then press the right button over the required printer and select **Sharing....** Switch on **Shared As:** and give the printer a new **Share Name:** and **Password:** if you wish.

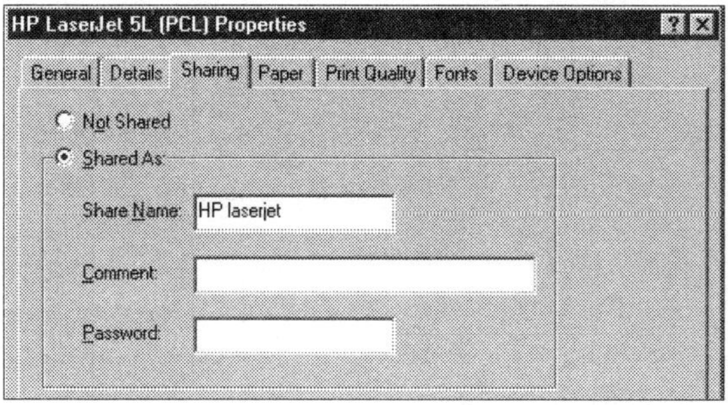

Identification

Before you can connect two computers on this simple network each machine must be identified uniquely with a **Computer name:** and **Workgroup:**. Each computer is set up using the **Identification** tab in the **Network** dialogue box accessed from **Start**, **Settings**, **Control Panel** and **Network**.

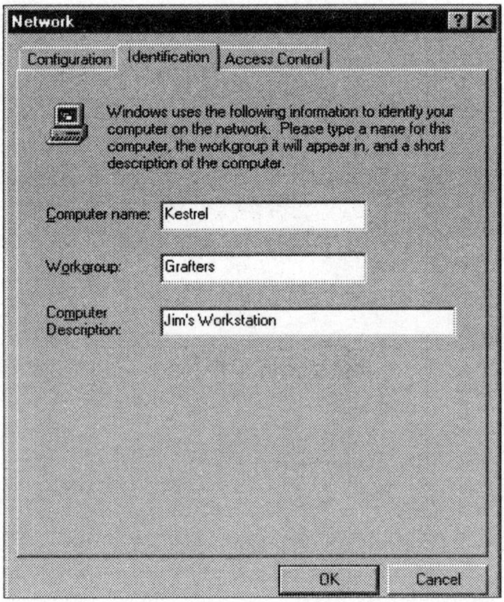

Computer name: is compulsory and identifies the machine on the network. The computer name can be up to 15 characters with no blank spaces.

Workgroup: should be the same for both computers and identifies a group of users wishing to access the same disc drives, files or printer.

Computer Description: is optional, but allows additional information to be given about the computer, such as its geographical location, in the case of a large network. (These network features are set up in a similar way if you are installing computers on a full blown network.)

Making the Connection

We are now ready to make the connection between the two computers. The network software components in Windows Me should have been set up, as well as the sharing of the required resources such as disc drives, folders and printers. The basic arrangement is that one machine acts as the *Host* and the other is designated the *Guest*. The Host is the machine containing the shareable resources - disc drives, folders and printer(s). Either machine can act as the Host during a particular session provided the necessary resources have been set as shareable as previously described. Obviously the connecting cable must be in place and if you are using a parallel cable, you will need to fit a second parallel port if you are intending to share a printer.

When you launch the **Direct Cable Connection** from **Start**, **Programs**, **Accessories** and **Direct Cable Connection**, a wizard allows you to set the machine as Host or Guest.

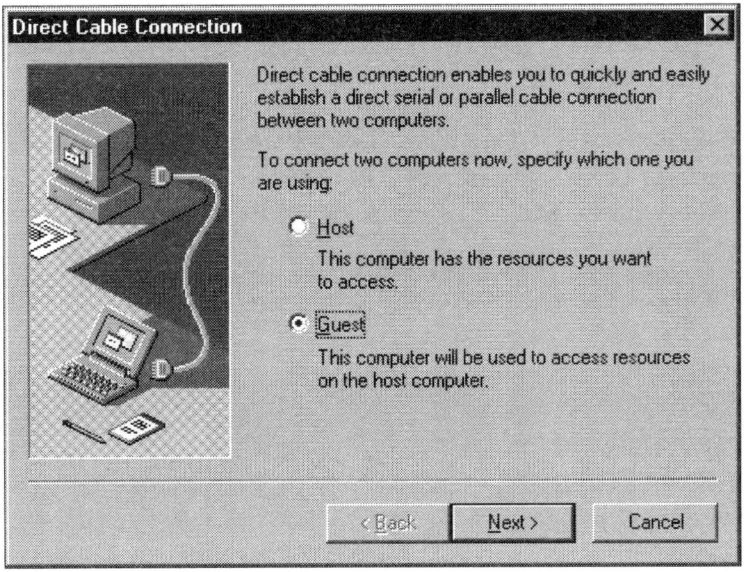

Then you have to select either the parallel port or the serial port to match your particular cable connection.

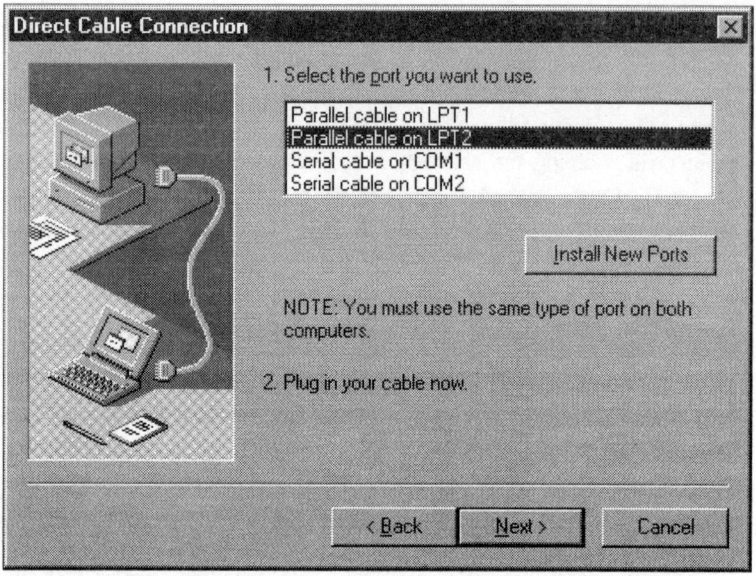

You must complete the wizard for both Host and Guest computers. Then the Host computer will **Listen** while the Guest makes a connection.

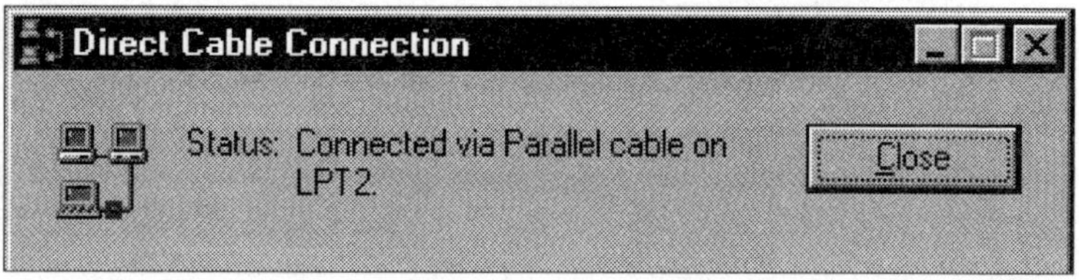

Once you are connected, the Guest machine displays in a window on its screen a folder containing the shareable resources from the Host.

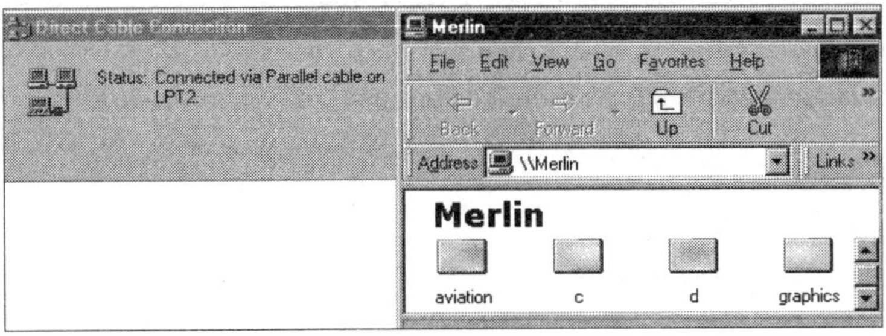

You can now open the Windows Explorer or My Computer and “drag and drop” folders or files from the Host machine to the Guest. Or you can use DCC to run Host-based programs on the Guest machine.

In future when you start up the Direct Cable Connection, the connection is made by clicking a **Listen** button on the Host machine and a **Connect** button on the Guest machine.

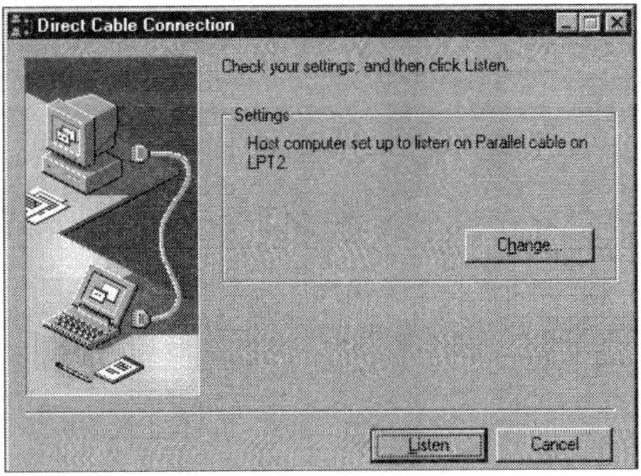

The **Change** button on each machine allows the Guest machine to be switched to Host and the previous Host becomes the Guest.

Sharing a Printer

Apart from sharing discs and folders, you can share resources such as printers over the **Direct Cable Connection**. The printer must be physically attached to the computer designated as Host. (You will need a second parallel port as described earlier). The printer must be set as shareable in the **Printers** folder of the Host machine (**Start**, **Settings**, **Printers**).

In my setup, the Host machine with the printer attached is identified as **Kestrel** while the Guest machine is **Merlin**. After you make the connection, the Guest **Merlin** displays a window showing the shareable resources of the Host **Kestrel**.

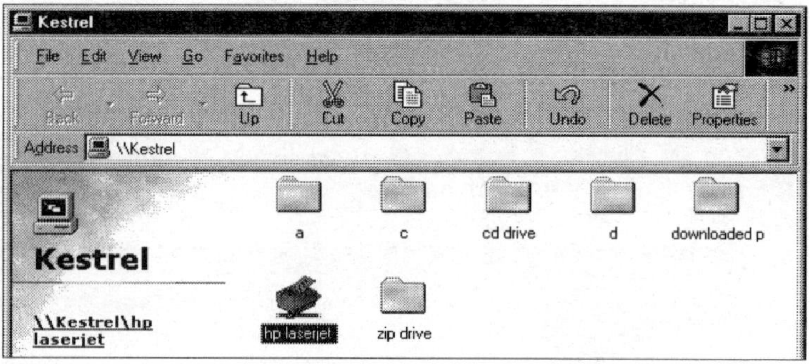

Included in the window on Merlin is the printer **Kestrel\hp laserjet**, which is attached to the Host machine. Double click the icon for the printer to start the process of setting it up as a shared "network" printer.

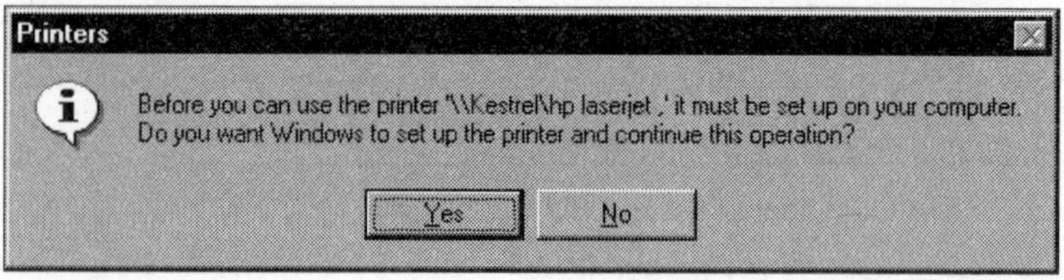

Clicking **Yes** starts the **Add Printer Wizard** which mainly requires you to click **Next**. You will be asked to select the model of printer and to provide the printer driver files either from your Windows Me CD or from a disc supplied by the manufacturer of your printer. You are given the opportunity to change the name of the printer (as it appears on the Guest machine) and print a test page before clicking **Finish**. You should now be able to use the printer on both machines by selecting it in **Print** in applications such as Word or Paint.

The **Print** dialogue box displayed on the Guest machine Merlin is shown below. The full path of the network printer attached to **Kestrel,** the host machine, is given i.e. **\\Kestrel\hp laserjet**.

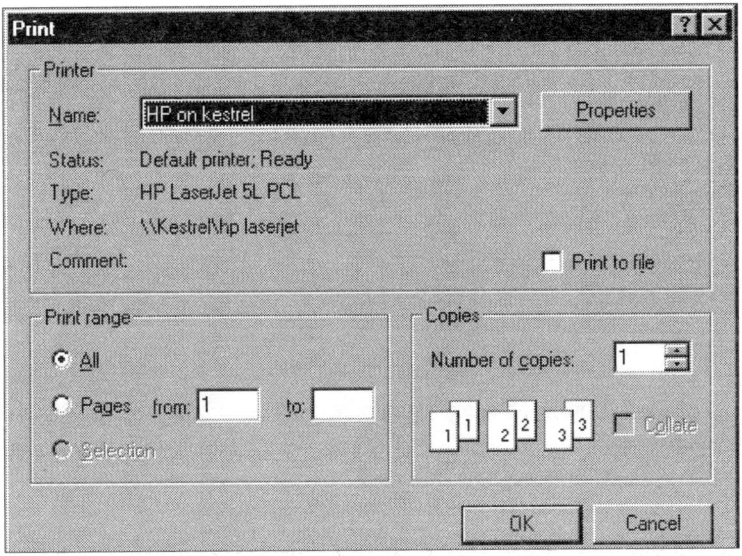

As mentioned previously, the Direct Cable Connection is an economical method of linking two computers, since all you need is a cheap cable - Windows Me does the rest. However, better performance, albeit at greater cost, can be obtained by creating a peer-to-peer network, as discussed later in this book. This is suitable for connecting a cluster of 2-10 machines in the home, office or primary school, for example.

Summary: Simple Cable Connections

- A rudimentary network of two computers can be made economically by connecting their serial, parallel or USB ports with a short cable. This link can be used for sharing disc drives, folders and printers.
- Windows Me contains all of the software needed to manage this system - known as the Direct Cable Connection. DCC and several essential software components must be installed from the Windows Me CD.
- In the Direct Cable Connection, one machine is designated as the Host and the other as the Guest. The Guest displays, in a window on its screen, the *shareable* resources from the Host computer, permitting operations such as file transfer and printer sharing.
- Disc drives, folders and printers must be set as *shareable* in My Computer, the Windows Explorer or the Printers folder.
- A special cable is required for data transfer operations - a normal printer cable will not work.
- If connecting machines via a parallel cable, the fitting of an extra parallel port is desirable.
- Data transfer over a cable linking the parallel ports is several times faster than using a cable connecting the serial ports.
- Third party software such as Traveling LapLink from Traveling Software offers enhanced features for file transfer and remote computing. This includes support for a connection using a special cable between the USB (Universal Serial Bus) ports. This is much faster than both the parallel and serial connections.
- The Direct Cable Connection can perform a useful function if cost is a major consideration. Otherwise the building of a peer-to-peer network (described in later chapters) should be considered for connecting a small number of computers (2-10 approximately).

9

Connecting with LapLink Gold

Introduction

The last chapter discussed the Direct Cable Connection used to link two machines by their serial or parallel ports. One of the main reasons for connecting computers is to enable files to be copied between machines. For example, users of portable computers who spend time working away from their office-based desktop machine. A vast amount of data may accumulate and the files will need transferring to the office machine as quickly as possible. The transfer could be done on returning to the office using a short cable (about 2 or 3 metres long) to connect the two machines.

While the Direct Cable Connection, a component of Windows Me, is quite adequate for basic copying work, there are some very useful third party software packages which provide additional facilities. These include enhanced **File Transfer**, **Remote Control** of distant computers and **Print Redirection** (printing involving remote computers). LapLink Gold is one of the leading packages in this aspect of computing.

If you need to connect two machines which aren't on a peer-to-peer or client/server network or fitted with modems, packages like LapLink Gold can use a serial, parallel or USB cable. So you can make a simple network using the cable provided to link two machines in close proximity (typically 2 or 3 metres apart).

LapLink in its various versions is a well-established tool used by computing professionals for copying large quantities of files between two standalone machines (as an alternative to swapping floppy, ZIP or JAZ discs or CDs.)

A typical situation would be when an office computer is replaced, posing the problem of how to transfer hundreds of files from the old machine to the new. The solution is simple - connect the two machines by a LapLink cable via their serial, parallel or USB ports and install the LapLink software on both machines. It's then just a case of selecting some or all of the files and starting the copy process.

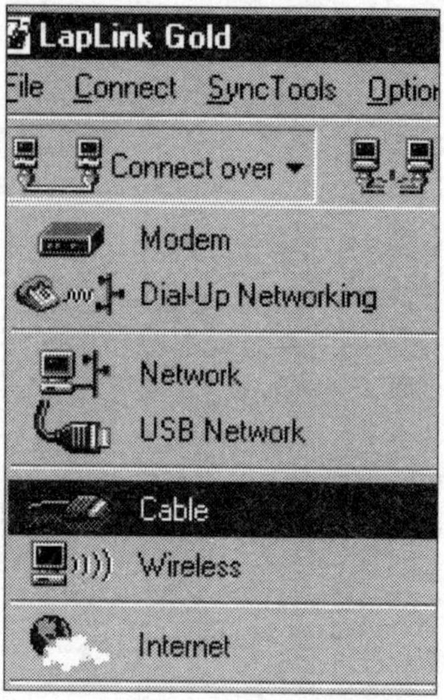

LapLink Gold has a wide range of services for use with computers linked by a variety of connection methods. Apart from the short cable linking serial, parallel or the latest ultra fast USB ports, they may be connected remotely via modems, Dial-Up Networking and the Internet. Additionally LapLink Gold may be used to facilitate communication between workstations on a local area network, such as the peer-to-peer network described later. Laptop machines are often fitted with *infra-red* ports. They can use the **Wireless** connection to communicate with other machines also fitted with an infrared device.

The LapLink Gold software can be purchased on CD together with an instruction manual, from LapLink.com, Inc., or from the usual suppliers. Serial, parallel and USB cables can also be bought separately.

You can also obtain a free Trial Version of the software by downloading an evaluation copy from the Web site at:

www.laplink.co.uk

Downloading the LapLink software from a Web site and installing on your hard disc is simply a matter of following the on-screen instructions. This topic is described elsewhere in this book.

Installation of LapLink Gold from a CD starts automatically when you put the CD in the drive. You need to enter the serial number found on the CD case and there is a choice of an **Express** installation which includes all the common options or **Custom** installation which allows you to select the options to install. Then the files are copied from the CD to your hard disc and you are given the opportunity to set up **Print Redirection** either immediately or later.

After restarting the computer, LapLink Gold can be launched from the **Programs** menu off **Start**.

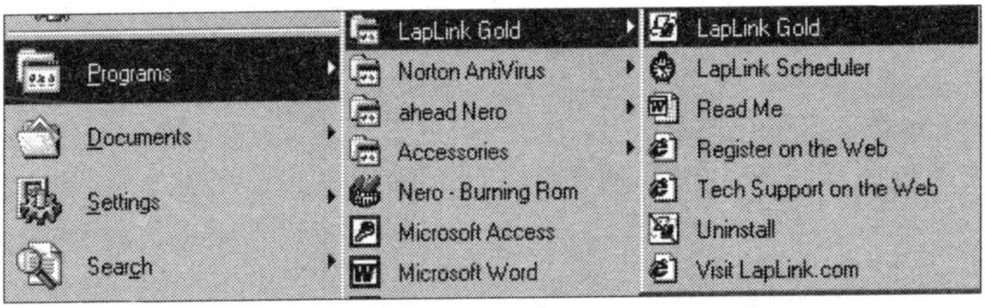

When you first run LapLink Gold you are presented with the main window with the **LinkBar** across the top, as shown below.

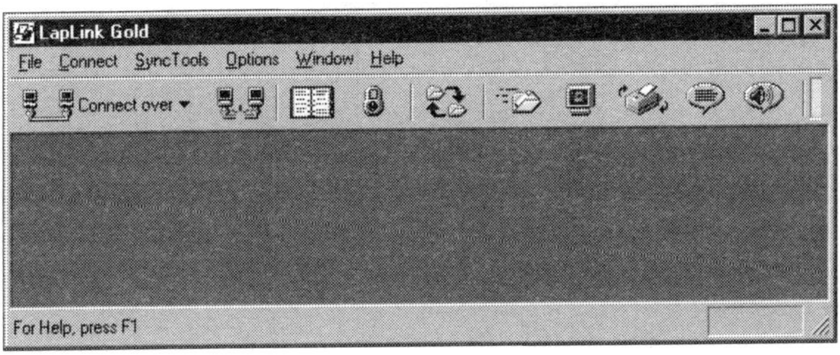

Security Options

No one can make a LapLink connection until suitable security options have been set. These are accessed by clicking on the padlock icon on the **LinkBar**.

The **Security** window opens as shown below.

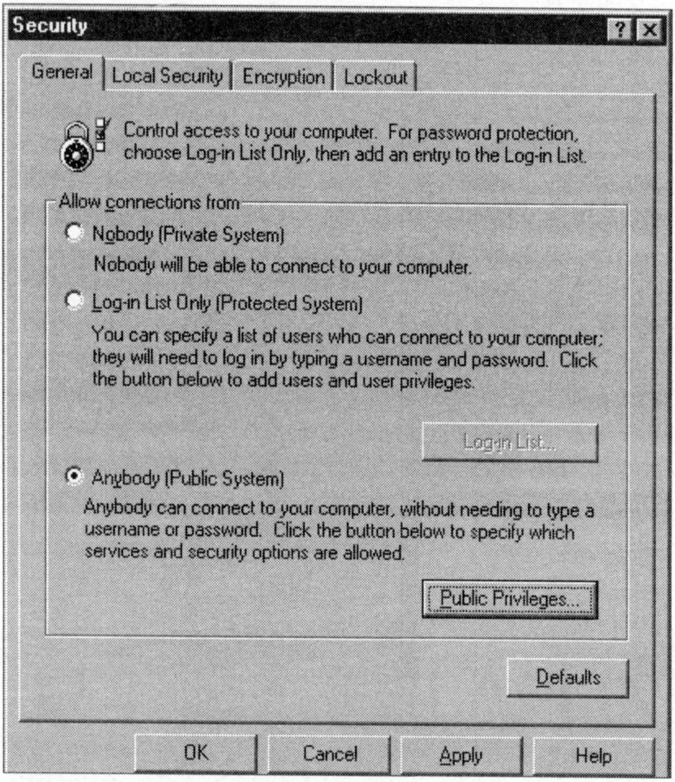

Nobody (Private System) - you can connect out to other machines, but no one can connect to yours.

Log-in List Only (Protected System) - you compile a list of log-in names and passwords for people allowed to connect to your machine (and potentially copy or delete files and alter settings).

When adding users to the Log-in List you can control which of the services (**File Transfer**, **Remote Control**, **Print Redirection** and **Text and Voice Chat**) they will be allowed to use, as shown below.

Anybody (Public System) - With this security option set, anyone can connect to your machine, so you should only switch on those services (**File Transfer**, **Remote Control**, **Print Redirection**, **Text Chat**) which you are happy for them to use.

The **Locking** options, when switched on, allow someone calling into the computer to blank the screen and disable the mouse and keyboard. If you want to work on a host, i.e. remote computer, you could arrange for the **Locking** options to be enabled on the host so that you could prevent other people using the keyboard or looking at your work.

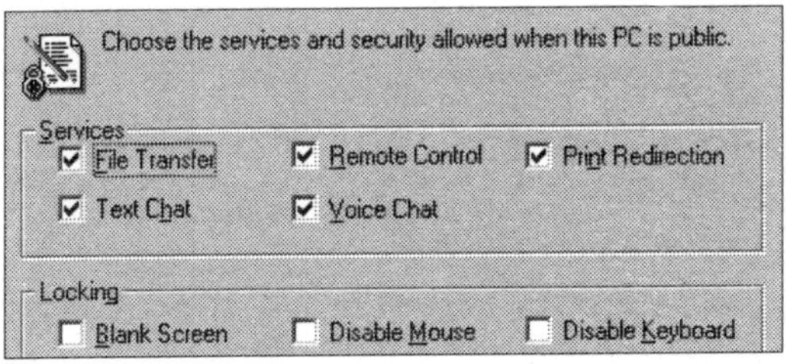

Making LapLink Connections

Once the security options have been set, you are ready to make a connection to another computer. Both machines must have LapLink running before you try to connect. Click the connection icon, then select the method you wish to use, such as **Cable** shown in the menu below:

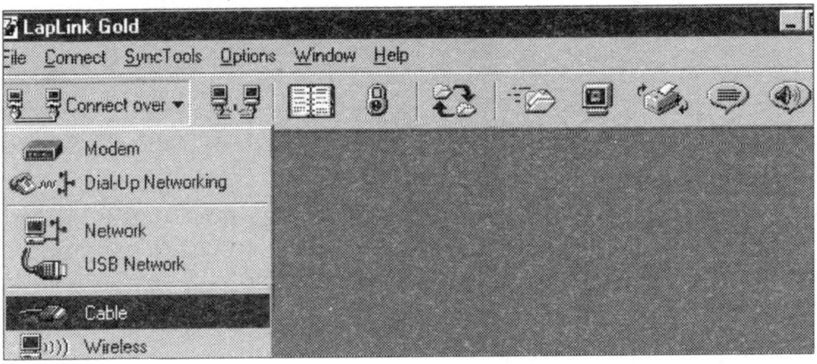

Cable Connections

Two local stand-alone machines (about 2 or 3 metres apart) can be connected using the **Cable** option, with either a serial, parallel or USB cable as supplied with LapLink or available from computer stores. This method would be useful, for example, when you returned a laptop from your travels or had two standalone machines between which you want to transfer a substantial amount of data. To avoid having to disconnect devices such as mice, printers and scanners to free up ports, it's worth considering the fitting of additional serial or parallel ports. The parallel cable will give better performance (faster data transfer) than the serial cable, but the USB cable far outperforms both.

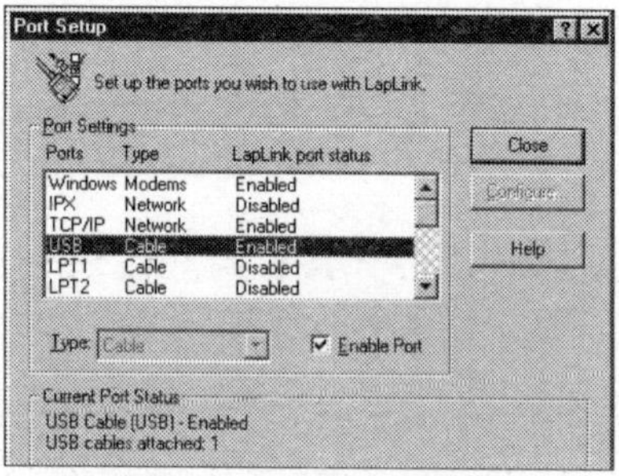

Before making the connection you need to set up the port you are going to use. If using a serial cable, select COM1 or COM2, etc., or LPT1 or LPT2, etc., in the case of a parallel cable. (A USB connection is shown). Also tick the **Enable Port** check box.

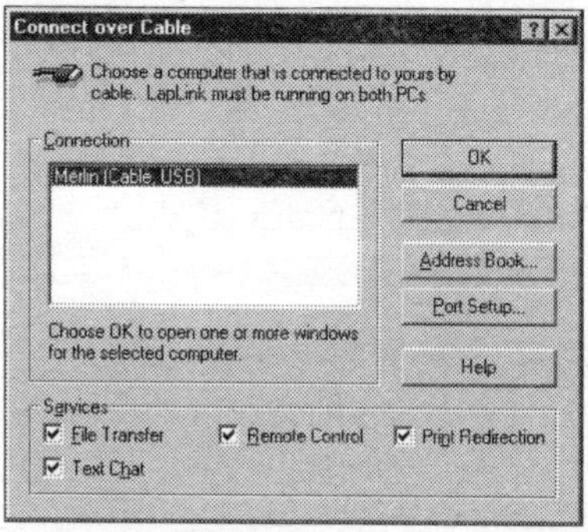

Once you have set up the ports on each machine with LapLink running on both, your computer should detect the available connection, in this example a USB cable connecting to my remote computer named Merlin.

Now select with a tick the services which you wish to use (**File Transfer**, **Remote Control**, etc.). Click **OK** and the machines should beep to announce that the connection has been made. LapLink is now ready to run the selected services (discussed later).

Using LapLink Gold

Whichever connection method you are using to connect the two machines, the basic services (**File Transfer**, **Remote Control**, **Print Redirection** and **Text Chat**) are the same. Obviously operations such as transferring very large folders between machines will be faster on devices such as the peer-to-peer network and the USB cable than over a serial cable or a telephone line.

All operations are controlled from the **LinkBar** across the top of the LapLink window.

Before you click **OK** to make your selected connection you should ensure that you have chosen the LapLink services you will need during the session which is about to start.

The next section gives an overview of the main LapLink services.

File Transfer

The file transfer service would typically be used by someone returning to their office (or connecting remotely), having accumulated a lot of new files on a laptop during their travels or when working at home.

Clicking on the **File Transfer** icon opens up Explorer-like windows for the two machines displayed side-by-side with their names across the top of their respective windows.

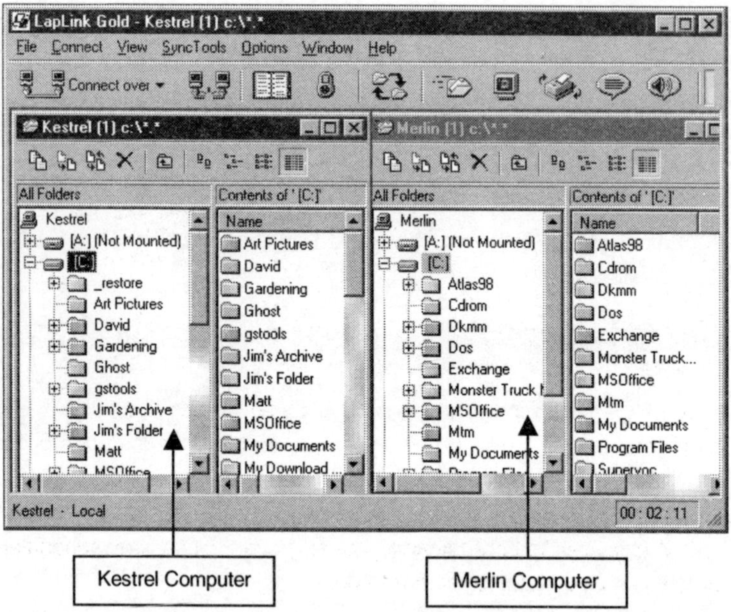

Copying can be achieved by dragging and dropping the required folders and files. Simultaneously holding down **CTRL** during the drag operation ensures that files are *copied*, while holding down **SHIFT** has the effect of *moving* files. Alternatively the **File** menu contains a full range of options which include copying, moving, deleting and renaming selected files and folders.

By default the **SpeedSync** feature is switched on. This ensures that whenever files are transferred from a source folder to a target folder of the same name on the other machine, only the data which has changed is transferred. There is also a **Clone Folder** tool which makes sure that source and target folders are identical. This includes removing from the target folder any files which do not exist in the source. Older versions of files in the target folder are overwritten by newer copies from the source.

Xchange Agent

This icon opens an **Xchange Agent**, also accessible from the **SyncTools** drop down menu on the **LinkBar**.

An Xchange Agent is an automated copying operation between two computers running LapLink. This can be saved and run manually when required or at a scheduled time. Synchronization ensures that corresponding folders on both machines have the latest versions of files. A preview feature allows you to confirm that the scheduled operation is what you really want to do.

Remote Control

When you click this icon from the **LinkBar**, the desktop of the remote machine appears on your screen. This gives you complete control of the remote machine, using your mouse and keyboard, just as if you were sitting in front of the remote machine. This enables you to carry out management and maintenance tasks on the remote machine. If you don't want anyone to use the remote machine or look at the work you are doing on it, there are options which enable you to lock the keyboard and mouse and blank the screen.

While you are working at your machine, a person can sit at the remote machine and both of you can alternately operate the host machine. This would, for example, allow you to collaborate on a joint document in Word or some other Windows application. Alternatively you could carry out interactive training and support with the person sitting at the remote machine.

Print Redirection

This service allows you to use printers attached to remote computers, for example because they offer colour or higher quality than any printers available locally. This would be particularly useful using LapLink Gold across the Internet or a local area network. You could prepare a document on your computer at home or out on your travels, then while still away from base, use Print Redirection to produce high quality output on the machine back at the office. Alternatively if you are away from your main place of work you could print locally a copy of a document stored on the office machine. So Print Redirection allows you to print documents on printers attached to computers at either end of a LapLink connection.

Before you can print using a printer attached to a remote machine, you must have your local machine set up with the printer software just as if the printer were attached to the local machine. To start this process, select **Options** and **Print Redirection Options...** from the LinkBar in LapLink Gold. Then select **Setup...** as shown below.

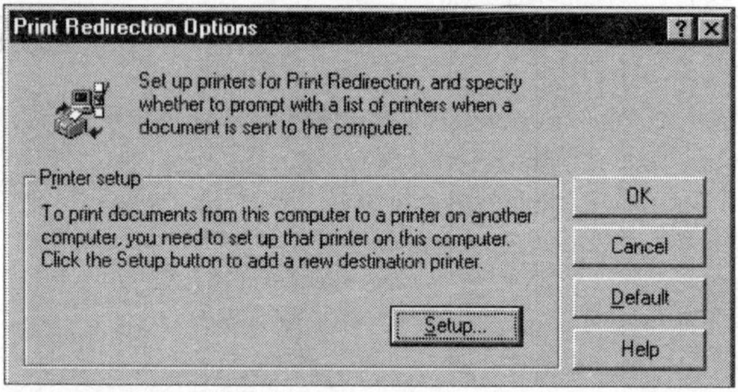

For this you will need to have your Windows CD or the driver discs provided by the manufacturer of the printer. Once you have made a connection, you simply run the application and open the document to be printed. Then using the standard **File/Print** command in the application you select, from the list of available printers, the required printer (it should have **LapLink** after its name).

Text Chat

This service allows you to send short messages to a colleague running LapLink on a remote machine. **Text Chat** could be used, for example, while giving support or training to someone using modems over the only available telephone line - so that no other method of two-way communication is possible. Ensure that **Text Chat** is ticked when you make the connection.

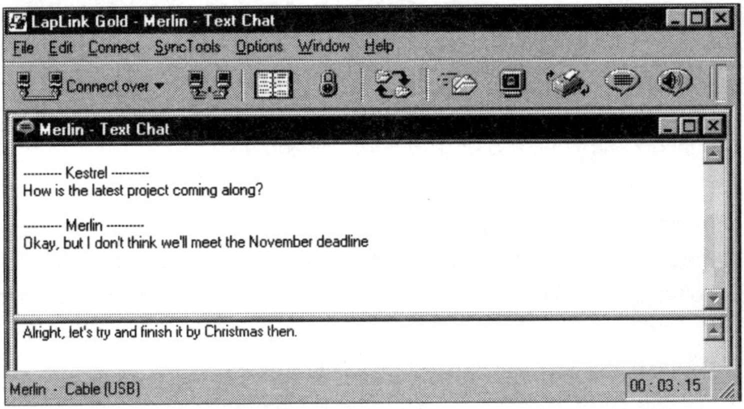

Text is typed in the lower panel, then sent when you press **Enter**. The **Text Chat** window will pop up in the foreground of the remote machine, displaying your message. Your messages and the replies appear in the top panel of your computer, under the names of the computers they were sent from.

Messages can be prepared offline in advance of making a Laplink connection using a Windows Me application like **Notepad.** Then it is copied to the clipboard using the **Copy** command in the Windows application. After the connection has been made, use **Edit** and **Paste** in **Text Chat** to place the text into the bottom panel in the **Text Chat** window. In a similar fashion, text can be copied from **Text Chat** into another Windows application.

Summary: Connecting with LapLink Gold

- LapLink Gold provides a range of services between computers which have been connected locally via a short cable or local area network and remotely via a modem/ISDN.
- LapLink enables large quantities of data to be copied between two computers and is much more efficient than disc swapping methods.
- File transfer using a USB cable connection is very much faster than with a cable connecting parallel ports, which in turn is faster than the serial cable. Please see **Appendix A: The Universal Serial Bus** for more details. This describes how to check your computer for USB support and the fitting of USB ports, if necessary.
- LapLink Gold has many additional features designed to enable mobile laptop computer users to communicate with their desktop machines and office networks. Equally to enable the home user to communicate with their work computers or those of friends and colleagues in distant locations. Apart from File Transfer, these features include Remote Control, Print Redirection and Text Chat.
- Remote Control allows the user to take over a distant computer and use and manage the machine just as if he or she were sitting in front of it. This enables training and support at the remote machine.
- Print Redirection enables documents to be retrieved from remote computers and printed locally. Alternatively documents stored on a local computer may be output on a remote printer when there is no suitable printer available locally.
- Text Chat is used to send and receive messages during a LapLink session such as training or online support.
- Xchange Agent allows the scheduling of file transfers and *synchronization* ensures that folders contain the latest files.
- Speedsync saves time by only copying the changed parts of files.
- Security features built into LapLink include an option to prevent unauthorised access to a computer. Access to the LapLink services (File Transfer, Remote Control, etc.) can also be controlled.

10

Building Your Own Network

Introduction

A network allows many people to access the same information and to share expensive software and peripheral devices such as printers and centralised backup facilities. Large networks can be used for internal communication by e-mail and to host an Intranet (an in-house Internet).

The benefits of networking need not be confined to the large organization with hundreds of workstations. Many homes now have two or more computers and lots of small businesses, offices and primary schools have a cluster of several computers (2-10 say) which can benefit from networking, as follows:

1. Expensive printers, CDs and scanners, etc., can be shared by all of the computers.
2. A single telephone line, modem and Internet connection, can be accessed by every workstation.
3. Files can easily be copied between computers - much easier than swapping lots of discs.
4. You can communicate with people in different parts of your home, office, school or business premises.

Unlike large networks, which are extremely complex to install and manage, the small "peer-to-peer" network is quite simple - it's basically a case of installing network interface cards in the computers then plugging the cables and connectors together. Windows Me contains all of the networking software you need and introduces a new feature, the **Home Networking Wizard**, which greatly simplifies the task of setting up the network. Unlike Windows 95 and 98, this shields the user from some of the more technical aspects of networking.

Types of Network in Context

There are two basic network configurations - **client/server** and **peer-to-peer**. The peer-to-peer network is perfectly suitable for the home and small office user, for whom this book is intended, while larger organizations invariably use the client/server model. For completeness, a brief description of the client server network is given on the next three pages. The remainder of the chapter covers the setting up of a peer-to-peer network.

The Client/Server Network

The client/server model is used for larger networks - from about ten machines up to several hundred. These may be contained within a single room or scattered throughout a business site or college.

At the centre of the network is the server, often referred to as the *file server*. (You can also have *mail servers* and *print servers.*) The server is normally a more powerful computer than the users' workstations or *client* machines distributed around the network. The server and the clients must be fitted with network interface cards (NICs) and these handle the flow of data and provide the connections for the network cabling which links the computers. Networking hardware is discussed in detail later in this chapter.

The server normally has a more powerful processor, bigger memory and larger hard disc(s) than the workstations. This enables the server to carry out its demanding role dealing with the requests from the client machines. These will include running most of the applications software which is used around the network and dealing with printing. It will also act as a central store for everyone's work, in the form of wordprocessing documents, spreadsheets and other files produced by users of the client machines.

It is normal to buy a special network version of, say, a word processing or accounts program. This software is only saved on the file server machine, but you can run it from any of the client machines around the network. Licences should be purchased to run multi-user software on a large number of computers, according to the number of users.

In education or training a single CD may be licensed and made accessible to all of the machines on the network. This can be achieved using either a shared CD drive or by copying the entire CD onto a special dedicated hard disc, which acts as a CD server.

The server computer may also act as a *print server* to manage shared printing across the network, although nowadays this role is often performed by a dedicated print server - a separate small hardware device which is plugged into the network in a suitable location.

It's normal for the server machine to be left running continually, including weekends and holidays. This enables users to go online at any time, perhaps from another building on the site. When the server is eventually shut down, this must be done according to a certain procedure. If the server were to suffer a sudden power failure, the resulting unsupervised shut down may damage the server and its contents. Servers on essential networks are fitted with an Uninterruptable Power Supply (UPS). This keeps the server powered up long enough for a shut down to be carried out according to the correct procedure.

As the server may contain all of the data files for an entire business, security is vitally important. When a server goes down, the whole network is immediately out of action. All data files should be backed up onto magnetic tape every day, with several tapes used in rotation and stored separately.

The client/server model is very efficient for the larger organization, with its centralised resources. However, the client/server model is expensive and a large network (with *hundreds* of computers) requires highly trained IT professionals as network administrators. It really is too complex for enthusiastic amateurs to dabble in. The administrators' work includes the management of users and their login names and passwords, the installation of software and the scheduling of backups. Also the setting of access rights to files and directories, the removal of obsolete files and protection against virus infection. Apart from troubleshooting any hardware problems there is also the task of staff training. In large organizations, the network staff might also design and maintain a company Web site or create an in-house *intranet*.

Even a client/server network with a small number of machines (10-20 say) will require at least one well-trained member of staff and outside professional support for trouble-shooting and modifications.

The client/server model requires a dedicated network operating system such as Windows NT Server, Windows 2000 Server or Novell Netware and this can cost hundreds or thousands of pounds. Network operating systems provide sophisticated facilities for organising users with login names and passwords and for managing files and scheduled backups.

The cost of the server machine itself must also be considered, since in most cases it will be dedicated entirely to its role as a file server.

The client/server network is a sophisticated and powerful system giving high performance and security. However, it's expensive to manage and maintain and therefore not appropriate for many home and small business users. The next section describes the simple peer-to-peer network which is more suitable for the home or smaller organisation.

The Peer-to-Peer Network

The peer-to-peer network is eminently suitable for connecting a few machines (up to about 10) in the home, in a small office or perhaps a primary school. The peer-to-peer network uses the same basic networking hardware as the client/server model, i.e. cables connecting network interface cards in every machine. However, in the peer-to-peer network there is no dedicated server - all the machines have equal status. Also, there is no need for a special network operating system - everything you need is included within Windows Me.

When the peer-to-peer network has been set up, you can view the computers which are connected, using a feature called **My Network Places**. This can be launched from its icon on the Windows Me Desktop, as shown left. Each computer on the network appears in the workgroup window, as shown on the right.

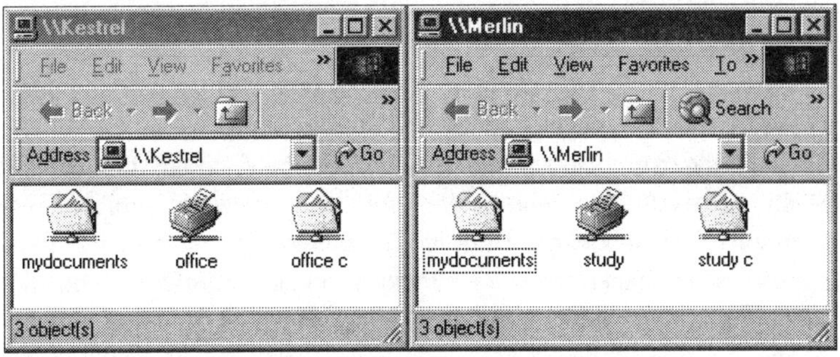

Shown above is a screenshot from the Kestrel computer, simultaneously displaying the shareable resources of both machines, identified as Kestrel and Merlin, on my peer-to-peer network.

Both Kestrel and Merlin are members of the same workgroup, Grafters. Double clicking on the icon for either machine opens up a window showing its shareable resources - discs, folders, CDs, printers, etc. Folders and files may be copied between machines by dragging and dropping. This is discussed in detail later in this book.

The peer-to-peer network enables operations such as file copying between computers to be carried out much faster than using a single cable linking the parallel or serial ports, as discussed in the previous chapter. Networking kits designed for the home or small business are becoming available very cheaply. The simplest consists of two network cards and the necessary cabling and connectors for under £20. Using the networking software provided free within Windows Me, this provides a very fast and efficient way of connecting two machines.

While it lacks the sophisticated management, security and backup facilities of the client/server network, the peer-to-peer network has several advantages. For a small number of computers, it's easier to set up and manage and doesn't require specialist computer staff. It is also cheaper since there is no need to dedicate a machine as a server. One disadvantage is that if one computer is used for printing, the person working at this machine may notice a loss of speed if several people are trying to print at the same time.

Ethernet

Ethernet is a networking standard (used by both client/server and peer-to-peer networks) developed by the Xerox Company in 1976. The Ethernet system includes the network interface cards, the cabling which connects the computers and the *network protocol* i.e. communication language. Data is transmitted around the network in *packets,* each packet also containing a unique address for both the sending and destination computers. Every packet is delivered to every station on the network. The network cards "listen" for packets containing their address. Only when the station's address matches the delivery address will the data be received by the computer.

The jargon surrounding cabling and connectors can be very confusing with several obscure names being used to describe the same object. Fortunately, with the increasing popularity of small networks there are now networking kits available which provide everything you need to connect two or three computers in a peer-to-peer network. Constructing a small peer-to-peer network is a task that anyone can tackle successfully and not nearly as complex as it might at first appear.

Thin Ethernet

The cheapest of these kits (under £20) includes two network interface cards and a **Thin Ethernet** cable to connect them. Also known as **Thinnet**, **Coaxial**, **Coax** and **10Base2**, this cable has a single copper centre and **BNC** bayonet connectors at each end. Although professionals use crimping tools to make up their own cables, ready-made cables can be purchased from computer suppliers. The cables are connected via T-pieces to the network cards at the back of the computer. In a Thin Ethernet network the computers are arranged along the cable in a line - a configuration known as the **Bus** topology.

This requires each end of the cable to be fitted with a special **terminator**. These should be included in a Thin Ethernet kit but otherwise they are available cheaply from computer stores.

Thin Ethernet represents fairly old technology and is limited to a data transfer rate of 10 Mega bits per second. (8 bits typically being used to represent an alphabetical or numeric character). However, 10Mbps is probably fast enough for most home networks - it seems stunningly fast when copying files. The T-pieces, each involving 3 bayonet connections, can be unreliable. In a network of many computers, with the bus technology, any break in the continuity of the cable will cause the whole of the network to fail. This can result in hours of "down time" until the break is detected. However, in a home environment, especially if cost is a factor, a cheap Thin Ethernet network consisting of two network cards, a Thin Ethernet Cable, two T-pieces and two terminators is all you need to start networking with two machines. The system will work perfectly well over the distances likely to be encountered in the home or small business.

UTP (Unshielded Twisted Pair)

Also known as **10BaseT, UTP** is a later design of cabling used in many modern networks and looks similar to telephone cabling. Plug-in connectors fit into ports in the network interface cards. These ports are known as **RJ-45**s. The core of the cable comprises two copper wires twisted together and this design gives higher performance. Standard UTP cable (**10BaseT**) operates at 10Mbps while a higher specification cable (known as **100BaseT**) has the potential to operate at the **Fast Ethernet** speed of 100Mbps. For operation at 100Mbps, a UTP cable classified as **Category 5** is recommended whereas 10Mbps systems can use **Category 3**.

If you are connecting only two machines you can manage with two network cards containing RJ-45 ports and a special UTP **cross-over** cable obtainable from computer stores.

However, a preferred solution is to connect the machines radially around a central **Hub** containing several RJ-45 ports. The computers are connected by individual cables like spokes around a wheel, an arrangement known as the **Star** topology. A major advantage of this configuration is that you can disconnect an individual computer and cable without disabling the rest of the network.

Complete kits can be purchased from networking giants like 3Com for under £100 and these include the network cards, cabling and a hub containing several RJ-45 ports. You simply plug the UTP cables into the hub in the way that telephone cables plug into a jack socket. (In large organisations computers may be up to 100 metres from the hub and extra hubs or **repeaters** can be inserted to increase the length of an arm of the network).

I have been using the 3Com OfficeConnect networking kit designed for the home and small business. It was easy to set up and is fast and reliable. The OfficeConnect hub has several LEDs which give diagnostic information such as the status of the ports and whether or not packets of data are being sent or received. If you wish to expand your network, more hubs can be connected at a later date.

The Network Interface Card

This is a small printed circuit board which connects each PC to the network cabling and handles communication with the other computers on the network. Also known as a *NIC* and a *network adapter*, the term *network card* will generally be used throughout this book. The network card is fitted to a spare expansion slot on your computer's motherboard (the main circuit board to which the principal components are connected).

Fitting the network card is a task which anyone can undertake, without special skills. It's just a case of removing the cover of your machine and plugging the card into one of the free slots on the motherboard. Network cards are available with either Thin Ethernet (BNC) connectors or UTP (RJ-45) ports. "Combo" cards allow both types of cable to be connected. If possible network cards designed for the computer's PCI slots should be obtained as these are easier to configure.

Before starting work you should rid yourself of any static electricity, as this can damage sensitive electronic components like the network card. You can earth yourself by touching a metal object such as the metal frame of your computer or part of a central heating system.

Alternatively you can wear one of the special earthing straps which can be bought cheaply from electrical component suppliers. A well-lit room is desirable: it's also useful to have a small torch handy to illuminate the hidden depths of your machine.

With the machine switched off, disconnect all of the cables from the back of the computer. The casing can then be removed, usually after taking out some small retaining screws. You should see several spare slots of various types on the motherboard as follows:

Long black slots:	ISA architecture
Long brown slots:	EISA architecture
Short white slots:	PCI architecture

The documentation accompanying your network cards should specify the type of slot required by your particular card.

If you have several spare slots all of the correct type, the card can be inserted into any one of them - position is not important. Now remove the blanking plate adjacent to the chosen slot by taking out and keeping safe the single retaining screw. Taking care not to touch the edges of the network card, firmly push it into the slot until the gold edge connectors are evenly engaged. Now secure the card by fitting the retaining screw. Replace the casing and reconnect the cables at the back of the machine.

You need to insert network cards in every computer which is going to be networked, before starting to connect the cables.

PCMCIA Network Cards

Anyone using a notebook (or laptop) computer on the move will probably want to connect to a network on returning to base. Special credit card size Network Interface Cards are available which plug into a tiny slot on the computer. These cards are termed PCMCIA (Personal Computer Memory Card International Association), after the computer industry group which agreed on a specification for upgrade cards for portable computers.

PCMCIA cards are very easy to plug in and remove and installation of the necessary software drivers should be automatic. Like many components for notebook computers, however, PCMCIA cards are more expensive than the equivalent ISA or PCI components for full-size desktop machines.

Connecting the Cables

Before you can configure the network cards you need to install the cabling which links the machines together. If you are using coaxial cable (Thin Ethernet) then you must connect the cable to each machine using T-pieces or Y-pieces and fit terminators to each end of the cable.

If you're using twisted pair (UTP) cabling then each cable should be inserted into the RJ-45 port in a network card, before inserting the other end in an RJ-45 port in the hub. When all of the cables have been connected, the power to the hub should be switched on. A constant green light (LED) against the number for each port on the hub indicates that the card and its associated cabling are correctly installed. There may also be a green light on the network card suggesting that all is well. If there is no green light at the appropriate port on the hub, check that the cables are properly connected and the network card is firmly and evenly located in the slot on the motherboard. Obvious though it seems, it may be necessary to check that the hub is actually powered up!

Configuring the Network Card

The latest Plug and Play technology should ensure that each new network card requires very little setting up before it is ready to start work. If you buy PCI cards then they should be self-configuring. Normally the card is detected automatically when the computer is restarted. Then you are asked to insert the Windows Me CD so that the appropriate drivers may be copied to your hard disc. All being well the network card is now ready for use, although the network software components in Windows Me still need to be set up on each machine.

However, you may encounter problems which prevent the seamless, automatic configuration of your network cards as described above. The following pages therefore discuss some of the alternative methods available for detecting, configuring and examining the new network cards.

If you have ISA cards or cards which are not compatible with Plug and Play, then a little more work will certainly be necessary. The process of configuring a network card sets various parameters so that the new device integrates smoothly without clashing with other devices already installed in the computer.

This includes allocating an *interrupt setting (IRQ)* to the network card. An interrupt setting is the number of a channel which the device uses to communicate with the central processor of the computer. This number must be unique to the device; Two devices (such as a modem and a network card, for example) cannot share the same interrupt number if they are to operate simultaneously. In the past this was frequently a problem during hardware installation, requiring manual adjustment to the interrupt settings. Plug and Play technology is intended to alleviate this problem.

Before fitting the network cards provided in the 3Com OfficeConnect Kit, you need to carry out a preinstallation procedure on each machine. Using software provided on floppy disc, the available interrupts are identified and a suitable one is assigned to the network card.

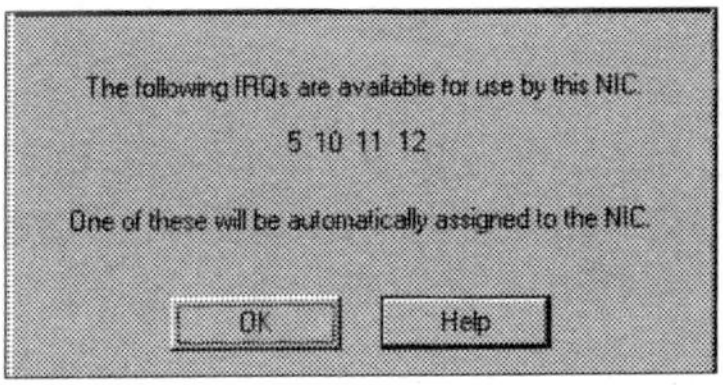

Before switching the computer on, you should make sure your Windows Me CD and any discs provided by the manufacturer of your network card are available. These will probably be requested during the installation process.

After startup, the computer should announce that the network card has been detected as a new piece of hardware.

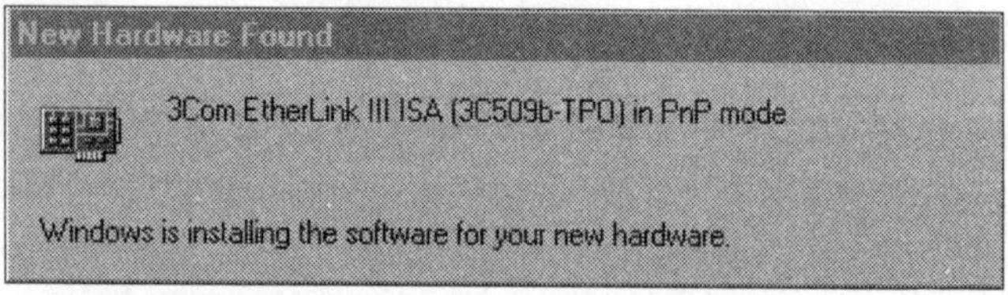

If the network card is not detected automatically you can start the process by selecting **Start**, **Settings**, **Control Panel** and double-clicking on the icon **Add New Hardware.**

If the **Add New Hardware Wizard** fails to detect the NIC, you can do a manual installation by choosing to select your hardware from a list.

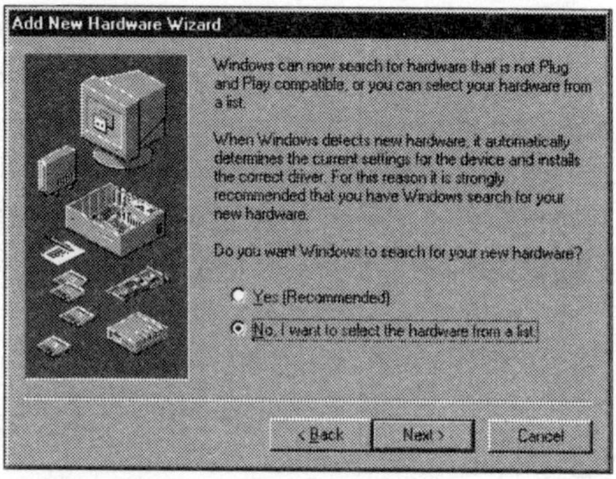

Then select **Network adapters** from the list of hardware types.

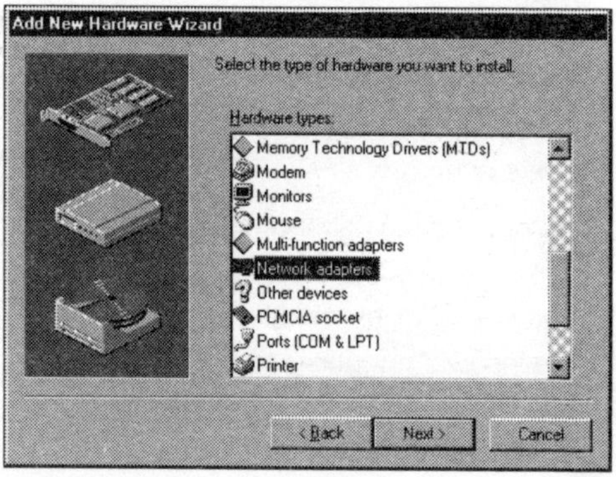

The **Select Device** window appears listing a range of manufacturers and models of network cards. You will need to select your particular card.

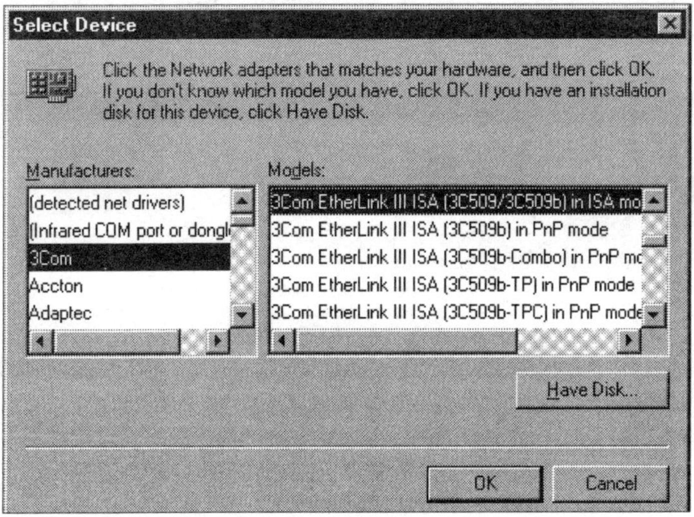

At this point you should click **Have Disk...** and you will be requested to insert the floppy disc(s) provided by the manufacturer of your network card.

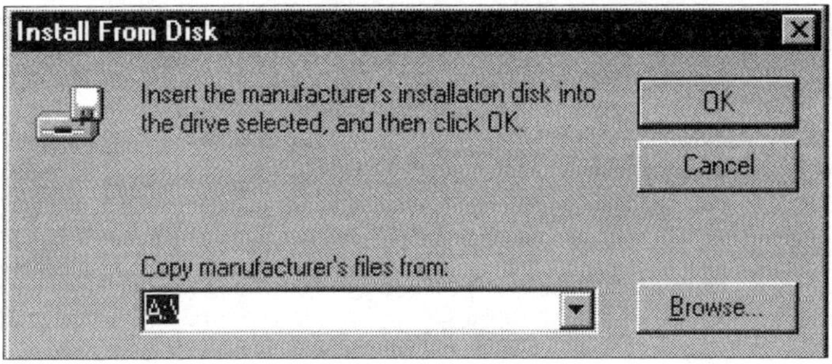

The remainder of the configuration procedure simply involves following the instructions on screen while the network is configured and the necessary files are copied to your hard disc.

In the 3Com OfficeConnect kit, an installation wizard automates the process and tests the card to ensure that it's working correctly.

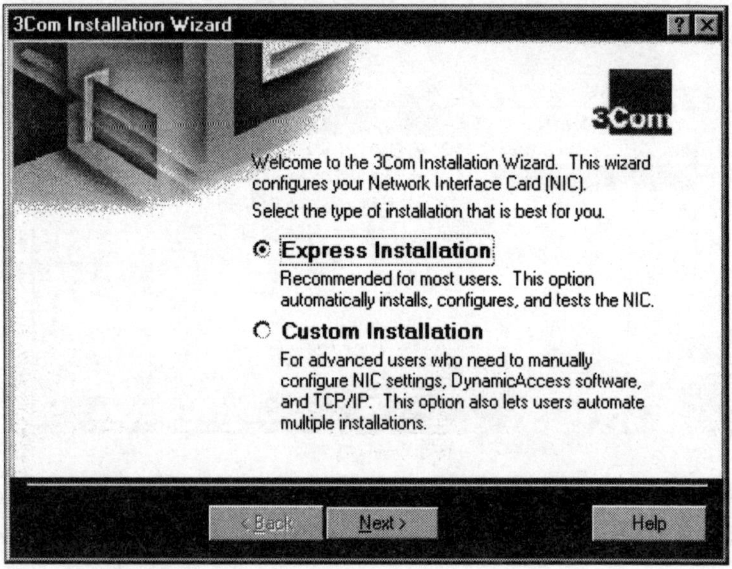

To complete the installation you will be prompted for the Windows Me CD and after copying the necessary files you will be instructed to restart the machine.

Identifying Network Computers

At some point in the installation process you will be required to enter some names to identify each of the computers or "workstations" on the network. You make up the names yourself, with a limit of 15 characters and no spaces.

Computer name: is compulsory and must be *different* for each computer on the network.

Workgroup: is compulsory and must be the *same* for every computer in a group which are to share the same files or resources on the network

Computer Description: is optional.

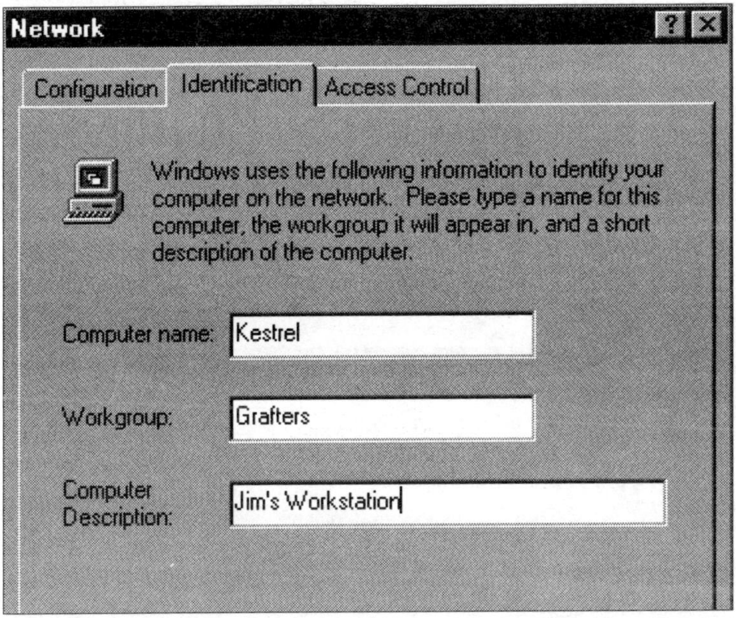

These names can be altered at any time by selecting **Start**, **Settings**, **Control Panel**, double-clicking the **Network** icon and selecting the **Identification** tab.

Examining the Network Card

You can check that your network card is working correctly using the **Device Manager** in the **Control Panel**. This is accessed by selecting **Start**, **Settings**, **Control Panel** then double-clicking the **System** icon before selecting the **Device Manager** tab.

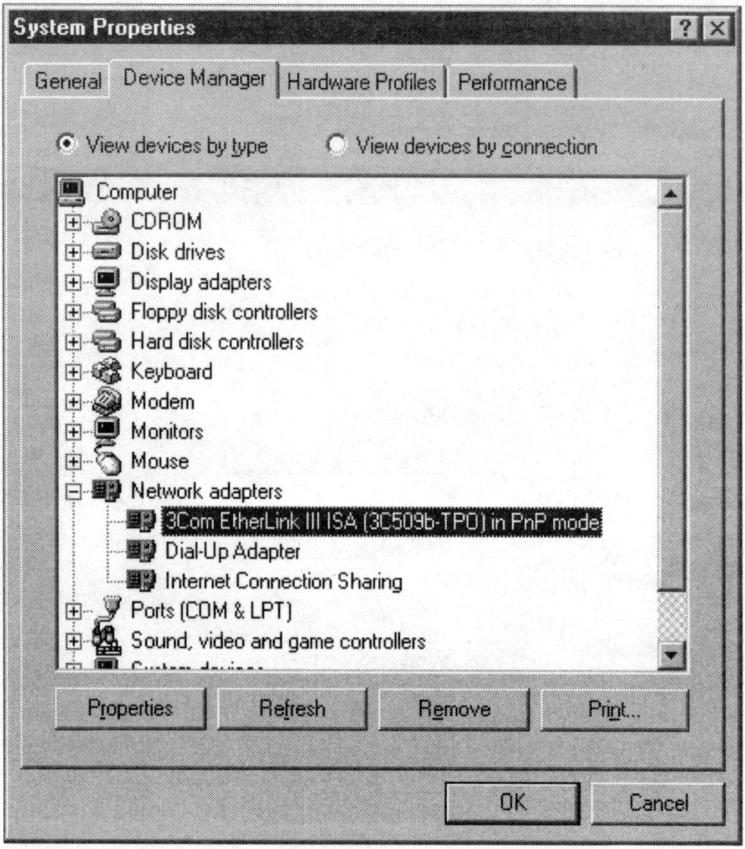

Selecting **Network adapters** should show the name of the network card which you have just installed. If there is any problem with the network card an exclamation mark in a yellow circle will appear through the icon for the device next to its name in the list.

With your network card highlighted in the device manager, clicking the **Properties** button should lead to the **General** tab and a message stating **This device is working properly**.

An unwanted network card can be deleted by highlighting and clicking the **Remove** button shown above.

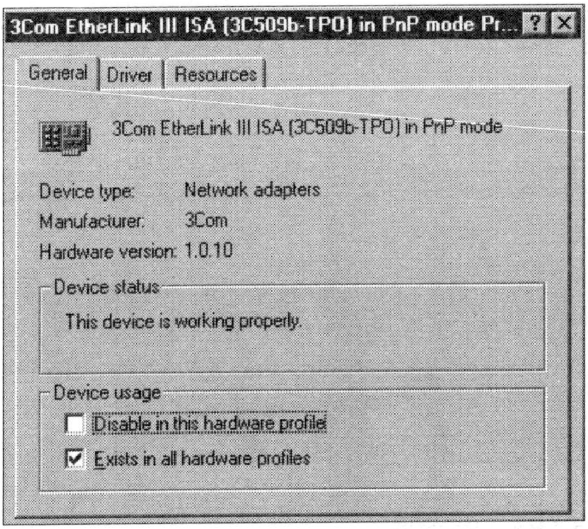

However, if an error is reported, selecting the **Driver** tab should provide help and the opportunity to re-install the network card driver software.

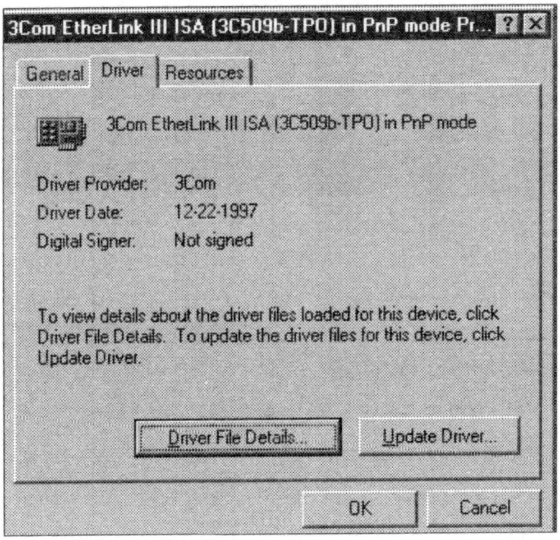

Buttons are provided to check the **Driver File Details...** or to **Update Driver...**.

If there is a problem with the IRQ (interrupt) setting on your network card, it may be possible to alter this after selecting the **Resources** tab for the network card.

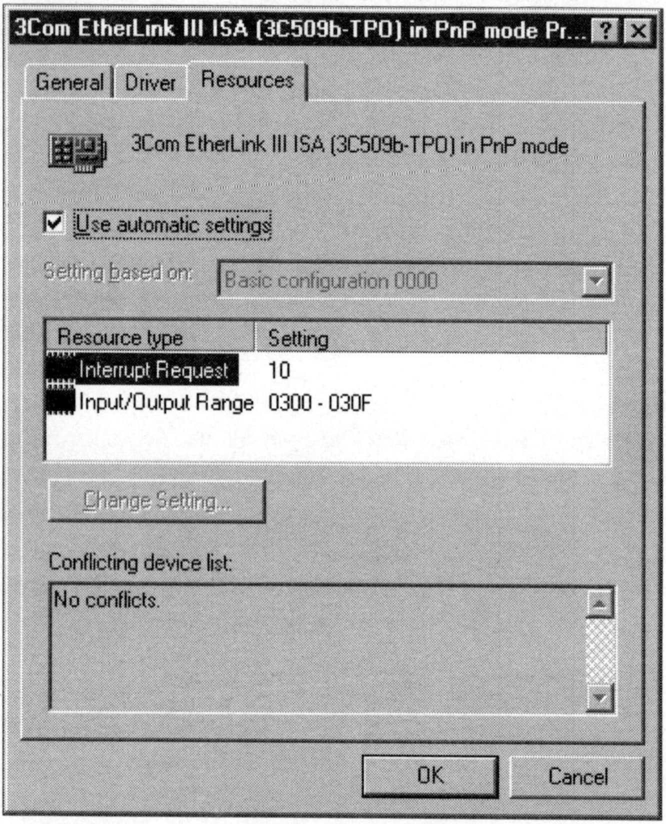

This should, all being well, display **No conflicts.** but if there are conflicts you can experiment with other settings by first switching off **Use automatic settings**. Now click **Change Setting...** and scroll through alternative values for **Interrupt Request**, **Memory Range** and **Input/Output Range** until **No conflicts.** appears in the **Conflicting device list:**.

The Windows Me **Home Networking Troubleshooter** accessed from **Start** and **Help** gives good diagnostic support for any remaining obstinate problems.

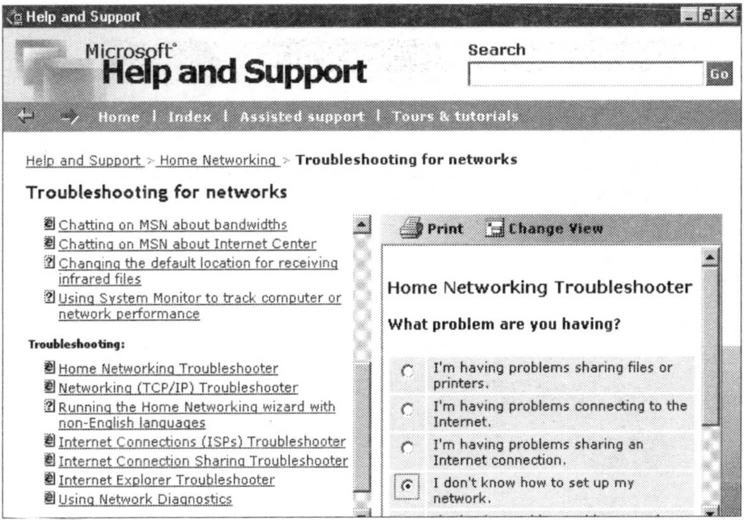

If you buy a 3Com network card, the **3COM NIC DOCTOR** diagnostic software is added to the Windows Me **Start/Programs** menu as part of the installation process.

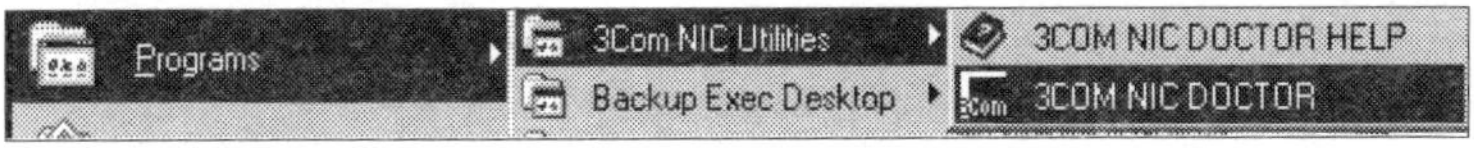

This includes utilities which test both the network interface card and the integrity of the network itself. Amongst other things it is also possible to alter the configuration of the 3Com card.

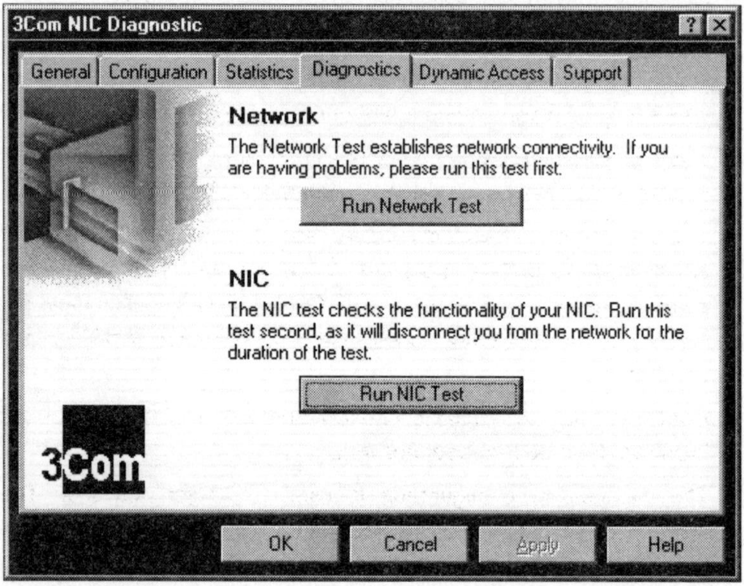

Before you can start to use the new network there is still some setting up to do in Windows Me. Fortunately Windows Me introduces the **Home Networking Wizard**. This makes sure that the correct Windows Me network software components are installed. You also need to ensure that users of the network will be able to share folders and devices such as printers. These topics are covered in the next chapter.

Summary: Building Your Own Network

- Networking enables two or more computers to share expensive resources such as data files, applications software, printers, and CDs. Also to carry out tasks such as file transfer and backups.
- Windows Me contains **Internet Connection Sharing,** software which allows several networked computers to share an Internet connection using one modem and one telephone line.
- The peer-to-peer network connects all machines as equals; they can access each others' applications and data files and share a printer.
- The peer-to-peer network is relatively easy to set up and manage for small networks of 2-10 machines. Windows Me contains all of the software needed to set up a peer-to-peer network, including the newly introduced Home Networking Wizard, which simplifies the process.
- Complete kits are available cheaply and these contain all of the hardware for a peer-to-peer network.
- The client/server configuration is used for larger networks. The server is a powerful machine dedicated to the management of the network and used as a central store for the applications software and data files. A special network operating system is required such as Windows 2000 Server or Novell Netware.
- The client/server network has sophisticated software for security and file management, including backups. These require the skills of a trained network administrator.
- Ethernet is the dominant standard for network technology such as network interface cards and cabling. Thin Ethernet is an older and slower type of cabling which requires computers to be connected in a continuous line, known as the Bus topology.
- UTP is a newer Ethernet specification, with the potential for faster operation, in which computers are connected around a central hub in the Star topology. The hub has diagnostic facilities and allows individual cables and machines to be removed without disabling the rest of the network, unlike the Bus configuration.

- Fitting network cards and connecting the cabling is a simple task which anyone can accomplish.
- If a computer has been previously fitted with a network card, the old card should be physically removed before starting to fit the new network card. The entry for the old card in the **Device Manager** should also be removed, after clicking **Start**, **Settings**, **Control Panel** and double-clicking the **System** tab. Highlight the name of the network card in the **Device Manager** and click the **Remove** button.
- The installation process involves the copying of driver software for your particular brand of network card. Also the setting of various parameters such as interrupts, to avoid conflicts with previously installed devices.
- PCI network cards are recommended as they are self-configuring and therefore very easy to install.
- The new network card should be detected automatically but if not, Windows Me provides manual methods of detection and installation.
- To complete the installation you will need your Windows Me CD and any discs provided by the manufacturer of the network card.
- All computers on the network must be individually identified with a unique *computer name.*
- All computers sharing the same drives, folders and resources must be members of the same *workgroup.*
- The status of the network card can be examined in the **Device Manager**, accessed by **Start**, **Settings**, **Control Panel** and **System** icon. This reports on any problems/conflicts and allows alternative settings to be tried. A yellow circle containing an exclamation mark indicates a fault with a device.
- Windows Me includes the **Home Networking Troubleshooter** which diagnoses and suggests solutions for a wide range of network problems.

11

Windows Me Home Networking

Introduction

This chapter describes the final setting up of the Windows Me software in order to run a small peer-to-peer network. Before starting work you should have already installed network cards in all of the computers, as described in the previous chapter. Then you should have examined the **Device Manager**, accessed from the **System** icon in the **Control Panel**. The name of your network card should be listed under **Network adapters**. If it is not working correctly the card's name will appear next to a circle containing an exclamation mark. The name on its own without an exclamation mark indicates that the card is installed correctly. This is described on page 196.

You should also have connected all of the network cards to a hub in the case of a UTP network or to each other in the case of Thin Ethernet cable (pages 186-187). If you are using UTP cabling with a hub, the hub should be switched on and you should see lights corresponding to each network card.

The next part of the work was quite complex in the past and involves checking that each machine has certain networking software components installed. These components have jargon names such as "TCP/IP", "NetBEUI" and "IPX/SPX-compatible protocol". Fortunately, Windows Me introduces the **Home Networking Wizard**, which guides you through the setting up of the networking software and shields you from the more technical jargon. The Home Networking Wizard is described shortly.

Internet Connection Sharing

During the execution of the Home Networking Wizard, you are given the opportunity to set up Internet Connection Sharing. This facility is now one of the main reasons for setting up a home or small business network. Internet Connection Sharing allows all of the computers on the network to access the Internet through one modem, one telephone line and one Internet connection.

The machine with the physical Internet connection is known as the *host* or *gateway* computer and relays Internet information back to the *client* computers around the network. Internet Connection Sharing is a software component of Windows Millenium, and *should only be installed on the host machine*. To make sure ICS is installed, select **Start**, **Settings, Control Panel** and double click the **Add/Remove Programs** icon. Now select the **Windows Setup** tab, highlight **Communications** and click the **Details...** button. You may need to scroll down to see **Internet Connection Sharing**, which should be ticked as shown below.

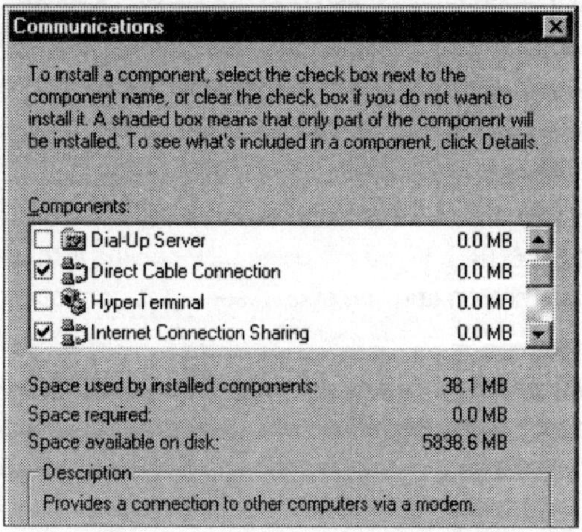

After clicking **OK** and **Apply**, you may be asked to insert the Windows Me CD so that the necessary files can be copied to the hard disc. More work is needed before you can use Internet Connection Sharing to connect all of the client computers to the Internet. This is covered later in this chapter.

The Home Networking Wizard

The Home Networking Wizard can be launched from the **My Network Places** icon on the Windows Me Desktop or from the menu system using **Start**, **Programs**, **Accessories**, **Communication** and **Home Networking Wizard**.

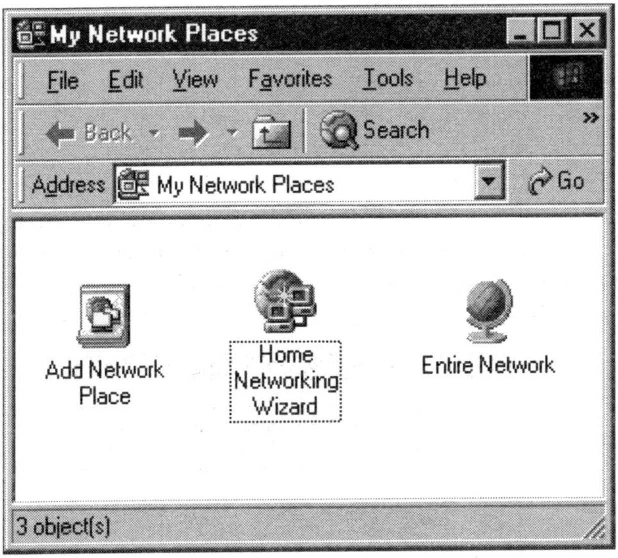

If you are going to set up Internet Connection sharing, the computer containing the direct physical Internet connection, i.e. the modem or other device, is designated as the *Host* and must be running Windows Me. If the other machines on the network are running Windows 95 or 98, the Home Networking Wizard will allow you to create a floppy disc version of itself. This is then used to run the Home Networking Wizard on all of the client machines on the network.

After creating the floppy disc you are asked whether the computer is to connect directly to the Internet Service Provider (ISP) or via another computer on the home network, as shown on the next page.

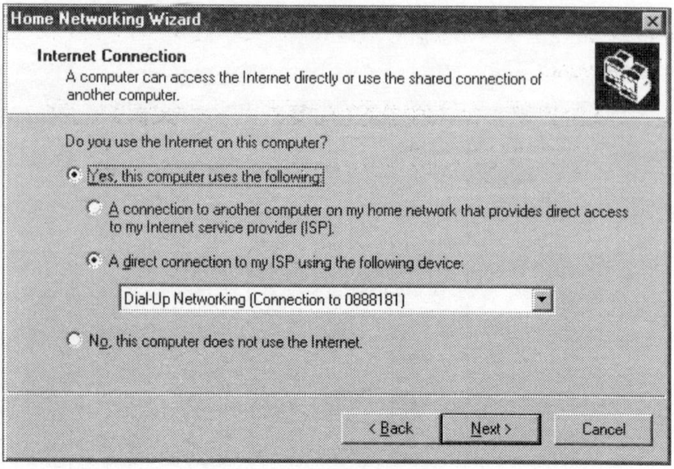

In the above example, the host machine is being set up, so the direct connection to the ISP is selected. In the next window, you can agree to let other computers use the Internet Connection on this computer. Please note that the Home Networking Wizard has automatically picked up the 3Com EtherLink network card which connects this computer to the network.

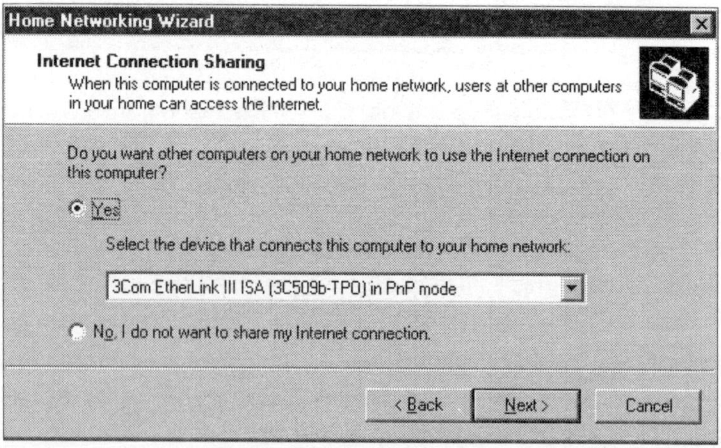

The next window requires you to enter identification for each computer on the network.

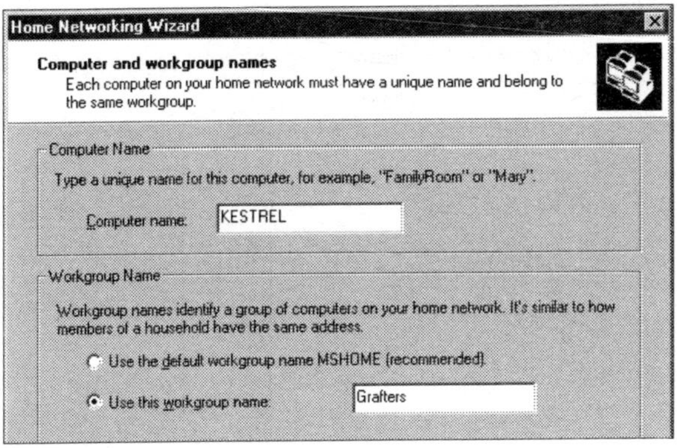

Computer Name must be *different* for every computer on the network. **Workgroup Name** must be the *same* for all of the computers on the network wishing to share the same files and printers.

After clicking **Next**, you can opt to share files and printers on the host machine with other computers on the network.

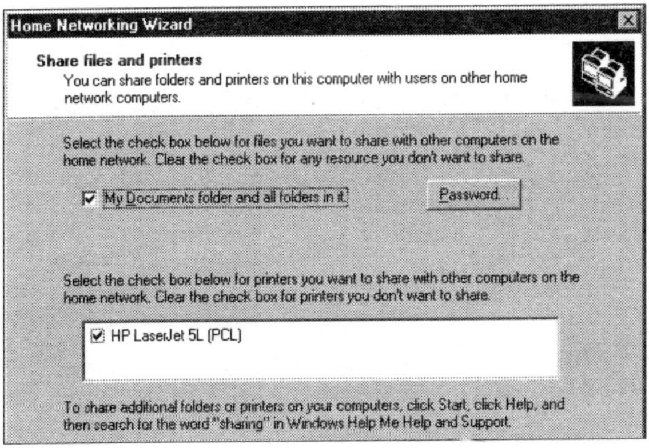

At this stage you should enter a password for the shared folder. You may wish to make other resources (folders and printers) shareable, with passwords, as discussed later in this chapter.

The Home Networking Wizard finishes by asking you to restart the computer and, all being well, you are congratulated on successfully setting up Home Networking on this computer, the network *host* .

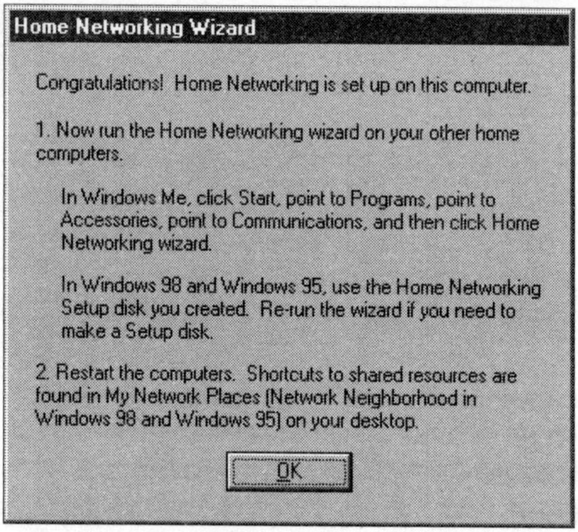

The Home Networking Wizard must now be run on all of the *client* machines on the network. Computers running Windows 95 or 98 will need to launch the home Networking Wizard using **Start** and **Run** and the floppy disc created earlier as follows:

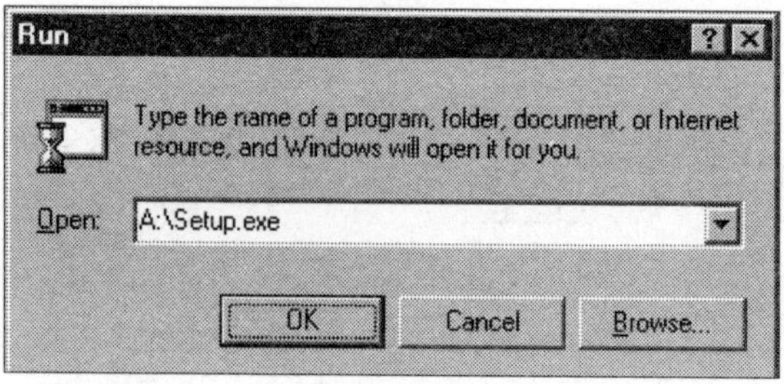

Completion of the Home Networking Wizard for the client machines is very similar to the method described on the previous pages for the host machine. The main difference is that the client uses the home network to connect to the host computer and thence out to the Internet.

My Network Places

You should now be able to examine your new network by double clicking the icon for **My Network Places** on the Windows Me Desktop. This corresponds to the **Network Neighborhood** feature on Windows 98. All being well the window for My Network Places will open as shown below.

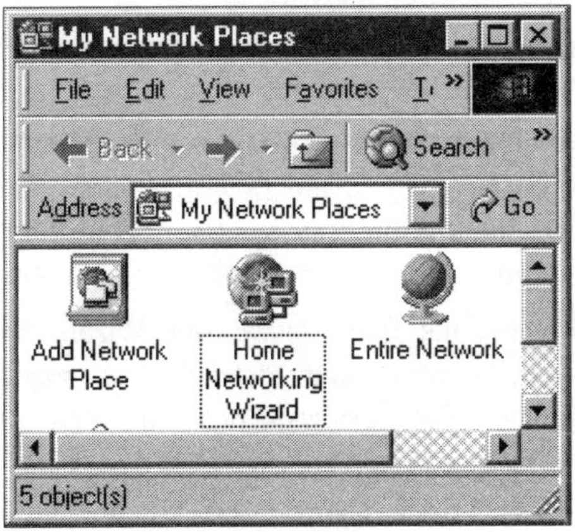

Double clicking on the **Entire Network** icon opens up the workgroup window, in this case **Grafters**, as shown below on the left. Double clicking on the icon for the workgroup **Grafters** reveals the two computers, **Kestrel** and **Merlin**, connected to my two-machine network, as shown below on the right.

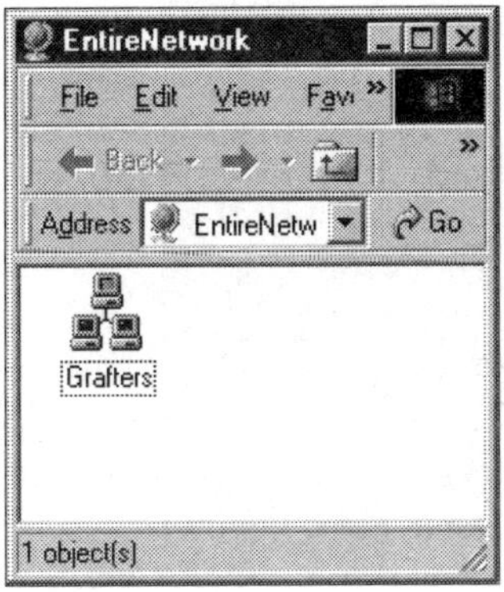

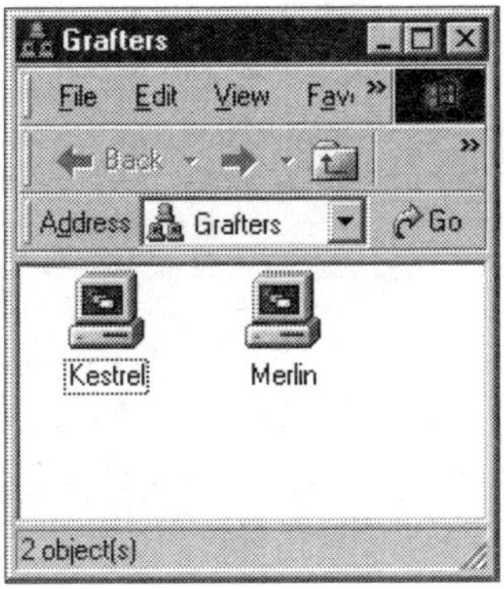

Troubleshooting

Double clicking on the icons for each machine should open up the shared resources which are available. Then you can copy files and folders between computers. This is discussed later. However, if all of your networked machines are not shown in the My Network Places window as shown at the bottom of page 209, here are a few things to check:

- Make sure that all of the network cables are connected to the network cards and to the network hub, if fitted.
- Ensure that every computer is fitted with a correctly functioning network card. Check in the Device Manager in the Control Panel that there is no error symbol next to the name of the network card (please see page 196 for more information).

You may need to run the Home Networking Wizard again on any machines which will not connect to the network. If you suspect there is a problem in the setting up of the networking components, performed by the wizard, these can be inspected "manually" by double clicking the network icon (shown left) in the Windows Me **Control Panel** (**Start**, **Settings**, **Control Panel**). Select the **Configuration** tab as shown below.

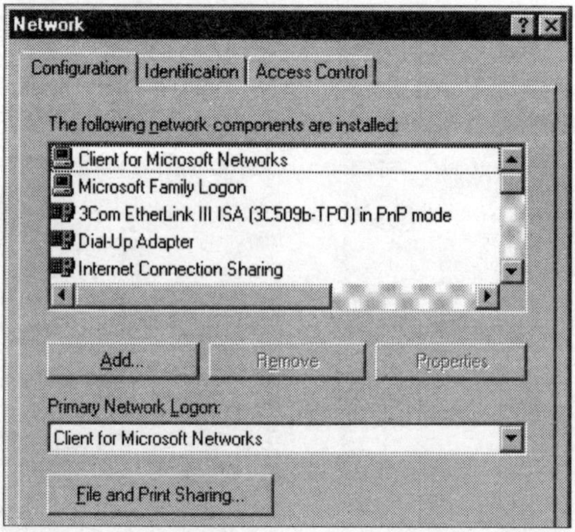

The Home Networking Wizard should have made sure that the necessary Windows Me components were installed. However, you may wish to check that the following components are present in your own Network window, like the one shown on the previous page (scroll down the list if necessary):

- Client for Microsoft Networks
- TCP/IP – The Internet Protocol
- Dial-Up Adapter
- Internet Connection Sharing (host machine only)
- File and Printer Sharing for Microsoft Networks
- The name of your network card, e.g. 3Com EtherLink II ISA

Select **Client for Microsoft Networks** as the **Primary Network Logon:** in the **Network** window as shown on the previous page.

Any items which are missing from the list can be installed after clicking the **Add...** button. Adding networking components in Windows Me is discussed in the Direct Cable Connection on page 158.

Clicking the **Identification** tab on the **Network** window allows you to edit the name of the computer and the name of the workgroup.

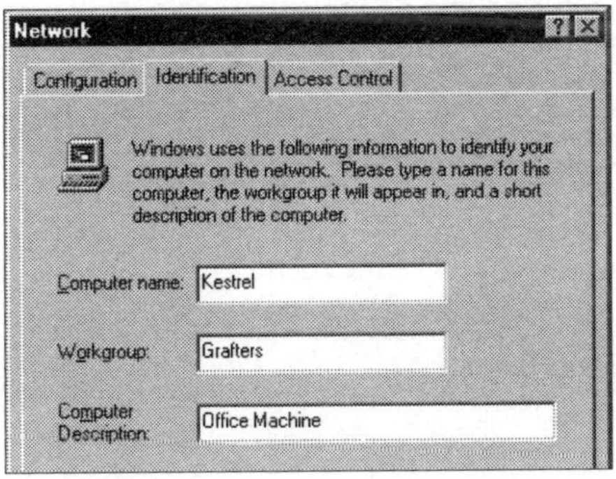

The machines will not be recognized by the network unless:

- Each machine has a *different* **Computer name.**
- All machines have the *same* **Workgroup.**

Now click the **Access Control** tab and set the access to **Share-level access control**. This will allow you to put a password on each of the resources (folders and printers) to be shared on the network.

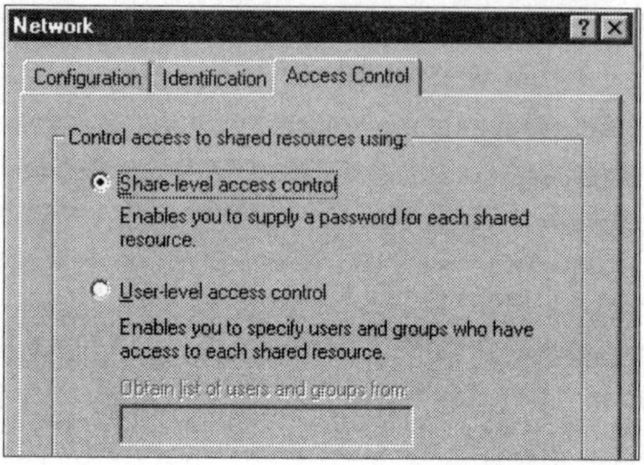

You should now be able to open the folder **My Network Places** and see the icons for your individual machines on the network. Double clicking the icon for any of the machines will show the *shareable* resources on that machine. These are the hard discs, folders and printers which have been designated as shareable after right clicking over their icons in My Computer. Making files and printers shareable is discussed in detail on pages 159-161 of this book. At the same time you can set passwords for the resources according to the level of access, **Read-Only** or **Full**. You should also give the shared resource a meaningful name to identify it on the network.

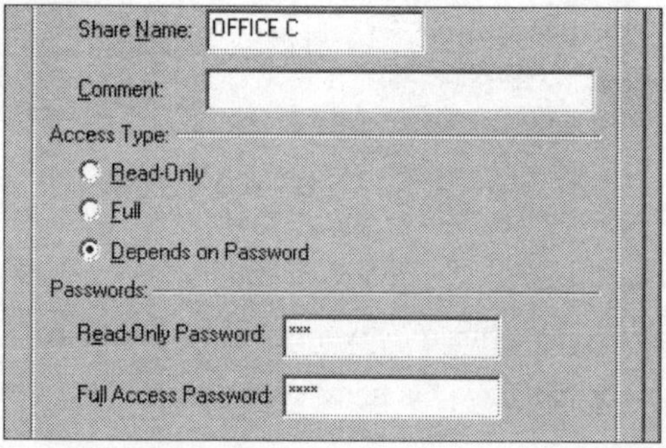

Sharing a Printer on the Network

If you've bought an expensive printer you may as well make it available to all computers on the network. Otherwise people have to use a floppy disc to move their work to the machine attached to the printer, or copy it across using the network. It's quite easy to give each machine on the network direct access to a remote printer attached to another computer.

First make sure the printer is shareable. Working at the machine with the printer attached, select **Start**, **Settings**, **Control Panel** and **Printers**. Then right click over the printer and select **Sharing...** as described on page 161 of this book. Give the printer a **Share Name**.

The next step must be completed on all of the computers which are not attached to the shared printer. In this example, the computer called **Kestrel** is to share a printer attached to the computer called **Merlin**.

Working at **Kestrel**, open the **Printers** folder from **Start**, **Settings** and **Printers**. Now double click the **Add Printer** icon to start the **Add Printer Wizard**. Click **Next** and then select **Network printer**, before clicking **Next** again. The next window requires you to browse for a path to the shared network printer. When you click **Browse...** a window appears showing **My Network Places**.

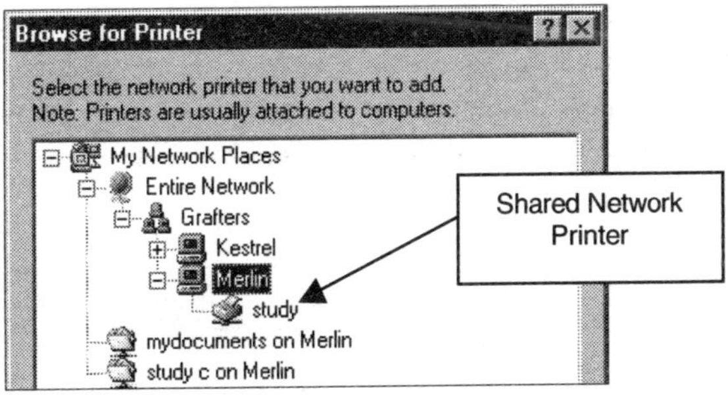

You may need to click on the workgroup icon and the icon for the computer with the printer attached, to reveal the shared printer on the network. In this example the shared printer is named **study** and is physically attached to Merlin, but shared remotely across the network by the **Kestrel** computer.

If you now highlight the printer and click **OK** in the **Browse for Printer** window shown on the previous page, the path of the shared network printer **\\Merlin\study** appears in the **Add Printer Wizard**.

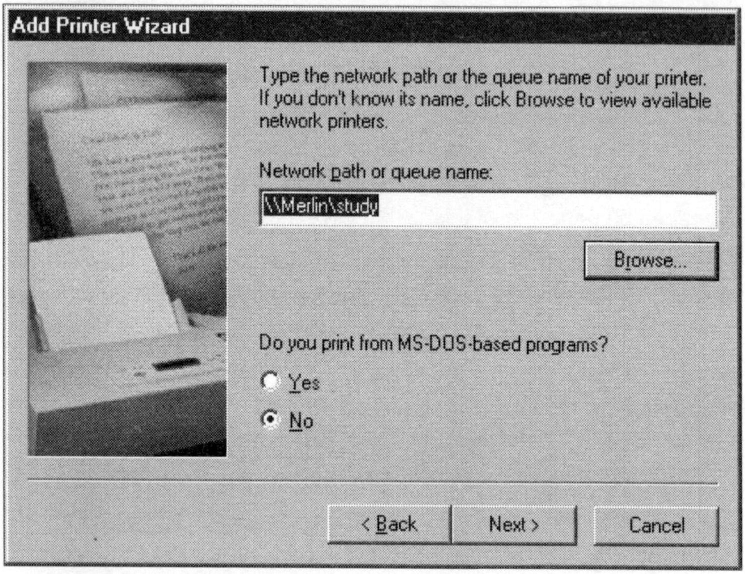

If you wish to print from MS-DOS programs (i.e. programs using the text-based operating system which preceded Microsoft Windows), click **Yes**. This option requires you to select a button marked **Capture Printer Port...** in order to print from MS-DOS programs.

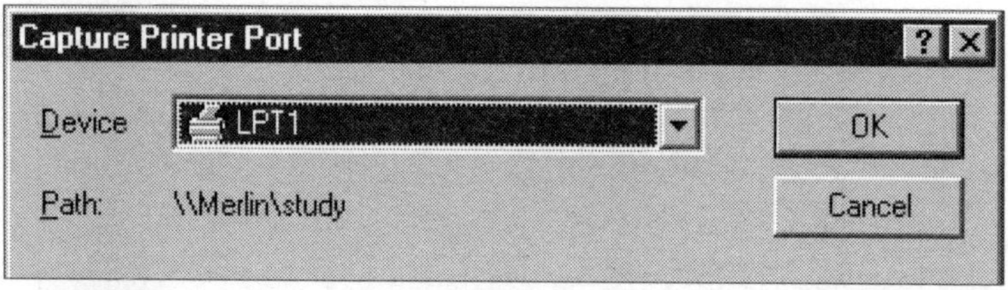

Clicking **OK** to **LPT1** (or whatever is your printer port), returns you to the **Add Printer Wizard** where you will be required to select the type of printer.

If the machine you are working on doesn't already have the necessary "driver" software to make the printer work, you will be required to install it in the **Add Printer Wizard**. You should be able to select the brand of printer from a list and it may be necessary to insert your Windows Me disc or a disc provided by the manufacturer of the printer.

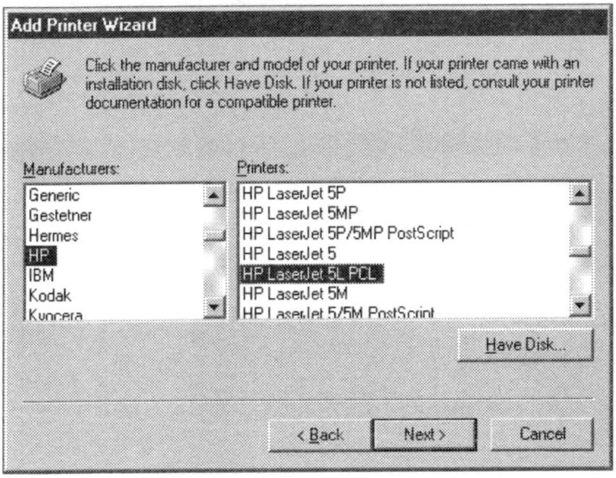

Then you can give the shared printer a name which will appear in the **Printers** folder and after selecting **File** and **Print** in applications.

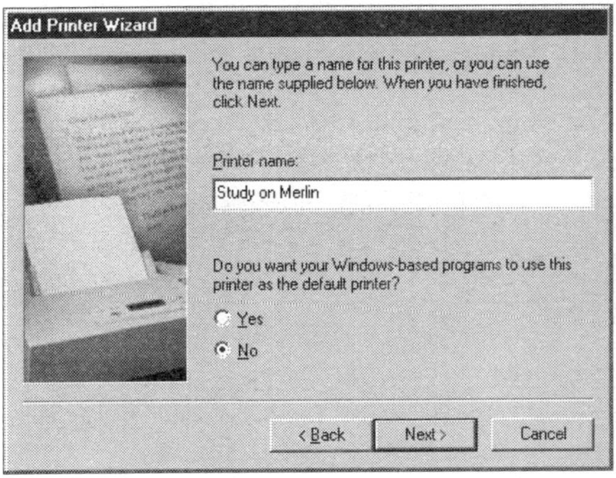

You are given the chance to print a test page and afterwards are asked if the page printed correctly. If you answer **No** to the question, the **Printing Troubleshooter** window opens as shown below, to help you diagnose and fix any problems.

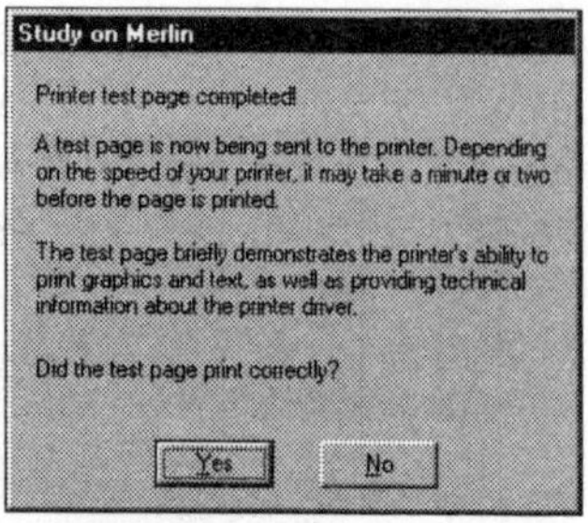

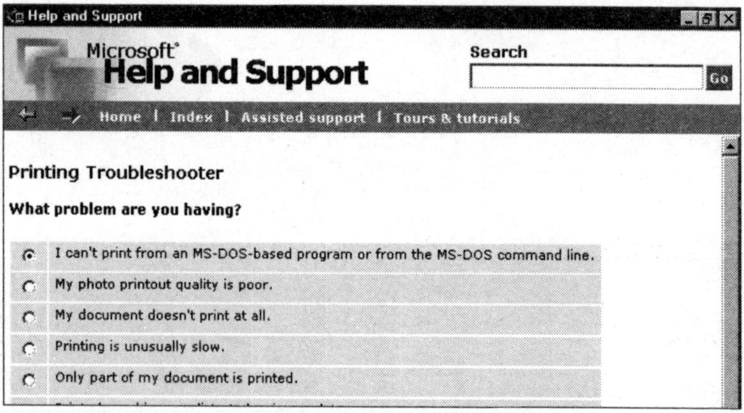

Assuming the network printer has been successfully set up, it will now appear alongside of any local printers in your **Printers** folder, opened by clicking **Start**, **Settings** and **Printers**, as shown below for the **Kestrel** computer.

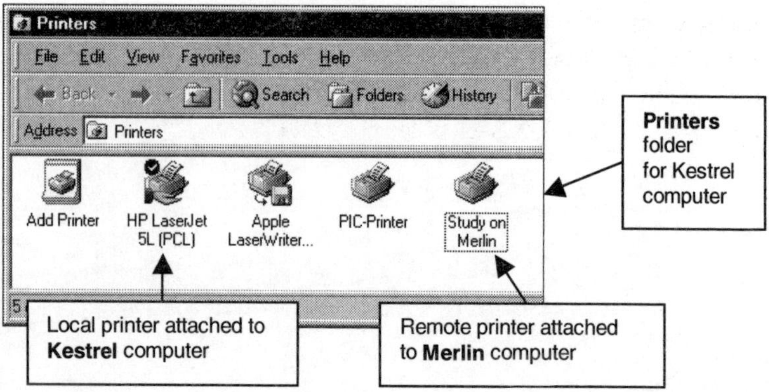

The networked printer, **Study on Merlin** in this example, must be set up as just described, on all of the computers to which it is not physically attached. Then it can be used from within applications such as Word 2000, by selecting **File** and **Print** in the normal way.

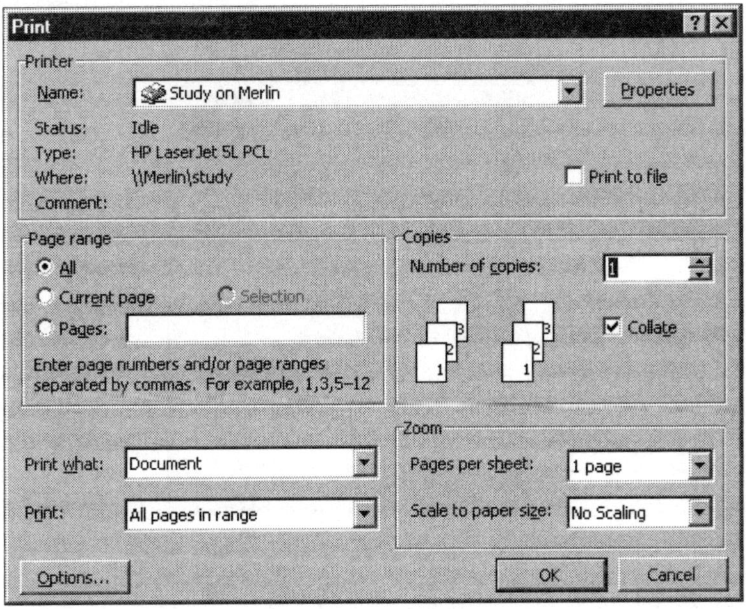

In the above extract from the print dialogue box, the remote printer **Study on Merlin** has been selected in the **Name:** bar. The path to the remote printer, **Merlin\Study**, is given next to **Where:**. In the case of a local printer this would normally say **LPT1**, i.e. the printer port used to attach the printer to the back of the computer.

Using the Network

Open **My Network Places** from the Windows Me desktop as discussed previously. Now double click first on **Entire Network** and then on the name of your workgroup, in this example called **Grafters**. In my example icons for the two machines **Kestrel** and **Merlin** appear.

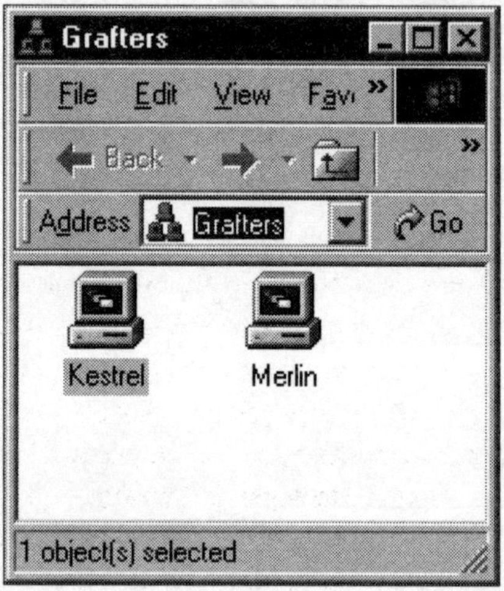

Now double click, successively, on each of the icons for the two machines, **Kestrel** and **Merlin** in this example. The two windows open up showing the shareable resources for each machine.

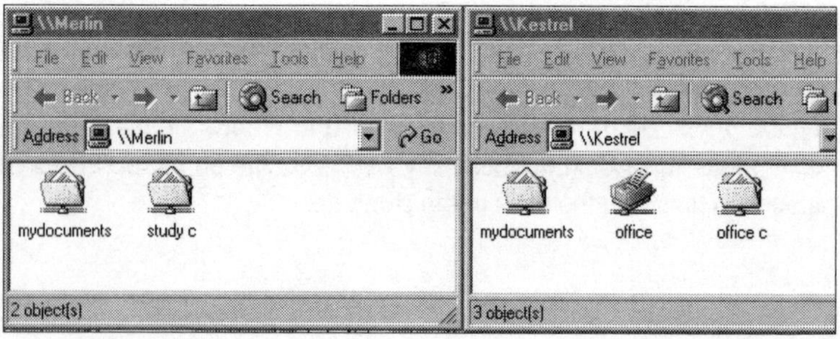

The two windows on the previous page have been *tiled vertically* by right clicking over an empty spot on the Taskbar at the bottom of the Windows Me screen.

If your networked computers are not shown in their own separate windows, you can switch this on in **My Computer** from **Tools** and **Folder Options....**

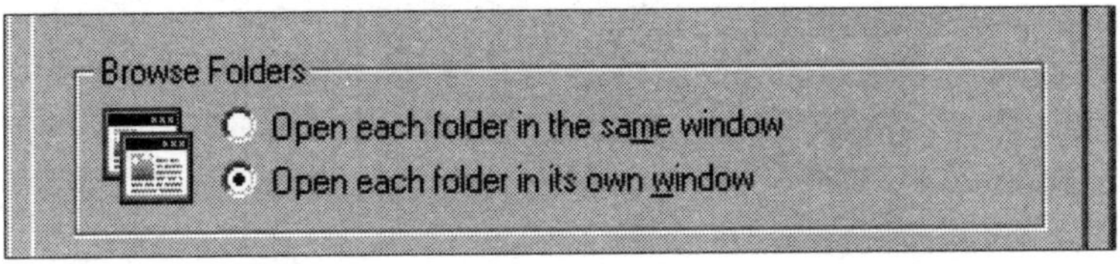

Make sure that **Open each folder in its own window** is switched on. Otherwise you will not be able to open the windows simultaneously and carry out copying operations directly using "drag and drop" with the mouse. You can see in the two windows at the bottom of page 218, that apart from the **mydocuments** folder on each machine that was set as shareable in the Home Networking Wizard, the other shareable resources are the **C:** drives on the two machines (**study c** and **office c**) and the printer called **office** attached to the **kestrel** computer. The names for the hard discs and printer were given during the process which made them shareable, as discussed previously.

Copying between Computers using the Network

In the example below, I have opened up the **C:** drive on **Kestrel** (called **office c**), in order to copy the folder **David** to the **C:** drive (called **study c**) on the other computer, **Merlin**.

Then I copied the folder **David** to the **C:** drive on **Merlin** by dragging and dropping. The whole process is carried out at a very impressive speed. Please note that a folder cannot be copied unless it is set as **Full** access, using **Sharing...** in **My Computer** on the machine containing the folder, as shown on page 212. If you drag and drop a folder using the *right* button on the mouse, on dropping the folder onto its destination you are given a menu to choose either *copying* or *moving* the folder.

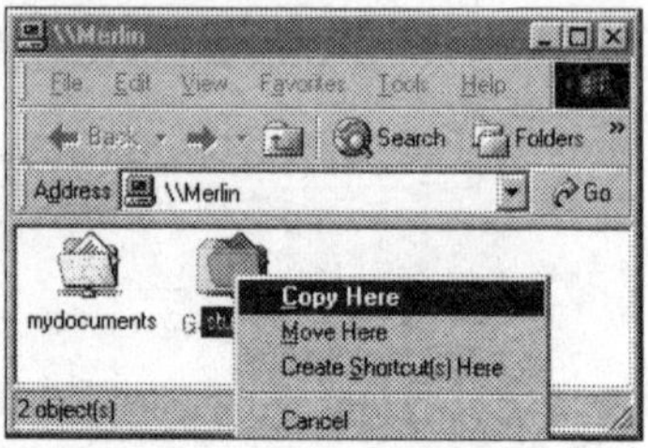

Sharing Files on Another Computer

While working in a program like Word 2000, for example, you can open files from another computer and edit and save them on your machine. (provided you have **Full** not **Read Only Access).** If you have **Read Only Access**, you will be able to edit the document on screen but you will not be able to save the modified document.

To open a file from a folder on another machine on the network, for example using Word 2000, select **File** and **Open...**, then **My Network Places**.

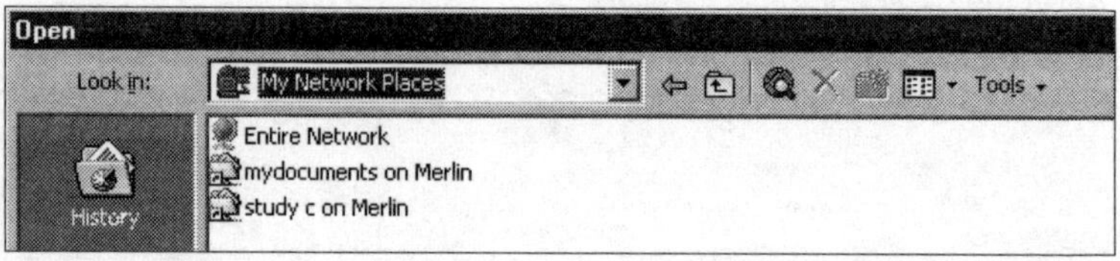

You now have access to the hard disc on the other networked computer, and can open any of its shareable files into Word 2000 (or any other application) on your machine.

WinPopup

When your network is up and running you may need to communicate with other people who are not within speaking distance - in another room in the house perhaps or in a different part of a business. Windows Me includes the utility WinPopup which allows the sending and receiving of short text messages around a network.

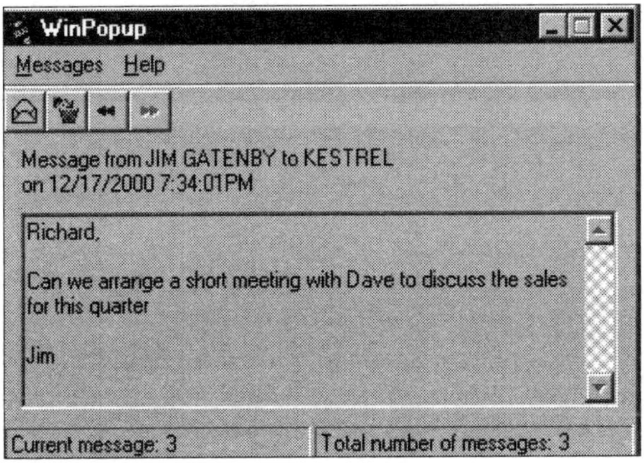

WinPopup is supplied on the original Windows Me CD but may not have been included in the list of optional components when Windows Me was installed on your machine. You can see if WinPopup is installed by selecting **Start**, **Settings**, **Control Panel** and double-clicking on the **Add/Remove Programs** icon. Select the **Windows Setup** tab, scroll down and highlight **System Tools** and click **Details....**

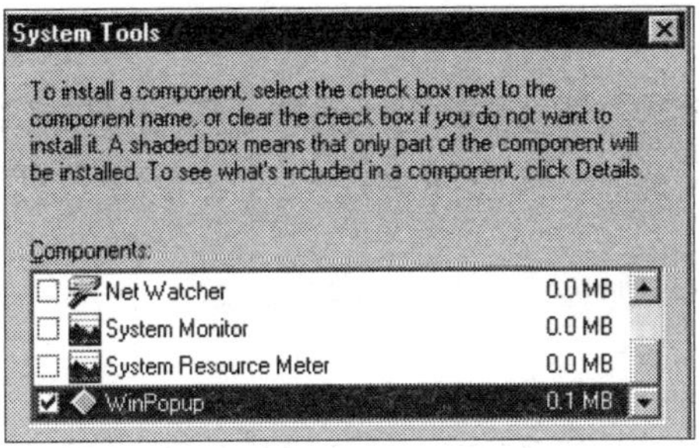

You should see a tick in the box next to **WinPopup**. Make sure WinPopup is ticked and click **OK**. If necessary, you will be asked to insert your Windows Me CD so that the essential files can be copied.

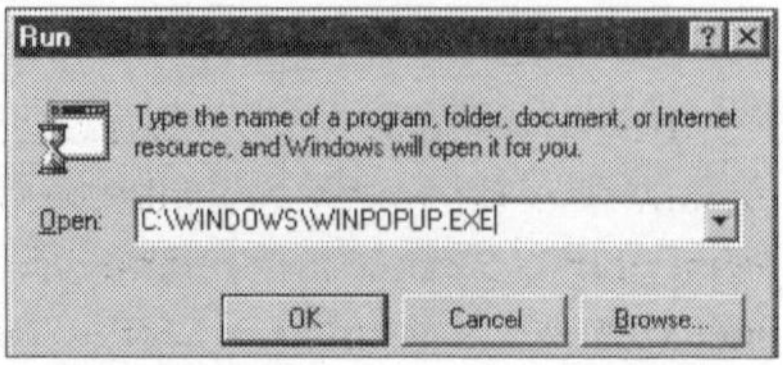

Once installed, WinPopup can be launched by selecting **Start** and **Run...** and entering its name in the **Open:** bar. Or you might create a shortcut icon for WinPopup on the Windows Me Desktop as discussed elsewhere in this book.

Wokstations which are to receive messages must have WinPopup already running - unobtrusively minimised on the taskbar. To send a message, first click the icon representing an envelope.

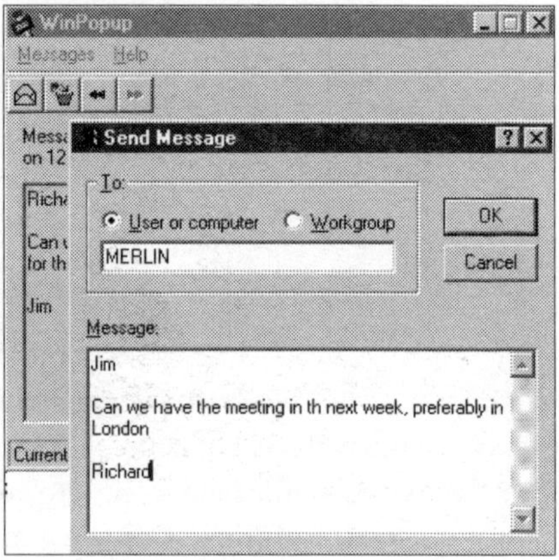

This opens a window in which you can type a short message. The radio button **To:** allows messages to be sent either to a named user or computer on the network or to everyone in a particular workgroup.

After entering the text, click **OK** and you should be informed that the message was successfully sent. The recipient workstation(s) may emit a beep (optional) to announce the arrival of the message as it pops up in its own window on the screen.

An optional dialogue across the top of the message window gives the sender, the date and the time. There are buttons to scroll through the accumulated messages and an icon for deleting messages. **Options...** allows you to specify the way a message is announced and displayed when it arrives at its destination.

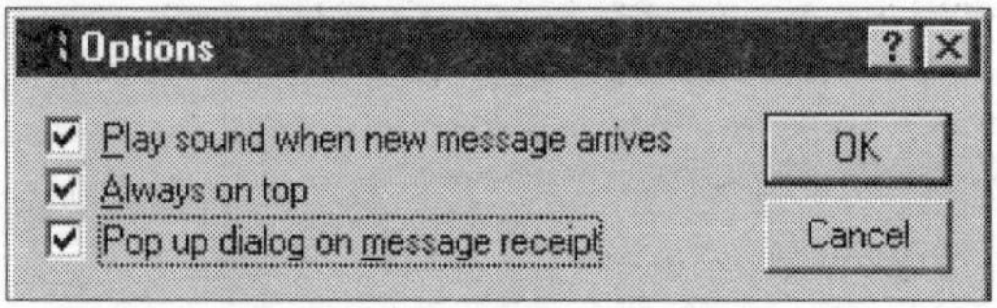

Launching WinPopup Automatically on Startup

To receive messages, all workstations must have WinPopup currently up and running, probably minimised on the taskbar. If you wish to have WinPopup running every time Windows Me starts up, it must be included in the **StartUp** folder. This is achieved by selecting **Start**, **Settings**, **Taskbar and Start Menu....** Select the **Start Menu Programs** tab, click **Add...** then **Browse....**

You need to locate **WINPOPUP.EXE** - it should be in the **Windows** folder. Click the file name and **Open** to place the path to WinPopup in the **Create Shortcut** dialogue box.

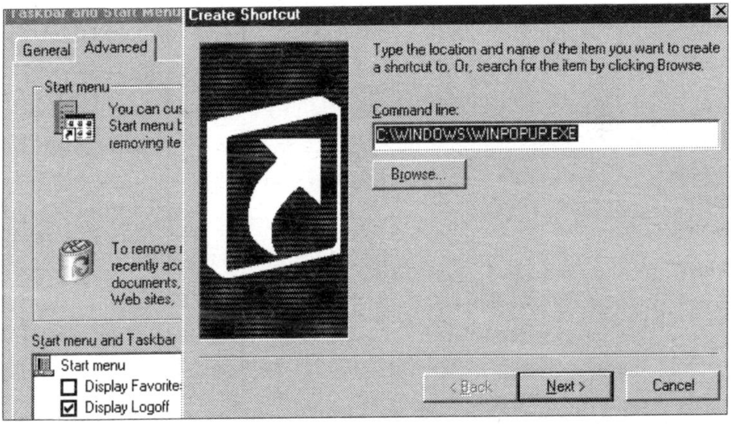

Click **Next** and then highlight the **Startup** folder. Click **Next** and enter the name that you want to appear on the **Startup** menu and then click **Finish**. WinPopup should now run automatically whenever the computer starts up. This procedure needs to be repeated on all of the machines on which WinPopup is to start up automatically.

The same method can be used to launch any program automatically, provided you can browse and locate the program or executable file such as **WINPOPUP.EXE** in the above example.

Connecting Client Computers to the Internet

This section describes how the client machines around the network, which don't have their own direct connection to the Internet, can share a connection on another computer. The machine with the modem (or other device) is known as the host machine and manages requests for information from the client machines. When this information is received from the Internet it is relayed from the host back to the clients.

The main language or *protocol* used for Internet work is known as TCP/IP. Each machine on the network is identified by a unique IP number which acts like an address for the delivery of information. IP numbers are allocated automatically to the client computers by the host machine, although they can be entered manually, as discussed later in this chapter.

Before you can connect a client machine to the Internet via your host computer, you must be sure that the following work (described in the previous chapters) has been successfully completed.

- The host machine (but not the clients) has the Windows Me component Internet Connection Sharing installed.
- The host machine and all of the client machines are connected on a functional Local Area Network, consisting of cabling and network cards.
- The Home Networking Wizard has been run on the host computer and all client machines. In the wizard, the appropriate type of Internet connection (direct or via the LAN) should have been selected for the host and client machines.
- Each machine should have been identified with a *unique* Computer Name and a *common* Workgroup Name.
- The host machine has a connection to the Internet via a modem or other device and this is working correctly.

The pages which follow describe the use of the Internet Connection Wizard to connect the client computers to the Internet via the host computer which contains the modem or other Internet connection.

The Internet Connection Wizard must be repeated on all of the client machines. There should be no need to alter any of the settings on the host machine.

Making an Internet Connection

The Internet Connection Wizard can be started from its icon (if available) on the Windows Me Desktop or from **Start**, **Programs**, **Accessories**, **Communications** and **Internet Connection Wizard.**

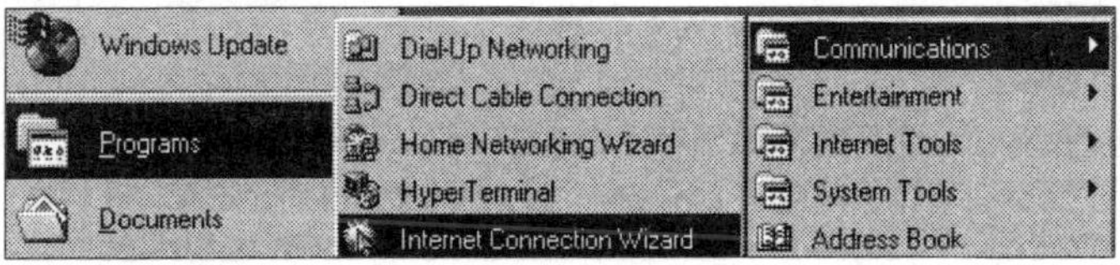

The Welcome screen for the wizard presents a number of choices involving new and existing accounts.

The last option should be chosen, i.e. **I want to connect through a local area network (LAN)**

The next dialogue box gives a choice between a modem connection to the Internet and a connection through a local area network (LAN).

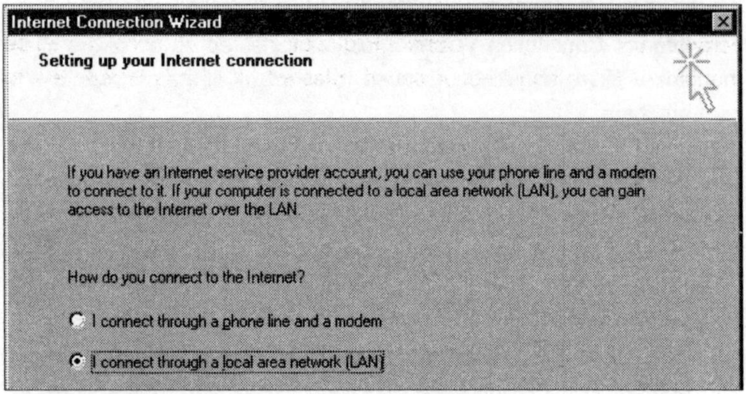

Choose the second option **(LAN)** and click **Next**. You are then advised to select **Automatic discovery of proxy server** and clicking **Next** again should cause the computer to launch your Web browser such as Internet Explorer 5.5. If you are near to the host computer you may hear the modem dialling the number of your Internet Service Provider then all being well you will be logged on to the normal Home Page.

The above procedure needs to be carried out on all of the client machines. Then you will be able to connect to the Internet from any of the machines on the network, as if you had a direct Internet connection. If you are trying to connect while working at a client machine, the host machine must obviously be switched on, but it need not currently be on line to the Internet. When you launch a Web browser such as Internet Explorer 5.5 on the client machine, the modem on the host machine will dial the telephone number of the Internet Service Provider.

When finishing an Internet session, shutting down a client machine which has been connected to the Internet does not automatically shut down the Internet connection on the host machine. This needs to be done manually.

If you have any problems with Internet Connection Sharing, please check that the preparatory work on page 224 has been carried out.

IP Addresses

The next two pages describe how computers are identified on the home network and on the Internet. The IP address is part of TCP/IP, an acronym for Transmission Control Protocol/ Internet Protocol. It can be thought of as a language or set of rules which allows computers to communicate.

When we log on to an Internet computer using a *Domain Name* like **http://www.gatenby.co.uk/**, this is actually converted to an IP address having the form:

207.168.98.7 (Fictitious example)

We are spared the need to remember IP addresses by the use of the more user-friendly Domain Name for Web sites and e-mail addresses.

The computer hosting a Web site for an Internet Service Provider allocates an IP address to your computer every time you log on to the Internet. If a system known as Dynamic Host Configuration Protocol (DHCP) is used, a different address is allocated every time you log on. The host machine at the Internet Service Provider is often known as the **Gateway** computer.

The host machine on a home/small business network acts as a Gateway for the client machines around the local network. It has a fixed IP address (**192.168.0.1**) itself but allocates dynamic addresses to the other machines on the network. You can check the IP addresses of your computers by selecting **Start**, **Settings**, **Control Panel**, and double clicking the **Network** icon. On the host or gateway machine we have:

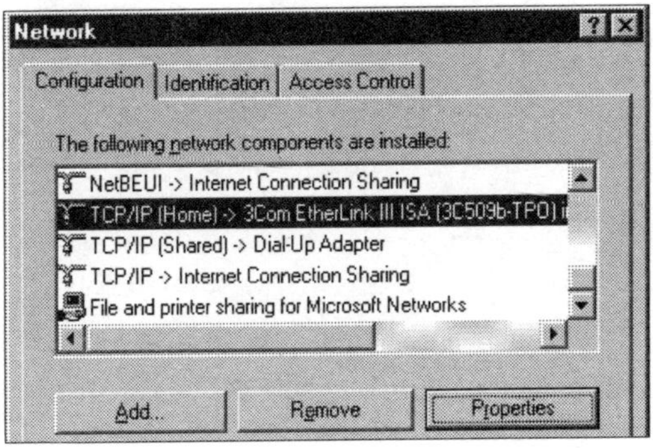

If you highlight the TCP/IP entry associated with your network card as shown on the previous page and click **Properties**, the **IP Address** should be as shown below:

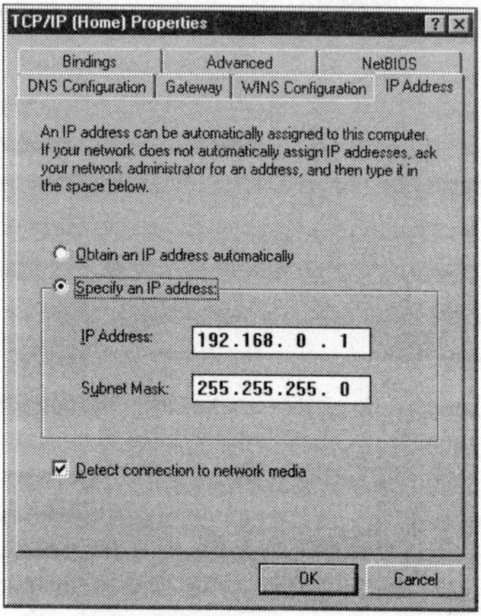

Now working at a client machine on the network, launch the **Network** window in the **Control Panel** as previously described. Then highlight the TCP/IP entry associated with the network card and click **Properties** and the **IP Address** tab. You will find that the option **Obtain an IP address automatically** is switched on.

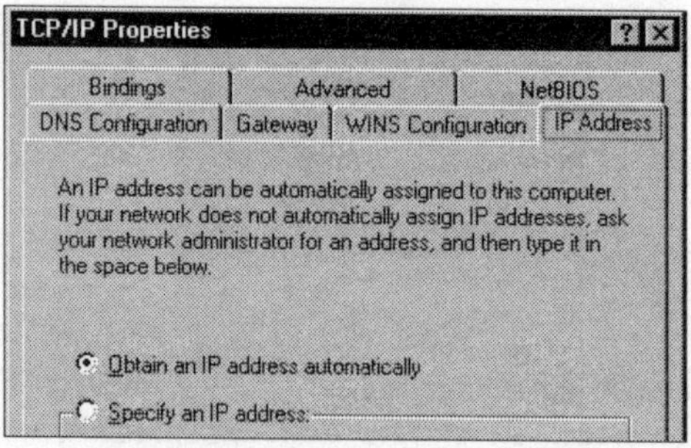

Specifying IP Addresses on Client Machines

If you are having problems or perhaps out of curiosity, you can specify your own IP addresses on the client machines, by entering them manually as follows:

- Select the **TCP/IP Properties** on the client machine as previously described.
- Select the **IP Address** tab and switch on **Specify an IP address.**
- Enter a unique **IP Address** in the range **192.168.0.2-192.168.0.254**.
- For the **Subnet Mask:** enter **255.255.255.0**.

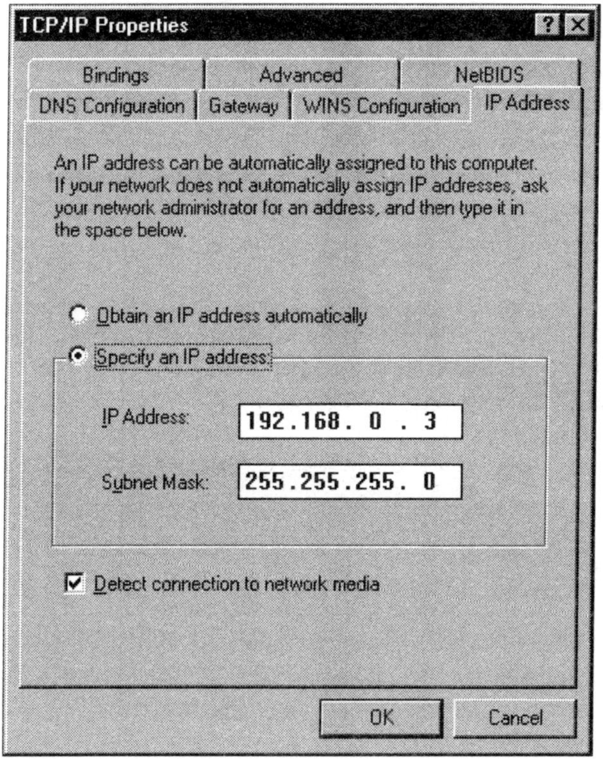

Now click the **DNS Configuration** tab and switch on **Enable DNS**. In the **Host:** box enter the name of the machine with a direct connection to the Internet. Enter **192.168.0.1** under **DNS Server Search Order** and click **Add**. The completed window is shown below.

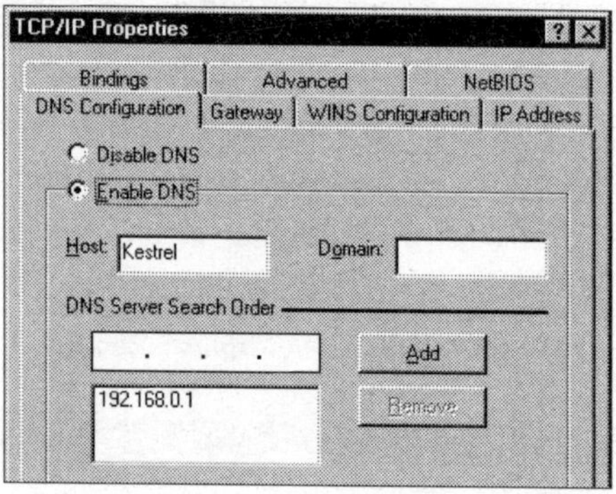

Finally select the **Gateway** tab and enter **192.168.0.1** and then click **Add**.

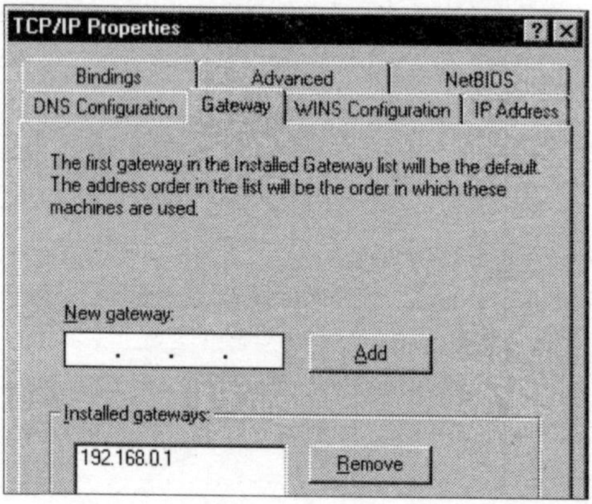

The procedure of specifying IP addresses on the last two pages should be repeated on all of the client machines on the network. The individual IP addresses must all be different, such as **192.168.0.2**, **192.168.0.3**, **192.168.0.4,** etc., up to a maximum of **192.168.0.254**.

Summary: Windows Me Home Networking

- Windows Me contains all of the software needed to set up and manage a home/small business network. This includes a new feature, The Home Networking Wizard. You must already have fitted network cards and cables to all of the computers.
- All of the computers on the network are shown in **My Network Places**, accessed from an icon on the Windows Me Desktop.
- Each computer and its shareable resources can be viewed in its own window on every workstation on the network. Resources can be set as shareable in My Computer.
- Copying files and folders can be carried out quickly and simply by "dragging and dropping" between the windows of different computers, displayed simultaneously on the screen.
- The WinPopup feature allows short text messages to be sent between computers and workgroups on the network.
- In order to share a single network printer, each workstation must be individually set up using the **Add Printer Wizard** invoked from **Start**, **Settings**, **Printers** and **Add Printer**.
- The network printer can be used from each workstation in the same way as a printer attached directly to the workstation, using **File** and **Print** from applications such as Word 2000.
- The Home Networking Wizard also sets up Windows Me Internet Connection Sharing. This allows several computers to use a single modem, telephone line and Internet connection.
- To use Internet Connection Sharing, each client machine is set up to connect to the Internet via the local network and the host machine, i.e. the computer with the modem directly attached.
- All machines connected to the Internet are identified by an individual IP Address. This is a number allocated automatically by the host or gateway computer, when you log on to the Internet. It is also possible to enter IP Addresses manually.

12

Installing a Modem

Introduction

The "56K" modem is the most popular method of connecting to the Internet, for home and small businesses. Although there are faster alternatives such as cable modems and ADSL (discussed later), currently these are relatively expensive and are being developed mainly in the business arena. Whereas the conventional 56K modem has a nominal data transmission rate of 56Kilobits per second, cable modems can exceed a rate of one Megabit per second.

Power hungry applications such as the streaming and downloading of video files require this extra speed. In the future therefore, the 56K modem is likely to be superseded by the more powerful "broadband" systems. ISDN provides some improvement in performance over the 56K modem and this technology is described later.

This chapter discusses some of the features of the latest modems and then describes fitting a modem to a computer. Windows Me makes this task much easier than previously and the work really can be carried out by anyone - you don't need any special skills or equipment.

With the latest modems, communications can involve much more than the transfer of plain text between computers. Apart from transmitting graphics, fax and sound, telephone messaging systems and video conferencing are now possible between two computers equipped with modems. Even if your computer already has a modem, it may be one of the earlier, slower models and you may wish to consider replacing it as described later in this chapter.

Choosing a Modem

One of the most important factors when choosing a modem is the speed of operation. Clearly, the faster the modem, the less time required to search the Internet or to download large audio, video or graphics files to your computer's hard disc. For a given communications activity, with a faster modem your connection charges should be lower.

The speed of a modem is normally measured in Kilobits per second (Kbps). (A bit is a binary digit (0 or 1) and 8 bits are used to represent a character such as a letter of the alphabet). Currently the "56K" modem is replacing its slower predecessors which evolved over recent years with successive speeds of 14.4, 28.8, 33.6K. (1"K" being approximately 1000 bits).

56K is a *nominal* data transfer rate - the actual rate may be less due to the telephone lines being busy and technical limitations. With the new 56K modems, *uploading* (or sending) from your computer is currently limited to 33.6K while *downloading* (or receiving) may achieve speeds closer to 56K.

At the moment there are two competing standards for the 56K modem; the x2 technology from US Robotics and K56flex from the Rockwell group. Initially these two standards were incompatible, but a recent agreement resulted in the V.90 standard. This resolves the conflict between x2 and K56flex.

56K modems can often be upgraded to the V.90 standard by downloading a *Flash Upgrade* from the Internet site of the modem manufacturer. This process is described in detail later, but briefly consists of replacing the modem's operating software, which is stored in a special bank of memory inside the modem. This "flash" memory can be overwritten with new program instructions whenever an upgrade is available.

When choosing a modem you should consider the functions you will need; the latest voice modems have answerphone and messaging facilities, in addition to fax and Internet access. You can also use a small microphone to enable complete hands-free voice communication, removing the need for a telephone handset. One small modem can therefore streamline your desktop by replacing several bulky devices.

Full duplex modems allow communication (voice or data) between two computers, in both directions simultaneously. The earlier *half duplex* systems could only communicate in one direction at a time. Full duplex modems therefore permit more natural conversations when used for voice communications.

Modems (together with a suitable camera) can be used for *video conferencing* and can distinguish between different types of incoming communication - data, fax and voice. Some modems can function independently when the computer is switched off - allowing faxes and voice mail to be dealt with at all times.

The External Modem

An external modem sits on your desktop and requires a plug for its own power supply lead. A disadvantage of the external modem is that it adds to the clutter on your desk. Fitting an external modem is easy, you simply plug it into the outside of the computer without the need to remove the metal casing. Most new computers are provided with two *serial* or *communication* ports - designated as COM1 and COM2. The ports have connectors at the back of the computer into which you plug the cables for peripheral devices like the mouse, and an external modem.

COM1 is often used to attach the mouse through a 9 pin connector. COM2 is located adjacent to COM1 and is frequently used with a 25 pin connector for an external modem.

The external modem has an array of indicator lights which report on the current activities - whether the modem is switched on, if it is sending or receiving data, fax or voice mail, etc. The external modem is portable - it can easily be unplugged and transferred to another computer.

The Internal Modem

This takes the form of an expansion card which fits inside of the computer. To fit an internal modem you therefore need a spare ISA slot inside the machine and to be happy to remove the casing of your computer and press the card into place. Since the internal modem has no case and fewer cables, etc., it is usually cheaper than the equivalent external device

The internal modem is tidier than the external model and shielded from accidental damage. Although it's not portable like the external model, it doesn't add to the bird's nest of cables at the back of the machine. Some internal modems have a bank of small DIP switches which you must set to configure the COM port. Internal modems contain their own COM port and this is often configured as COM4.

The Installation Process

The task of fitting a modem is not difficult nowadays and really can be carried out by anyone. Even the internal modem only requires you to undo a few screws to release the casing and then plug the modem card into a vacant ISA or PCI expansion slot. Fitting the external modem is even easier - you only have to connect a few cables between the modem and the back of the computer. If you are replacing an old internal modem with a new external one you need to remember to take out the old modem first. Then remove the software for the old modem using **Remove** in the **Device Manager** in the **Systems** applet of the **Control Panel** (discussed later). The modem manufacturers usually provide adequate instructions and it is virtually impossible to fit any of the cables the wrong way around.

Windows Me has been designed for *Plug and Play* installation. This means that newly fitted devices such as modems can be detected as soon as the machine re-starts and Windows Me takes command. In my recent experience of setting up several internal and external modems, Plug and Play has taken care of the entire setup process and it has not been necessary to get involved in the technicalities of COM ports, etc. However, these topics are covered in some detail later in this chapter, in case you are unfortunate enough to encounter problems.

When you re-start the computer after installing a new modem, a message should be displayed stating that new hardware has been found and Windows Me is installing the necessary software.

Installation of the device thereafter becomes automatic - you may at most be asked to insert one of the manufacturer's installation discs if Windows Me doesn't have the necessary "driver" programs from within its own resources.

Using the Control Panel

The **Control Panel** is an essential Windows Me tool for setting up and managing the devices such as modems, connected to your computer. To invoke the **Control Panel** first select **Start**, then **Settings** and click on **Control Panel**.

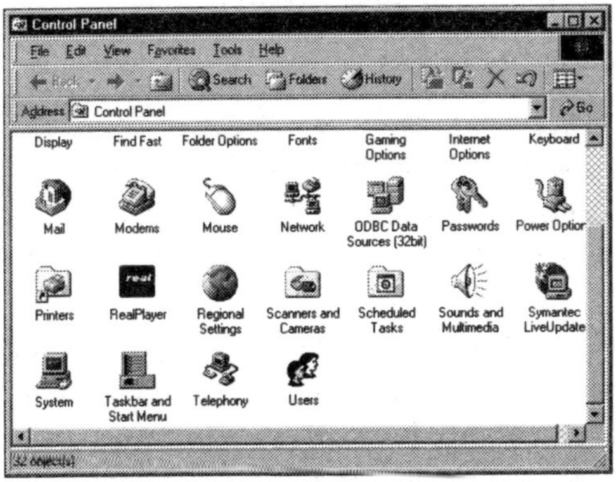

Two of the most useful **Control Panel** applets in the context of this chapter are **Modems** and **System**. You can check that the modem has been correctly installed by clicking **System**, then selecting the **Device Manager** tab in **System Properties**. You should see **Modem** listed and clicking this reveals your particular modem.

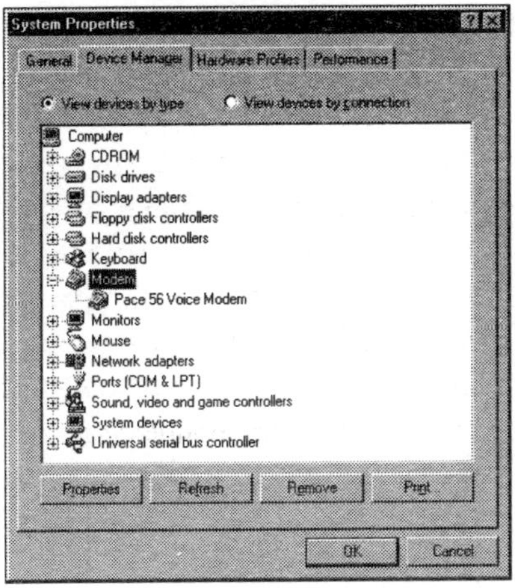

If you now highlight your modem in the list of devices and select **Properties**, the **General Tab** should confirm that the modem is working correctly.

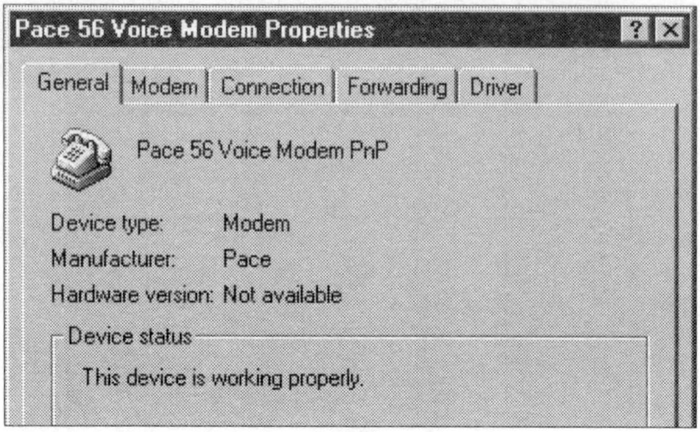

The manufacturer of your modem may also provide some diagnostic software on a floppy disc, to check that the modem has been installed correctly.

Plug but No Play

If your computer fails to detect the modem, it may be because the modem or the computer itself is not Plug and Play compatible. In this case you must use Windows Me to detect and install the modem manually. This is done using the **Add New Hardware** applet, found in the **Control Panel**, from **Start** and **Settings**.

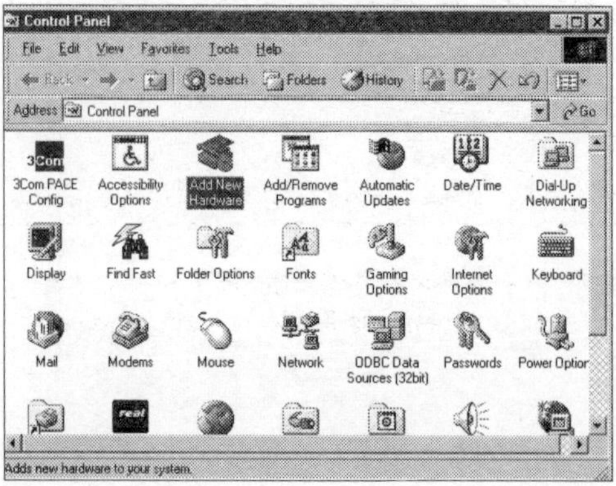

This invokes the **Add New Hardware Wizard** which will examine your machine for new devices.

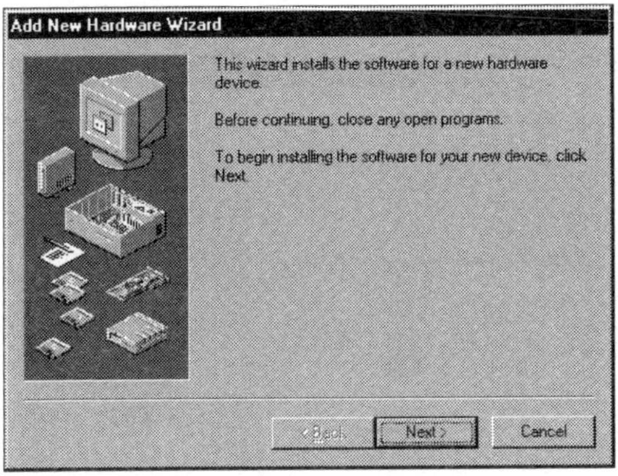

If new devices are found you will be prompted to insert the software to enable the modem to work. This may be contained on a floppy disc or CD provided by the modem manufacturer. Alternatively, suitable software may be available on your Windows Me CD.

The **New Hardware Wizard** should guide you through the installation of the software until the modem is finally up and running.

The Modems Applet

Another way to install a modem is by using the **Modems** applet in the **Control Panel**.

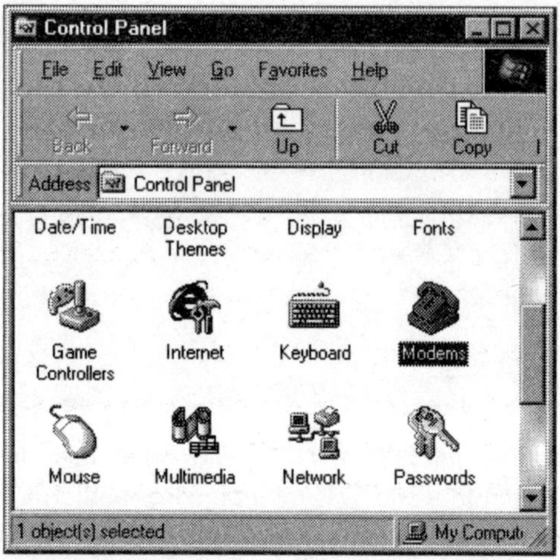

Clicking on **Modems** leads to the **Modems Properties** dialogue box from where you can select **Add** to install a new modem.

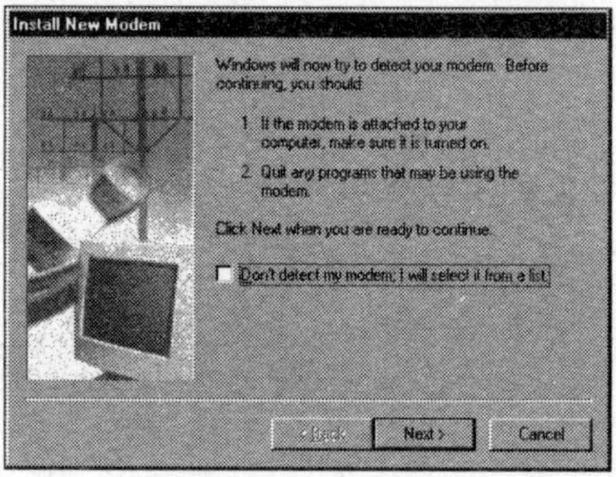

This will search for a new modem and then guide you through the process of installing the necessary software.

Once your modem is set up you can install any communication software packages which came with the new modem, such as fax and voice messaging. With Windows Me you already have Internet Explorer to browse the Internet; alternatively you may choose to install another browser such as Netscape.

If you are new to the Internet, you may also need to install software to connect you to an Internet Service Provider (ISP) such as the Microsoft Network (MSN) or America Online (AOL). This software may be included in the package with your new modem; alternatively it's often given away on the CDs on the front of magazines. These usually include a number of hours free Internet access time.

Testing a New Modem

If you've previously between connected to an Internet Service Provider such as The Microsoft Network or America Online then you can try to connect to them using your previous connection number. If you have not yet signed up with an ISP, then there are other ways you can check out the dialling capability of your modem.

Phone Dialer

This is a Windows Me accessory located in **Start**, **Programs**, **Accessories**, **Communications**.

If **Phone Dialer** does not appear in the **Communications** menu shown above, then it can easily be installed from your original Windows Me CD. From the **Control Panel** (described earlier in this chapter), select **Add/Remove Programs** then choose the **Windows Setup** tab. Now select **Communications** and **Details**. Make sure that **Phone Dialer** is ticked.

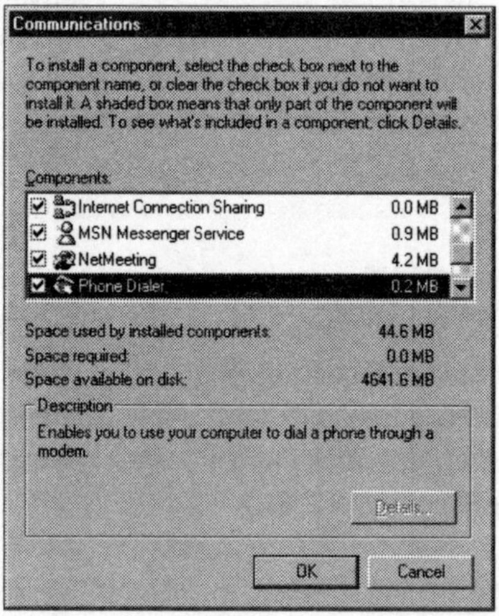

Click **OK** to install the new Windows Me component, in this case **Phone Dialer**. **Phone Dialer** is launched from **Start**, **Programs**, **Accessories** and **Communications.**

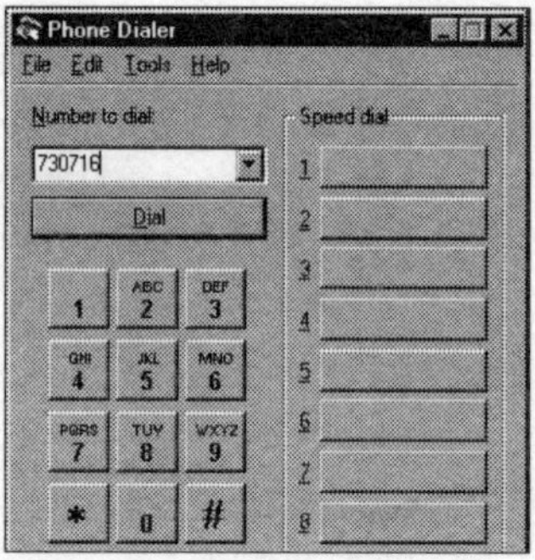

If you enter a telephone number, as shown above, then click **Dial,** you should hear the modem dialling the number.

Modem Troubleshooting

If the modem fails to dial, check all of the cabling according to the manufacturer's instructions. If there's a fault in the cabling between the computer and the telephone network, there will be no dialling tone when you try to connect. You will probably see an error message similar to the following:

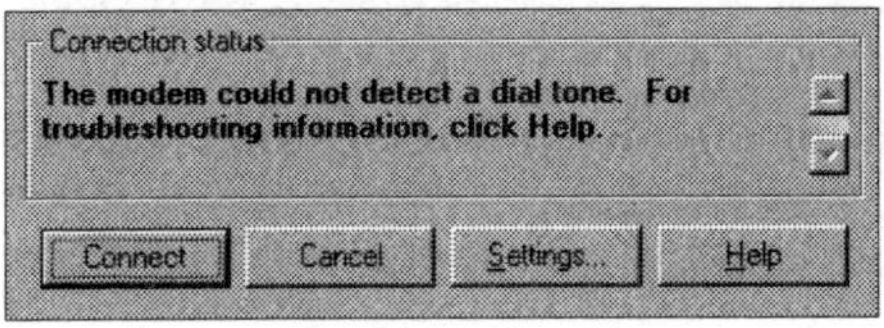

To check out the integrity of the cabling, attach a telephone handset to the telephone socket in the modem (if possible). You should hear a dialling tone and be able to manually dial up a telephone number, perhaps the connection number of an Internet Service Provider if you are already a subscriber.

Alternatively, with an external modem, the problem may be the COM port to which the modem 25 way connector is attached. Although there may be a physical 25 way connector on the rear of the computer, the ribbon cable from the back of this may not be plugged into the connector marked COM2 on the motherboard inside of the computer. (The motherboard is the main circuit board). This would result in an error message such as:

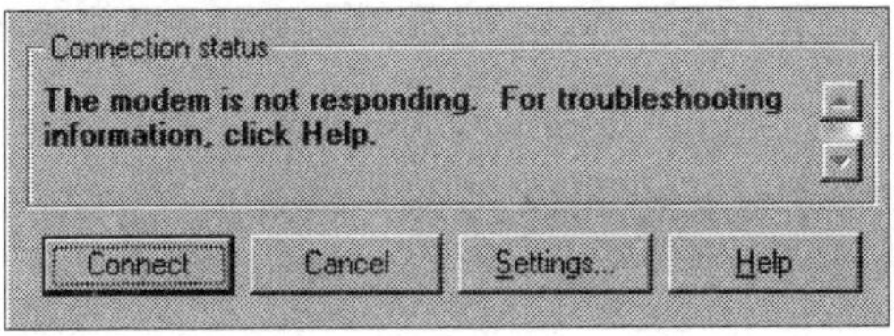

If you feel confident to remove the metal case of the computer you should be able to see the small ribbon cable connected to COM2 on the motherboard, next to the cable for the mouse attached to COM1.

If the cable for COM2 is not in place, then connect it, making sure the coloured stripe on its edge is in the correct position. (Copy the orientation of the mouse cable on COM1).

If you are still unable to dial with the modem, clicking **Help** from the **Connection status** window will open up the Windows Me step-by-step troubleshooter. This should lead towards a solution.

As stated previously, Plug and Play really does work with Windows Me and recent computers and modems. However, if there are any problems they are sometimes caused by conflicts between different devices trying to share the same resources. A common cause of conflict is the *Interrupt Request* setting of the communication port used for the modem, usually COM2 or COM4. These are discussed in the next section.

Interrupt Settings

An interrupt is a request from a peripheral device (like a modem) to the processor, asking the processor to give it some attention. Each device - modem, sound card, printer, mouse, etc., has a line along which it can send an interrupt request (IRQ). Each IRQ line is assigned a number in the range 0-15 (either by Windows Me during the Plug and Play installation or manually by the user).

The IRQ number is used by the processor to decide which request to deal with next. Consequently no two devices which are likely to be used simultaneously can have the same IRQ. This applies, for example, to devices such as a mouse and a modem. These conflicts are a common cause of newly installed devices failing to work.

You can check the IRQ numbers allocated to your devices (including the modem) using **Start**, **Settings**, **Control Panel, System** and **Device Manager**. Highlight **Computer** and select **Properties**.

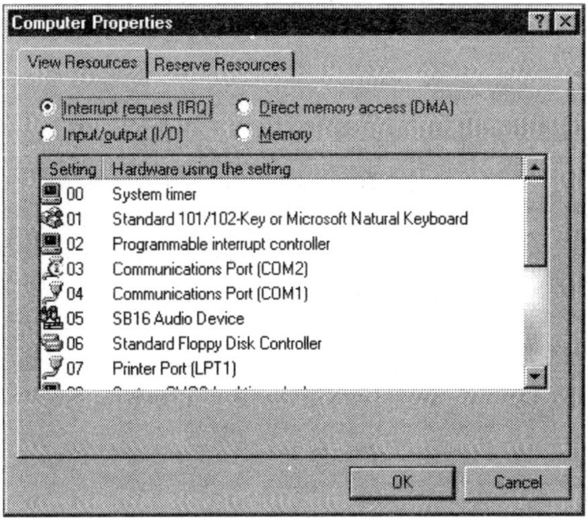

An exclamation mark against one of the devices indicates a problem in the interrupt settings. You can see that on my machine, the port COM2 (to which an external modem is connected) has an interrupt setting of 03. No other device uses 03 so there should be no conflict.

Some modems require the IRQ numbers to be set by manually altering the "jumpers" or links which connect pairs of pins on a circuit board. Rather than carrying out a physical modification, it may be possible to change the interrupt settings through software using Windows Me. First select the appropriate port (**Communications Port (COM2)** in this case) in the Windows Me **Device Manager** mentioned previously.

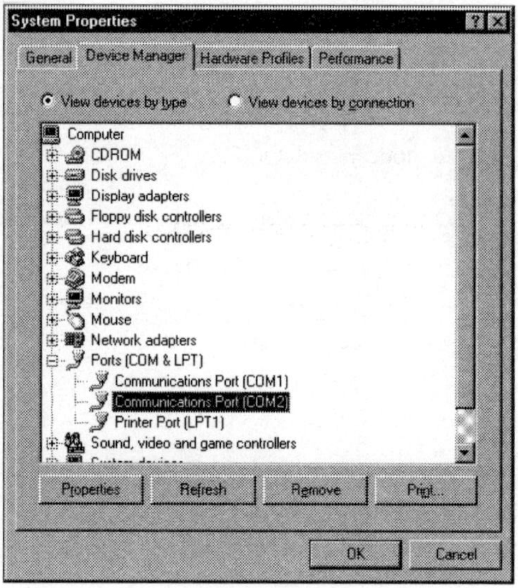

Now select **Properties** and **Resources** to reveal the settings for the port. If necessary it may be possible to alter the interrupt settings using **Change Setting...** or by experimenting with different settings for the **Basic configuration** in **Settings based on:**

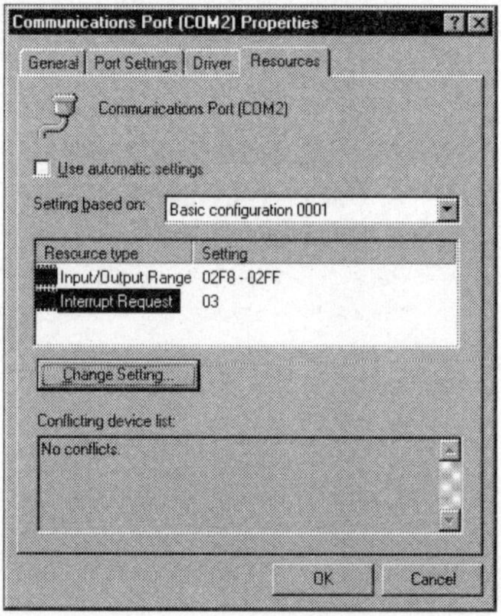

Internal modems have their own on-board communications port and this is usually configured as COM4. If necessary, you can alter the interrupt setting for COM4 after selecting **Change Setting...** in the **Resources** tab as described previously for COM2.

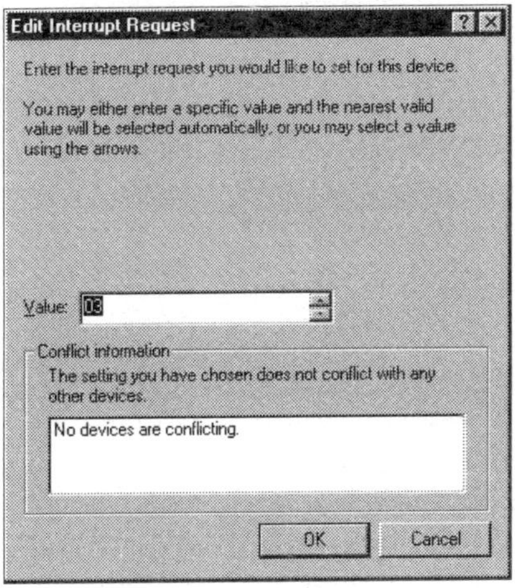

Flash Upgrades

Many of the developments in modem technology can be implemented by a software upgrade, i.e. changes to the built-in programs which control the modem. Traditionally this would involve replacing certain chips in the modem. However, a flash upgrade changes the instructions stored in a special area of battery-powered memory within the modem. The flash upgrades can usually be downloaded from the Internet.

For example, a flash upgrade is available to upgrade a modem from the 56Kflex standard to the newer V.90 standard. Before carrying out the V.90 upgrade you should check that your Internet Service Provider is using this standard.

The flash upgrade process is quite simple and the whole job can take less than half an hour. First you log on to the Web site of your modem manufacturer. (The address should be given in the modem documentation). Then you start the process by clicking the download button as shown below.

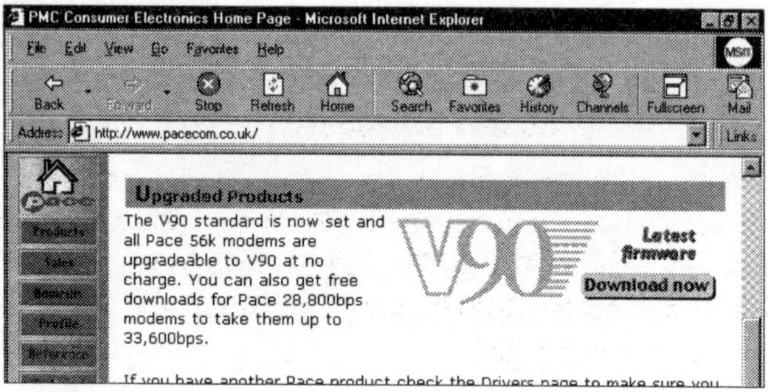

You will be asked to select the type of modem. The download only takes a few minutes, after which the upgrade program icon appears on the desktop. Starting this enables you to unzip the program and start the **V.90 Update Wizard**.

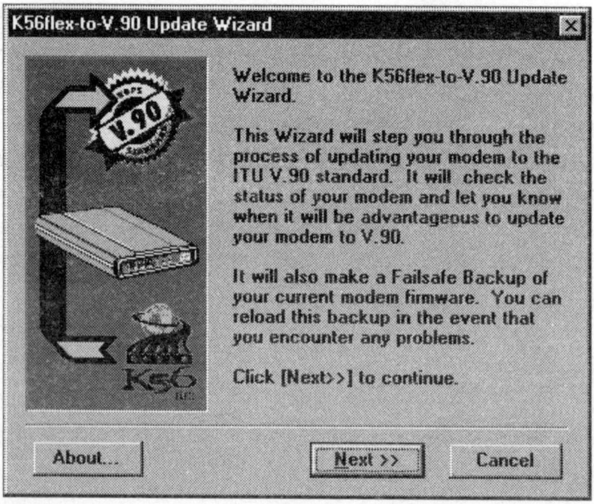

You are guided through the upgrade process with simple instructions and there is a fail safe procedure which allows you to revert to the original specification of modem if necessary. The whole flash upgrade process takes about half an hour or less and is straightforward.

A modem which is flash upgradeable is "future proof" to some extent. As new developments in modem technology evolve, some of them can be implemented by a flash upgrade to the modem software.

Checking the Speed of Your Modem

You can check the speed of your modem (*bytes received* and *bytes transmitted*) using the **System Monitor** (**Start**, **Programs**, **Accessories**, **System Tools**). This may need to be installed using the **Control Panel** applet **Add/Remove Programs** and the **Windows Setup** tab as described earlier.

The ISDN Alternative

As stated previously, the purpose of a modem is to convert binary digits coming out of the computer into analogue or sound signals for transmission along the telephone lines and vice versa when receiving data into the computer. This translation activity requires error checking and correction operations. The whole process is therefore slower than one in which the communication lines are able to handle data in digital form. Even with the fastest modems, demanding activities such as downloading very large data files from the Internet or video conferencing may be very time consuming.

ISDN (Integrated Services Digital Network) is one solution in the quest for higher speeds when transferring data, voice and video data across networks. ISDN is already in widespread use in businesses where large data and graphic files must be conveyed quickly and accurately. Until recently, the high cost of the equipment and running costs put ISDN out of reach for the home or small business user. Now, with schemes such as BT Home Highway, ISDN is becoming more affordable. The higher cost of ISDN relative to the modem is mitigated by the fact that communications activities are executed much faster, with a consequent reduction in connection charges.

There are two standards which relate to the speed of an ISDN network:

- Basic rate ISDN operating at up to 64Kbps
- Primary rate ISDN operating at up to 1.920Mbps.

The basic rate ISDN service is aimed at the home and small business user while larger organisations use the primary rate. It's possible to combine two 64Kbps basic rate lines to give communication speeds of 128Kbps, much greater than possible with the fastest modem.

Basic rate ISDN works by utilising your existing telephone cable link to the local telephone exchange. There may be problems, for example, if the cable is an older type made of aluminium rather than copper. (The higher speed primary rate ISDN used by large businesses employs optical fibres). Some telephone exchanges are not yet supporting ISDN. Therefore it's worth checking with your telephone company before spending any money to upgrade your system to ISDN. Also check that your Internet Service Provider is geared up to provide an ISDN service.

To connect to an ISDN network your computer must be fitted with either an ISDN Card (instead of an internal modem) or a Terminal Adapter (instead of an external modem). These can now be purchased for roughly similar prices to a modem.

A common problem in many homes is the single telephone line. If someone is reading their e-mail, surfing the net or sending a fax from the computer, the line can't be used for ordinary telephone calls. The BT Home Highway ISDN 2e scheme not only solves this problem but also provides the digital communication required by ISDN.

The original analogue phone line is converted into two lines which can each use digital or analogue data. The lines can be used in various combinations: one can be used as a conventional phone or fax line while the other acts as a 64K ISDN line. Alternatively you can integrate both digital lines to give an ISDN speed of 128K. Or both lines can be used for analogue phone or fax activities. A small amount of work by a BT engineer is required to install Home Highway.

The Future

The use of the Internet for streaming and downloading audio and video files is likely to increase in the future. Software like the Windows Media Player 7 described in Chapter 14 enables a PC to combine the roles of CD player, video player and Internet Radio Tuner. The 56K modem struggles when streaming moving video across the Internet and has probably reached the limit of its potential. The future is therefore likely to see a greater need for systems with higher data transfer rates or *bandwidth.* ADSL and cable modem are two high bandwidth (also known as *broadband)* systems currently being developed.

ADSL

This is an acronym for Asymmetric Digital Subscriber Line, a system which converts ordinary copper phone lines into high speed digital lines capable of handling demanding multimedia applications. You can talk on the phone line while simultaneously carrying out applications such as video on demand, multiplayer games and telecommuting with a corporate network. ADSL systems are always on-line to the Internet.

ADSL can download at speeds up to 8Mbps and upload at up to 1Mbps. This compares with a *maximum* of 56Kbps for the conventional modem and 128Kbps for ISDN. A major advantage of ADSL is that it utilizes millions of existing telephone lines, already in place.

Cable Modems

A cable modem is a special device which connects to cable television lines, rather than telephone lines. While potentially being a hundred times faster at connecting to the Internet, the main drawback compared with ADSL and the conventional modem is the limited number of TV cables currently installed. The higher speed for downloading video, graphics, photographs, etc., is coupled with better performance when moving about the Internet. Downloading (to your computer) using a cable modem can be carried out at 3-10Mbps. Uploading speeds (from your computer) are in the range 200Kbps-2Mbps. (Most Internet data traffic is in the downloading direction.) A file which takes 8 minutes to download with an ordinary modem takes 2 minutes on ISDN and 8 seconds using a cable modem. Cable modems are always on-line.

Summary: Installing a Modem

- A modem is a device for converting between the digital data used by computers and the analogue sound data traditionally conveyed by telephone cables.
- The latest modems conform to a standard known as V.90 and handle data at speeds up to a maximum of 56Kbps. Flash upgradeable modems can be modified by downloading software from the Internet.
- Modems now support sophisticated voice-mail, messaging and video conferencing, apart from e-mail, fax and accessing the Internet.
- The external modem is easy to install and is portable while the internal version is neater and cheaper.
- Windows Me offers Plug and Play, a system which greatly simplifies the installation of devices like modems. Both the modem and the computer must be of recent design and Plug and Play compatible.
- Modems are connected to the computer through devices known as communication ports or serial ports. External modems frequently use COM2 while the internal version often uses COM4.
- Problems occur when the modem conflicts with another device, by trying to use the same Interrupt Request Setting (IRQ).
- ISDN is a faster but more expensive alternative to the modem. Working entirely with digital data, it is popular with businesses. Most domestic telephone lines can be modified to use ISDN. The cost of converting to ISDN has fallen considerably in recent years.
- The increasing use of the Internet to download and stream (broadcast) massive audio and video files demands more powerful devices than the 56K modem. Fast broadband systems currently being introduced, primarily in business, such as cable modems and ADSL, should eventually become widely available and affordable to the general user.

13

Connecting to the Internet

Introduction

This chapter describes how a computer fitted with a modem or other device can be connected to the Internet. The computer might be used on its own to surf the Internet, communicate using e-mail or shop on-line, for example. This single Internet connection can be shared with other computers connected by cabling to form a home or small business network. Internet Connection sharing is a feature of Windows Me and is discussed in Chapter 11, Windows Me Home Networking.

Before starting the process to connect to the Internet, you must first choose an Internet Service Provider (ISP). This is a company with fast and powerful computers (known as *servers*) directly connected to the Internet. The ordinary user connects to the Internet via the ISP servers, using the modem and telephone lines. Part of the setup process includes the creation of a *dial-up connection* to enable your modem to dial the telephone number of the ISP's server computer. Your Windows Me Desktop probably already shows a number of Internet tools.

In the extract from the Windows Me Desktop shown on the previous page, Internet Explorer and Outlook Express are respectively the Internet browser and e-mail programs included with Windows Me. AOL (America Online) claims to be the "World's No.1" Internet Service Provider while MSN is Microsoft's own Internet Service.

Choosing an Internet Service Provider

Typically you pay the ISPs for their services by a monthly subscription, although recently there has been a spate of "free" connection services. These must be judged in the context of the quality of the services and support available. To avoid receiving enormous telephone bills, connection to the Internet must be available at the *local* telephone rate. When you start to set up a connection to the Internet using Microsoft's Internet Connection Wizard, you are presented with a choice of companies. These fall into two categories, **Online Services** and **Internet Service Providers**. The **Online Services** are provided by companies such as America Online, and The Microsoft Network (MSN). Apart from enabling you to browse the World Wide Web and send e-mails, these services contain their own closed news and information pages which are only accessible to subscribing members. You can see some of these companies by double clicking on the **Online Services** folder on the Windows Me desktop.

Double click on any of these icons to start the connection process.

Some **Internet Service Providers (ISPs)** offer a specialist connection service to the Web, without the news and information pages produced by the Online Services. Many of the Internet Service Providers offer a free evaluation period and you will normally have to give your credit card details at the outset. If you don't wish to continue at the end of the evaluation period you can cancel your membership.

You can often obtain CDs containing trial Internet connection software free on the front of magazines. Some of the larger players in the field such as AOL and The Microsoft Network (MSN) may send you a CD in the post, if your name and address have found their way onto the mailing list.

Some criteria for choosing an Internet Service Provider might be:

- Speed and reliability when connecting to the Internet.
- Telephone access numbers available at *local* telephone rates.
- The monthly or yearly subscription charges.
- The number of e-mail addresses per account.
- The quality and cost of the telephone support service.
- Support for the latest technology (such as 56K V90 modems)
- In the case of Online Services providing content, the quality and quantity of the pages of information - news, sport, travel, weather, etc., and their value as a research and learning facility.
- Parental controls over children's access to inappropriate Web sites.
- Amount of Web space available for subscribers to create their own Web sites and any charges for this facility.

It's very easy to be confused by the large number of competing deals offered by the Internet Service Providers. A good source of help is the computing press, which regularly publishes helpful comparisons of the various ISPs and their charges.

Making the Connection

This section assumes your computer has Windows Me installed and the modem is up and running. It is also assumed that you have set up an Internet browser such as Microsoft Internet Explorer or Netscape Navigator. There are several ways to launch the process of connecting to an Internet Service Provider or Online Service. Many of the services provide a free CD which just needs putting in the drive then you follow the instructions on the screen. Or you can open up the **Online Services** folder on the Windows Me desktop and start the process by double clicking on the service of your choice.

Windows Me provides the Internet Connection Wizard to simplify the process of connecting to the Internet. Double click the icon on the Windows Me Desktop, shown right, or select **Start**, **Programs**, **Accessories**, **Communications** and **Internet Connection Wizard**.

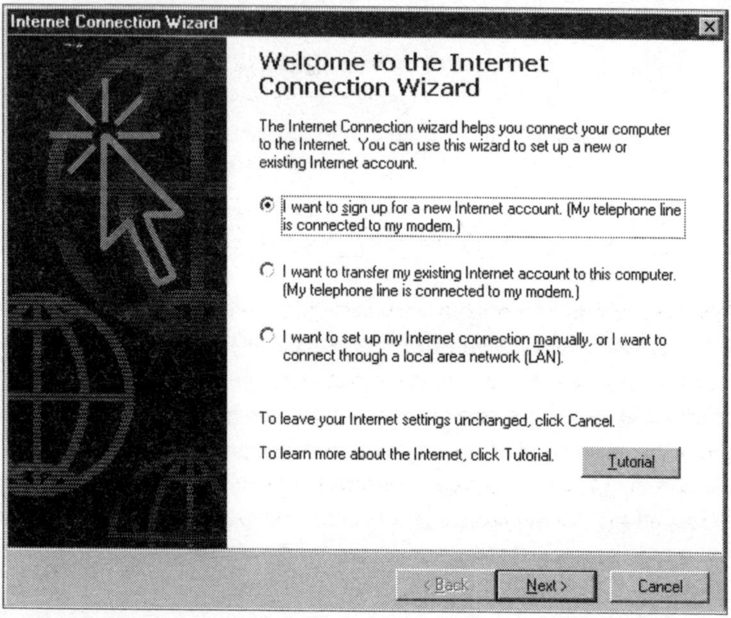

Apart from reminding you that your computer must be connected to the telephone line by a modem, you are given the choice of creating a new Internet account or transferring an old one. The third option includes a connection via a local area network. This was discussed in Chapter 11, and relates to Internet Connection Sharing by network client machines not fitted with their own modem.

If you choose to sign up for a new account, you will be connected to the Microsoft Internet Referral Service which presents you with a list of the available Internet Service Providers in your area.

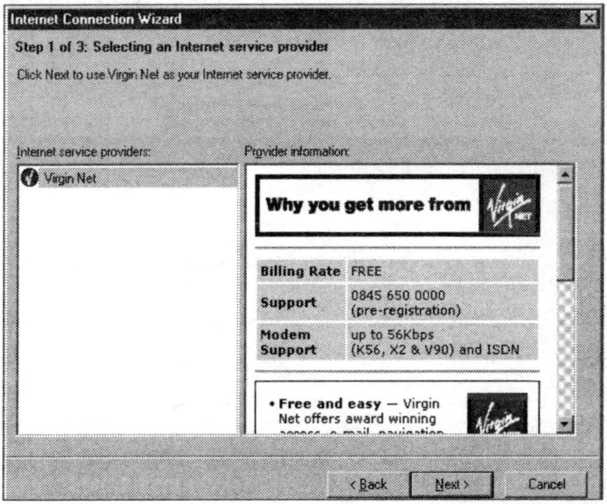

Selecting one of these leads onto a sign up process provided by the individual Internet Service Provider. This gives details not only of the monthly charges for the service but also any additional facilities provided. A telephone number is usually given, which can be used to cancel the account, if necessary, after the expiry of any free trial period. Whichever ISP you choose to subscribe to, you will be presented with dialogue boxes which require you to enter your personal details such as name, address, telephone number and the details of your credit card.

The next few pages give an overview of the process for connecting to AOL, the world's largest Internet Service Provider. After inserting the CD and starting the setup process, you are asked to close all other applications which are running. A welcome screen appears in which you select either **New Member** or **Current Member**. After clicking **Next** you can either accept the default directory into which the AOL software is to be installed or specify a different directory. You are then asked to select the method by which to connect to the Internet and in many cases this will be via a 56K modem on COM2 as shown below.

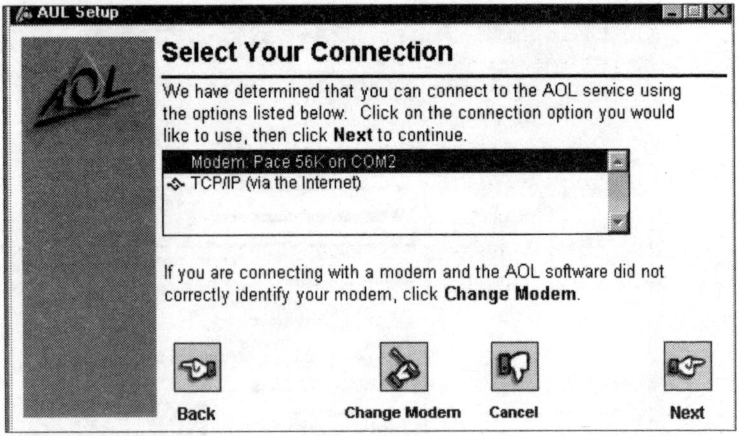

The next stage is to search for suitable Access Phone Numbers. You are advised to check with your telephone company that all Internet connections will be charged at the *local rate*. If you're a BT subscriber, you might wish to add your ISP's phone number to your list of BT Friends and Family frequently-used numbers attracting discounts.

After accepting United Kingdom or selecting another country from which you will be dialling, you are presented with a choice of available numbers from which you should select two. The two selected Access Phone Numbers are added to the **Selected Numbers** panel as shown on the next page.

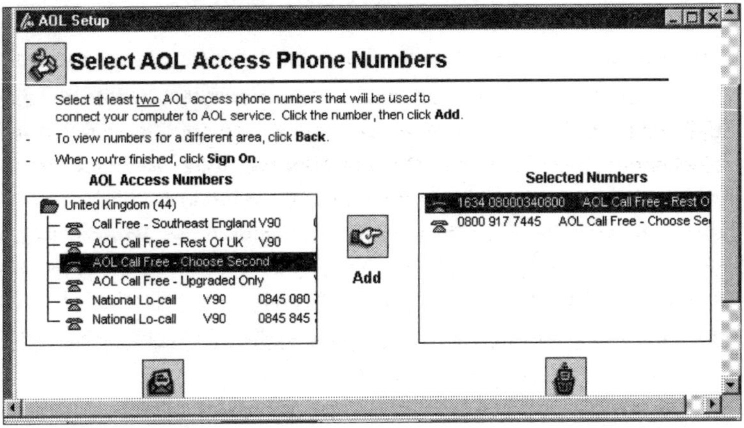

You are then asked to enter your **Registration Number** and **Password**. These are temporary names to get you started and can be found on the back of the free CD or somewhere on the accompanying packaging. You will be asked to make up your own "Screen name" and password later. Then you are required to enter your personal details as shown below.

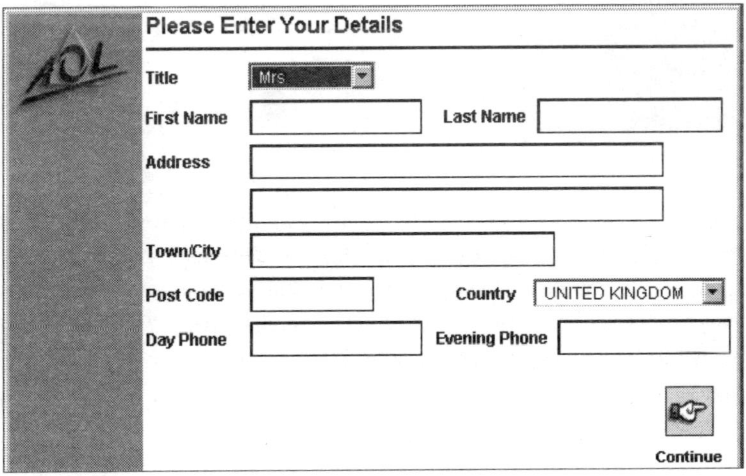

The next screen to appear explains the conditions of the AOL free trial. In this case, the monthly membership fee of £14.99 is waived and there are no Internet telephone call charges. The 50 free hours must be used in the first month online, after which you are charged the £14.99 membership fee, which includes the telephone charges using the AOL CALL FREE number selected earlier (shown on the previous page).

N.B. This screen provides a telephone number for cancelling the membership, which is worth noting if you decide not to continue with AOL. After selecting your method of payment from a number of credit card options you are asked to give details of your particular credit card.

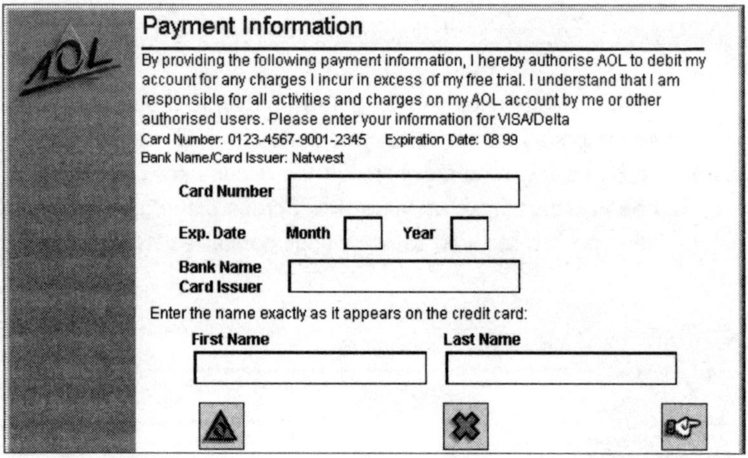

AOL
Payment Information
By providing the following payment information, I hereby authorise AOL to debit my account for any charges I incur in excess of my free trial. I understand that I am responsible for all activities and charges on my AOL account by me or other authorised users. Please enter your information for VISA/Delta
Card Number: 0123-4567-9001-2345 Expiration Date: 08 99
Bank Name/Card Issuer: Natwest
Card Number
Exp. Date
Month
Year
Bank Name
Card Issuer
Enter the name exactly as it appears on the credit card:
First Name
Last Name

Screen Names

After entering your credit card details you are required to enter a "Screen Name" which can be 3 to 16 characters long and may be a mixture of numbers and letters, if desired. The screen name serves both as your online identity and as your AOL e-mail address. Your full e-mail address (for Internet users not subscribing to AOL) is then something like:

screenname@aol.com

You can have a further 5 screen names on one AOL account, so that members of your family, for example, can receive their own e-mail.

AOL checks that the Screen Name you have entered is unique - if not you are asked to enter a different name.

Finally you are asked to enter a password, which should be between 4 and 8 characters long, difficult for anyone to guess and may contain both numbers and letters. The password must be entered twice and you are warned that AOL employees will never ask for your password. If you do tell anyone your password, you are responsible for any charges they run up on your AOL account.

The next screen to appear congratulates you on becoming AOL's newest member and you are given the chance to opt out of receiving mailshots from companies to whom AOL may supply the membership list. This is followed by the AOL Tour Guide which describes the main features offered by the world's largest Internet Service Provider.

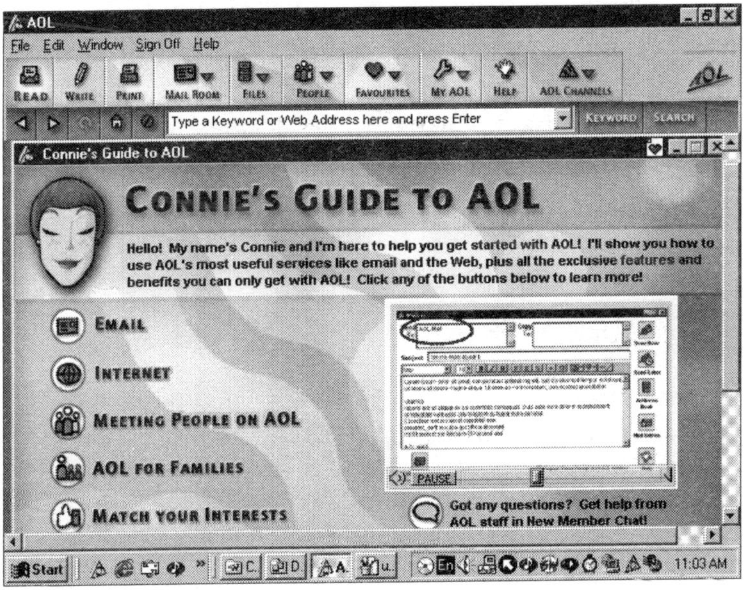

Once your connection to AOL is up and running it can be launched by clicking the AOL icon on the Windows Me Taskbar, then entering your password.

Then when you are connected on-line you are presented with the full range of AOL information services:

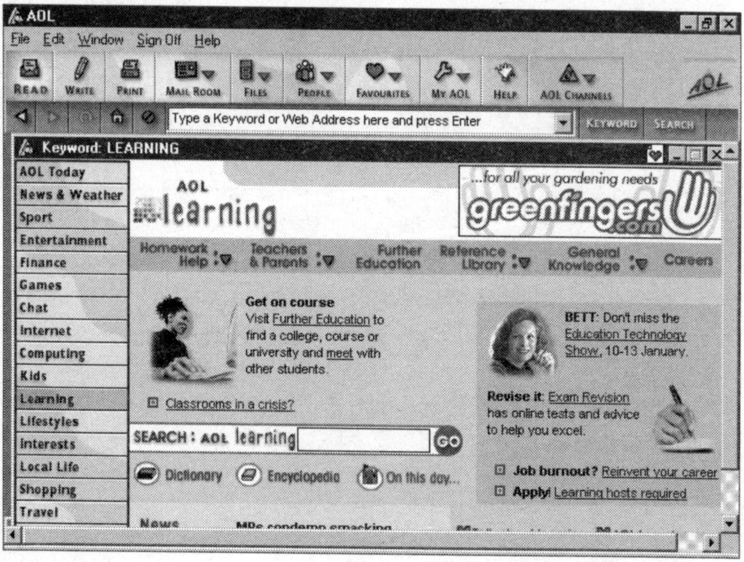

Apart from the vast library of information provided by AOL and available only to AOL members, you can click **Internet** to move onto the World Wide Web. Access a specific Web site by entering the Web address or start searching the Internet for sites containing particular words.

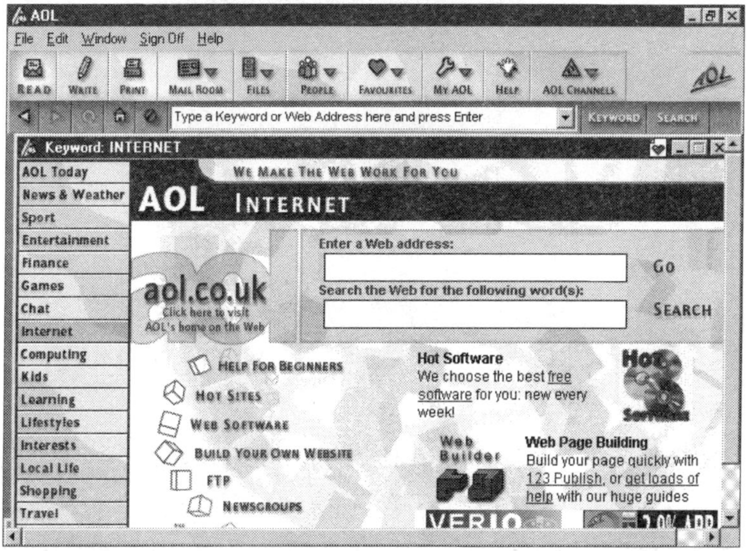

If, instead of AOL, you choose to subscribe to the Microsoft Network, for example, you will be asked to finish with the Internet Connection Wizard and start the MSN setup from its icon on the Windows Me Desktop. You are informed of progress at each stage. The software is copied to your hard disc and a connection is made to the ISP server. The system should offer a choice of telephone numbers giving charges at local rates. You are asked to provide personal information such as name, address and credit card details. Then you are asked to choose a user name (or screen name) and a unique password. The user name is also used as part of your e-mail address. At the end of the setup process you should be able to log on to the Internet with your own user name and password. You should also be able to send and receive e-mails.

If you choose to subscribe to the Microsoft Network (MSN) you will see the following **Connect To** dialogue box, where it is possible to edit dialling information, save your password and make the connection automatic.

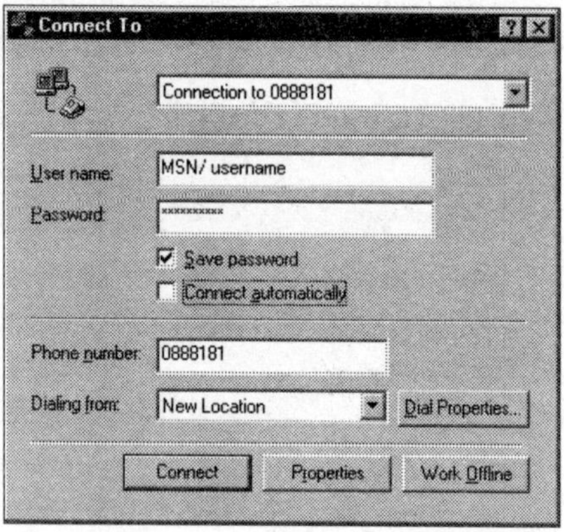

On connecting to MSN, you can click various on-screen links to a wide range of pages covering news, sport, weather, etc., or enter the address for a particular Web site. You can also choose from several Internet search engines which locate Web sites containing specified words.

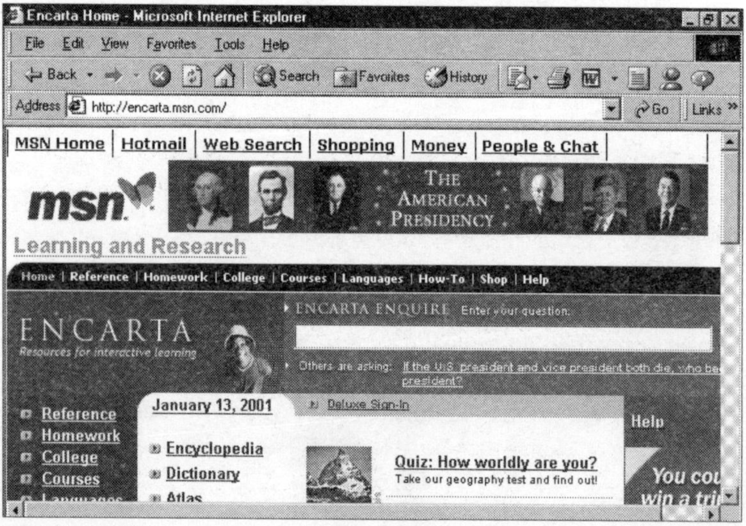

Dial-Up Networking

When you go through the connection procedure with one of the Internet Service Providers, you create a telephone dialling connection which is saved in a Windows Me folder called **Dial-Up Networking**. This can be opened by clicking **Start**, **Settings** and **Dial-Up Networking**.

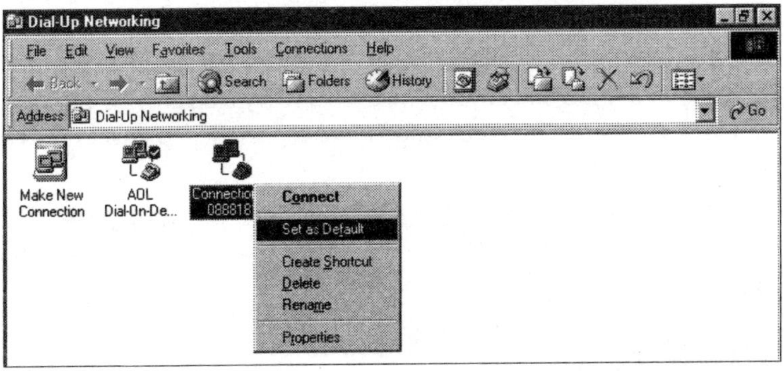

In the example shown above, there are two dial-up connections, one for AOL and the other for MSN. There is also an icon for creating a new dial-up connection by entering an ISP's telephone number. To set a dial-up connection as the default, right click over the icon and click **Set as Default** as shown above. This connection will then be activated when you launch the Internet Explorer or Netscape Web browser.

If you wish to use Netscape as your default Web browser, instead of Internet Explorer, install the Netscape software then in Internet Explorer click **Tools**, **Internet Options...** and select the **Programs** tab. Click the box to remove the tick against **Internet Explorer should check to see whether it is the default browser**.

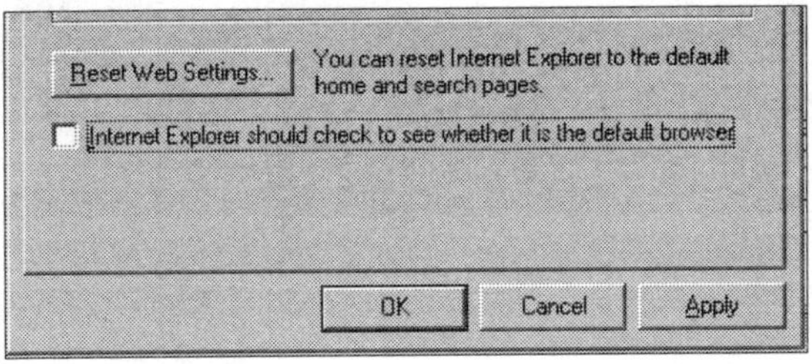

E-mail

The Internet connection process will have also set up your own e-mail facility, complete with one or more e-mail addresses, depending on your Internet Service Provider. All of the services provide e-mail facilities and the Online Services have their own built-in program. Popular packages are Microsoft Outlook Express which is supplied with Windows Me and Eudora Pro which is supplied as an independent package.

The main functions of the software are to handle the sending and receiving of e-mails and any attached files. They also provide a system for the management and archiving of messages and the creation of an electronic address book.

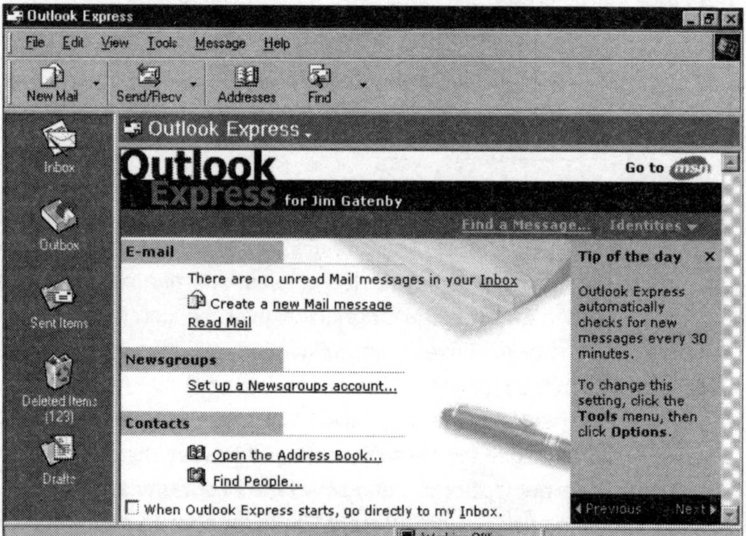

The main features of Outlook Express include the **Inbox** which stores all newly downloaded mail and the **Outbox**, which temporarily holds your outgoing mail before it is actually sent. Once sent the mail is removed from the **Outbox** and a copy placed in the **Sent Items** box.

To test your e-mail, try sending a message addressed to yourself. Click the **New Mail** icon shown previously, enter the e-mail address of the recipient, enter a **Subject** and start typing the text of the message. To save on-line time, you might consider typing the text of a long document with the e-mail program working **off-line**. Or type the text into a word processor then import the file into the e-mail program.

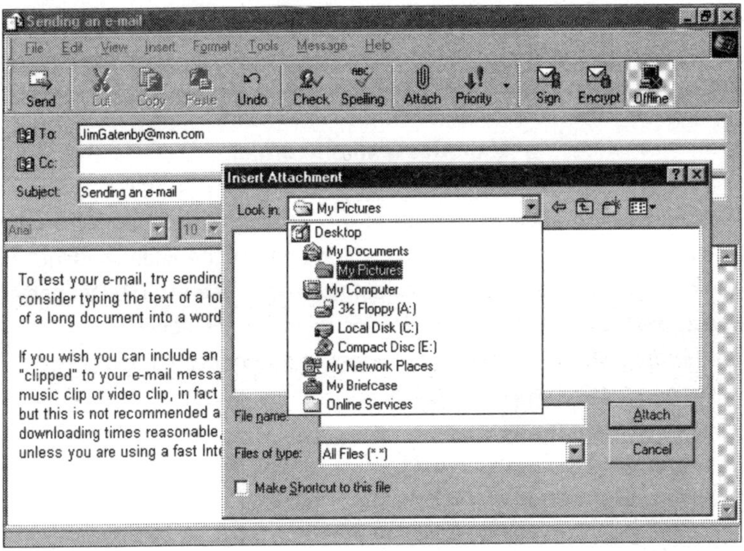

If you wish you can include an e-mail *attachment*. This is done by clicking **Attach** and selecting a file to be "clipped" to your e-mail message. The attached file can be a graphic, a photograph, a spreadsheet, a music clip or video clip, in fact any sort of file. I have even sent a complete textbook as an attachment, but this is not recommended as it takes ages to download by the recipient. To keep downloading times reasonable, it's probably best to restrict attachments to under 1 Megabyte in size, unless you are using a very fast Internet connection such as ADSL or Cable Modem. After you have finished typing the message click the **Send** button to upload the message to the mail server of your intended recipient. Next time your contact reads their mail it will be downloaded from the server to their computer.

E-mail Addresses

When you sign up for an Internet account you will be able to choose, or be given, your own e-mail address. This is a unique location enabling your mail to reach you from anywhere in the world.
Common types of e-mail address are as follows:

stella@aol.com

james@msn.com

enquiries@wildlife.org.uk

The part of the address in front of the @ sign is normally your *user* name or Internet *login* name. The second part of the address identifies the company or organization providing your mail server. The last part of the address is the type of organisation providing the service.
In the previous addresses **.com** refers to a commercial company, but other organisation types include:

.edu education
.gov U.S. government
.org non-profit making organisations
.co UK commercial company

Finally the e-mail address may end with a two digit code to denote the country, such as **uk** or **fr**.

Free E-mail Accounts

Some Internet providers only allow you to have one e-mail address unless you open and pay for further accounts. However, there may be a time when you need more than one e-mail address, perhaps for different members of your family or to separate business and social correspondence. A number of companies offer free e-mail accounts - the only obvious drawback being that you may be bombarded with advertising.

One of the well-known free e-mail services is Hotmail, operated by Microsoft and sponsored by advertising. This service is intended for people who are already paying for one e-mail account through their subscription to an Internet Service Provider or Online Service. It is extremely easy to set up a new Hotmail account - just fill in a few personal details after logging on to the Web site at:

www.hotmail.com

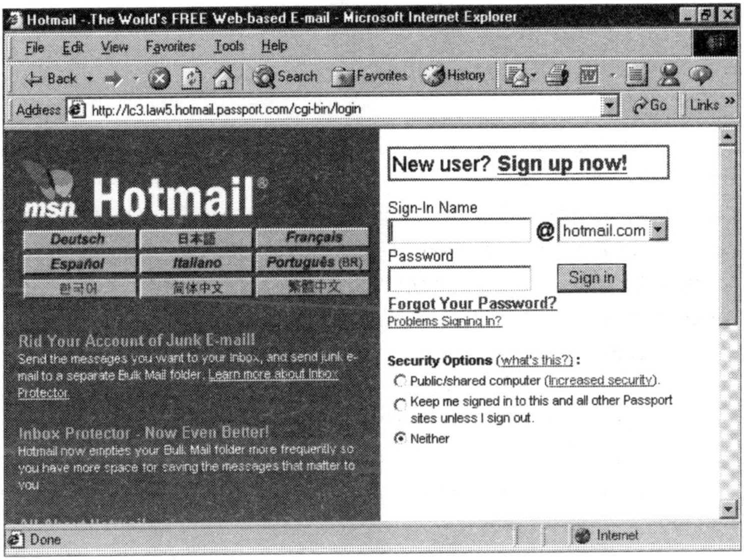

Hotmail is based on a World Wide Web site and uses an Internet browser rather than specialist e-mail software. Web-based e-mail provides easy access from remote locations anywhere in the world. So to access your e-mail all you need is any computer in any location, provided it's connected to the Internet. You can also use Hotmail to read the e-mail you have received through your conventional e-mail accounts with other services. Since Hotmail is based on the Web, it is possible to include links to Web sites in your e-mails.

Summary: Connecting to the Internet

- Getting on-line to the Internet requires a computer linked to the phone lines by a modem or other connecting device, together with an account with an Internet Service Provider (ISP).
- The choice of ISP involves considerations such as monthly subscription, charges for telephone support, information content provided and space for members own Web sites.
- The setup process is often carried out using CDs supplied free by the ISPs on magazines, in stores and by mailshots. Many of these offer a free trial for a limited number of hours on-line.
- The setup process includes the selection of a telephone number to connect to the ISP at the cost of a local call. Also the entry of personal details such as name, address and credit card details.
- A personal user name must be chosen and this is used both to log on to the Internet and as part of your e-mail address. A suitable password must also be chosen.
- Once the connection has been set up you can browse the Internet using Internet Explorer or Netscape, etc.
- Adjustments to connection settings can be made at a later time after selecting **Start**, **Settings** and **Dial-up Networking**.
- E-mails can be sent using programs like Microsoft Outlook Express or one provided by another ISP. E-mails can include *attachments*, which are files "clipped" onto the e-mail. An attachment can be any sort of file - text, spreadsheet, photographs, audio and video clips, etc. Very large attachment files take a long time to download and may cause inconvenience to the recipient.
- Hotmail is a free, Web-based e-mail service provided by Microsoft and giving access to your e-mail from any computer connected to the Internet and located anywhere in the world.

14

Windows Media Player

Introduction

Windows Me introduces a new multimedia feature, Windows Media Player 7. This has been very well received and may on its own be sufficient justification for upgrading from Windows 98 to Windows Me. The media player provides a stylish multimedia centre on your computer, enabling both sound and video clips to be played and managed. Windows Media Player 7 is a screen simulation having similar controls to a physical music centre or video player.

However, the Windows Media Player is a far more versatile and powerful tool than the conventional music centre or video player. The Windows Media Player can connect to the Internet to obtain both music, video and Internet Radio. You can also use the Media Player to transfer audio and video data between a range of local devices such as audio CDs, the hard disc of your computer and the small portable MP3 players which are becoming increasingly popular. The following is a list of some of the uses of the Windows Media Player:

- Play your favourite music using **CD Audio** while working normally at the computer on a task such as word processing.
- Copy music from CDs to your hard disc for convenience and to create personalised playlists.
- Obtain details of audio albums and video clips such as artist, track name and genre by connecting to the Internet. This information is entered automatically into the **Media Library** from the Internet using the **Get Names** feature in the Media Player.
- Copy music to portable devices such as MP3 players.
- Download and play latest audio and video clips from the Internet, using the **Media Guide**.
- Organise and manage audio and video files in the **Media Library**.
- Use the **Radio Tuner** to listen to radio stations on the Internet across the world.
- Search all of the disc drives on the computer for any existing audio and video files. These are automatically added to the Media Library.
- Choose from a range of **Visualisations** - animated patterns which move in time with the music. An ample number of visualizations are supplied and you can download even more from the Internet.
- Change the styling of your on-screen media player using the **Skin Chooser**.

Installing the Windows Media Player

The media player is part of Windows Me and a copy is certainly present on your Windows Me CD. However, as it's an optional component, the media player may not have been included when Windows Me was installed on your computer's hard disc. If the media player is installed, there should be a shortcut icon on the Windows Me Desktop, as shown on the right.

There should also be an entry for the media player in the menu accessed from **Start, Programs** and **Windows Media Player**.

If there is no sign of the Windows Media Player, it will need to be installed from the original Windows Me CD. Windows 98 users can download a copy of the Media Player from:

www.microsoft.com/downloads/search.asp

To install the Windows media Player from the Windows Me CD, select **Start**, **Settings** and **Control Panel**. Then double click over the **Add/Remove Programs** icon, shown right. Now select the **Windows Setup** tab, scroll down and select **Multimedia** and **Details....** A dialogue box opens as shown below. Make sure there is a tick next to **Media Player**.

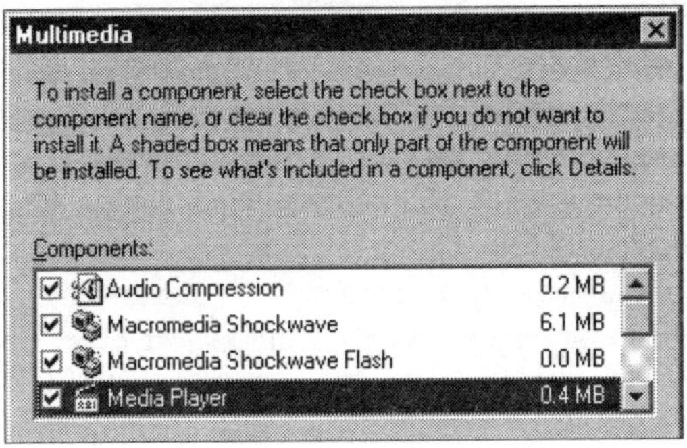

After you click **OK** you will be asked to insert the Windows Me CD to enable the relevant files to be copied and to complete the installation of the Windows Media Player.

Using the Windows Media Player

The media player can be launched by double clicking its icon on the Windows Me Desktop or by selecting **Start**, **Programs** and **Windows Media Player**, as shown on the previous page.

However, the media player can also be invoked by placing an audio CD in the drive. The media player opens in its own window occupying the whole screen. Down the left hand side are seven buttons used to select the main features of the media player. The buttons are **Now Playing**, **Media Guide**, **CD Audio**, **Media Library**, **Radio Tuner**, **Portable Device** and **Skin Chooser**. Only 5 buttons are displayed at a time – small arrows allow the other two buttons to be scrolled into view.

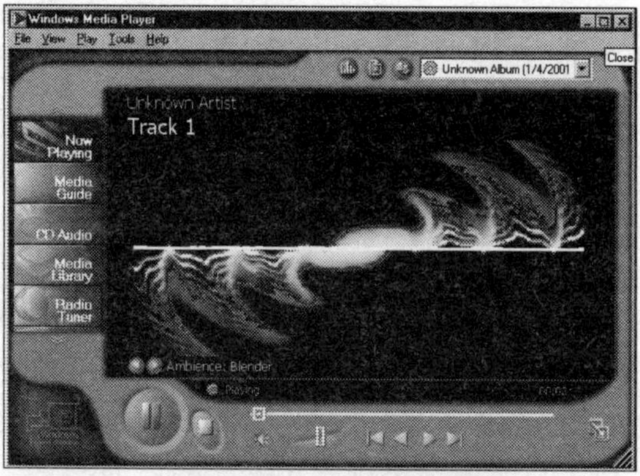

The Windows Media Player has the usual **Play**, **Stop**, **Forward** and **Reverse** buttons, etc. However, the centre of the **Now Playing** window is occupied by a constantly changing colourful display, which moves in time with the music. This display is known as a **Visualization** and a large number of alternative visualizations are provided. You can change the visualization by scrolling through the available list using the two arrows at the lower left of the **Now Playing** window.

Additional visualizations are available from the Internet after selecting **Tools** and **Download Visualizations**. This launches Internet Explorer.

If you wish to use the media player to provide background music while freeing the screen for other tasks on the computer, click the minimize button on the top right of the window. The media player will continue as an icon (shown right) on the Windows Me Taskbar at the bottom of the screen. Click the icon on the taskbar to restore the media player to its full size.

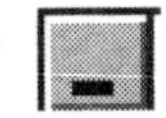

The media player can also be switched between the normal **Full Mode** and the **Compact Mode** shown below. This can be achieved either by selecting from the **View** menu across the top of the media player window in **Full Mode** or by clicking the arrow icon in the lower right of the media player window in either **Full** or **Compact Mode**.

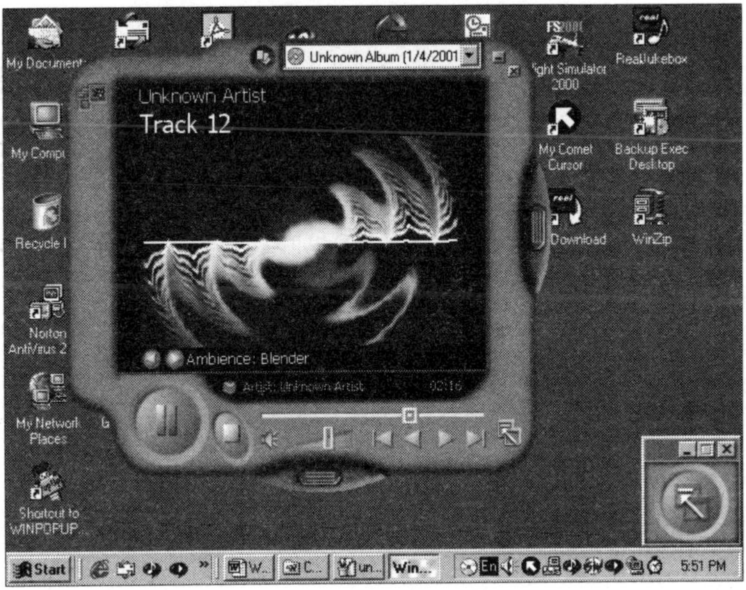

Please note that in **Compact Mode**, some of the media player's features are not accessible. To return to **Full Mode** click the arrow icon at the lower right of the Windows Me Desktop shown above.

Obtaining Details of CDs

When you place a new CD in the drive, the media player starts up and plays the tracks. If you switch to the **CD Audio** button, the window is mapped out to show all of the details of the CD. However, in the case of a new CD, the album is totally anonymous - the tracks and artist have no name and the genre is unknown.

However, if your computer is connected to the Internet, it's a very simple matter to obtain this information using the buttons **Get Names** and **Album Details** shown above.

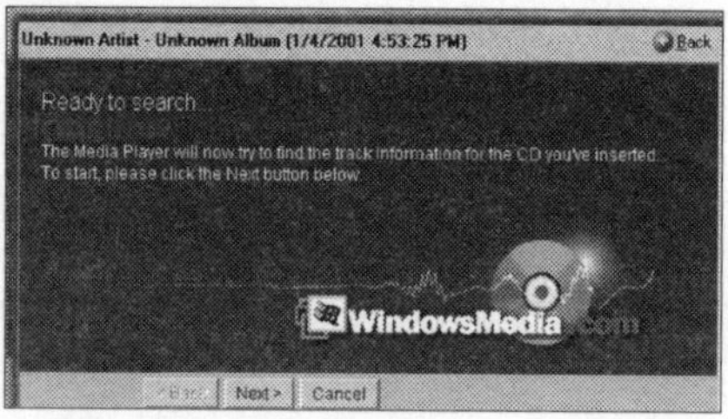

Once the album and track information has been found on the Internet it's automatically entered into the **Media Library** - there's no need to enter any information manually.

Copying Music from CDs to Your Computer

It's very convenient to make copies of your favourite CD tracks onto your hard disc. The advantages of this include the fact that the music is always available while you are working at the computer. You don't have to search around for CDs and keep swapping them in the drive. You can also copy just a selection of your favourite tracks, so that it's possible to create personalized playlists.

Before starting to copy a CD to your hard disc, you need to make sure that the option **Digital copying** is turned on. This can be checked in the media player by selecting **Tools** and **Options...** then clicking the **CD Audio** tab.

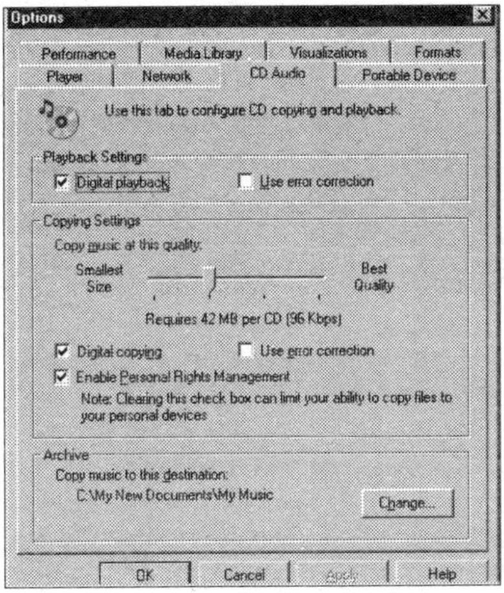

In the above dialogue box, apart from the need to ensure that **Digital copying** is switched on, you can move a slider to adjust the amount the music is compressed when recorded on the hard disc. There is a trade off between audio quality and disc space used. The smaller the size, the lower the audio quality. An entire audio CD containing several hundred megabytes of data can be saved using only 28MB of disc space, albeit with relatively low quality. The highest audio quality requires 69MB of disc space for an entire audio CD. You can change the destination folder on the hard disc from the default folder **C:\My Documents\My Music** using the **Change...** button shown above.

To begin the copy process, place the required CD in the drive and select the **CD Audio** button. By default, all of the tracks are ticked, but you can exclude tracks by clicking to remove the tick. Click the **Copy Music** button to start the copying process. The **Copy Music** button changes to **Stop Copy** as shown below.

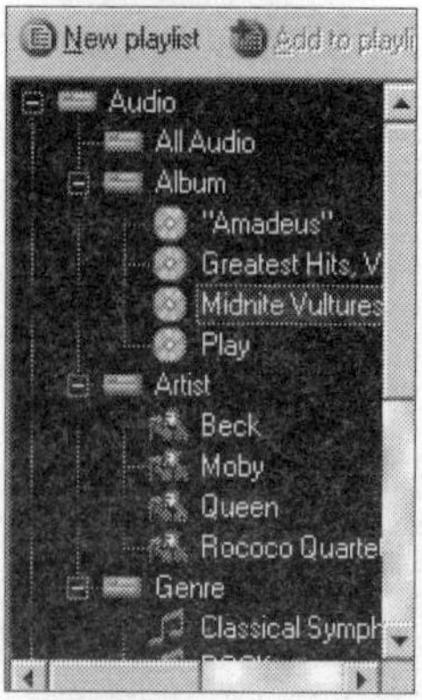

After you have copied the CD, its details are automatically added to the **Media Library**, shown left, accessed via its own button on the left of the media player. The Media Library lists all of your audio and video files and allows you to compile your own playlists. There is also a feature to search your hard disc for any existing audio and video files and add them to the **Media Library** under the headings **All Audio** and **All Clips**. This is discussed shortly.

Playing Music

To play music from a CD, simply insert the CD in the drive and the media player will start up automatically with the **Now Playing** feature selected. To play music which has been copied to your hard disc, start the media player, open up the **Media Library**. Select the required playlist or album and click the **Play** button to start the music.

The **Now Playing** feature gives access to a range of additional features and controls.

The centre of the window displays the currently selected visualization. You can cycle through the visualizations using the arrows, shown, in this example, next to **Ambience:Blender**.

Three buttons at the top of the window allow you to display a comprehensive range of settings.

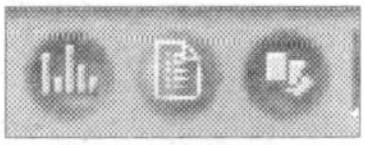

The left hand button presents a choice of audio and video controls.

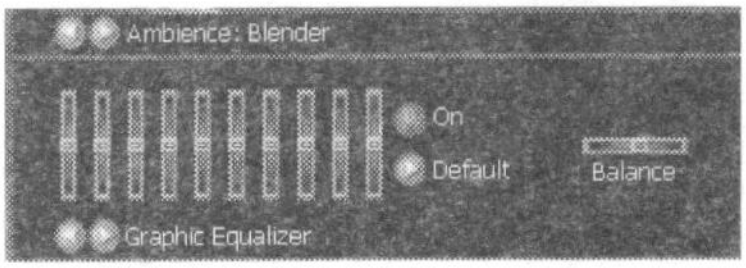

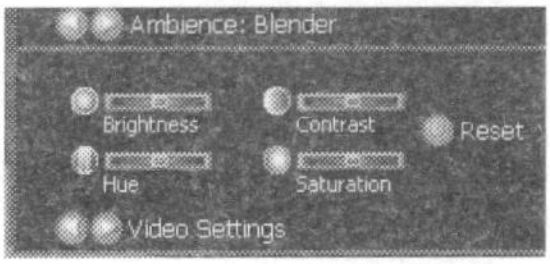

You can cycle through the various groups of settings, **Graphic Equaliser**, **Video Settings**, etc., using the arrows at the bottom left of the media player, just above the **Play/Pause** button.

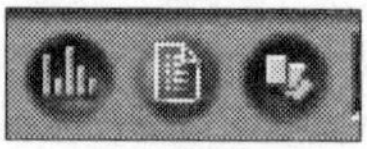

The middle button in the group of three shown left allows the playlist to be displayed on the right of the **Now Playing** window. The right hand button shuffles the items in the playlist.

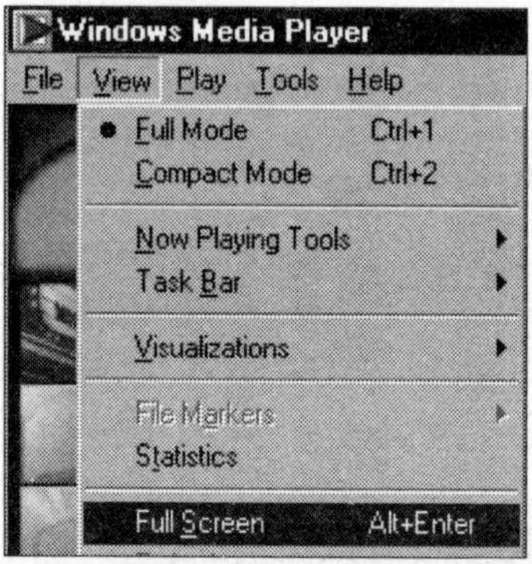

If you are using the media player with **Now Playing** selected, you can make the visualization fill the whole screen. Select **View** and **Full Screen** from the media player menu bar. To return to the normal view press the **Escape** key.

The **Visualizations** option on the **View** menu provides an alternative way to change the visualization. Further visualizations can be obtained from the Internet after selecting **Tools** and **Download Visualizations**. In order to see the visualizations, **Digital playback** must be switched on in **Tools**, **Options** and **CD Audio**.

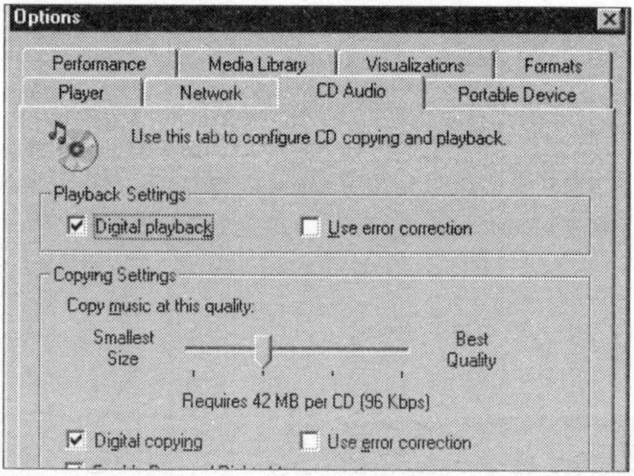

Changing the Media Player Skin

The **Skin** is the name given to the design of the media player, its case and controls, etc., as it appears on the screen. The **Skin Chooser** button is not always visible on the left hand side of the screen and you may need to use the scroll arrows to bring it into view. Click the **Skin Chooser** button and you are presented with a list of skins on the left hand side. On selecting a skin, its design appears in the right hand panel.

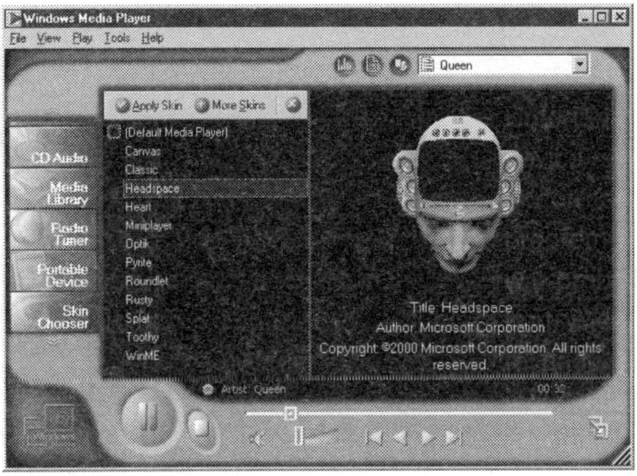

To change your media player skin to the one selected, click the **Apply Skin** button shown above towards the top left. Further skins can be downloaded from the Internet after clicking the **More Skins** button. This connects you to the **WindowsMedia.com** site.

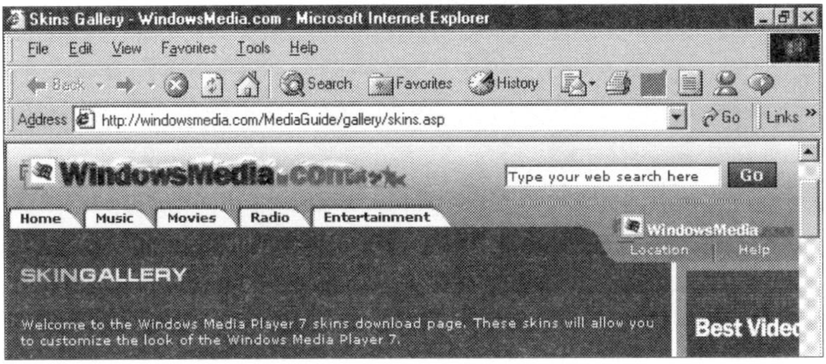

Searching Your Computer for Multimedia Files

Your hard disc(s) will almost certainly contain some audio and video files which can be played in the Windows Media Player. Perhaps you've downloaded multimedia files from the Internet and aren't sure of the location. The **Search Computer for Media...** option on the **Tools** menu can locate all existing audio and video files and add them to the **Media Library**.

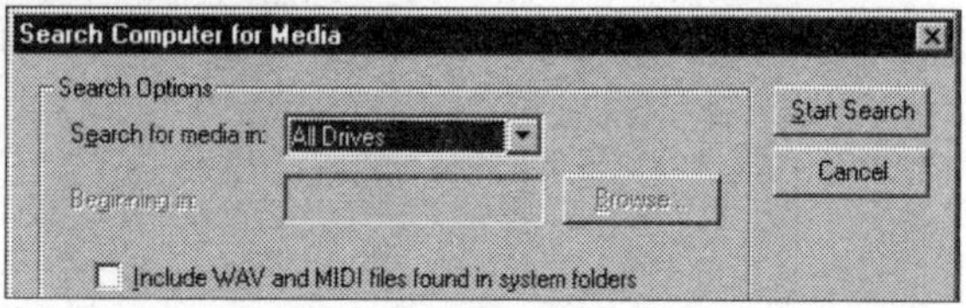

Before starting the search, you can decide which drive(s) to search and whether you wish to include the many **WAV** and **MIDI** files which Windows Me contains. This may result in the media library containing entries for a very large number of files. Entries for music files are added to the **All Audio** playlist while video files appear in the **All Clips** playlist.

In the example shown on the left, the search feature has picked up a clip from a flight simulator program. The entries in the **Media Library**, shown on the right of the media player, enable video clips to be selected and played. Towards the bottom left of the media player, the **Video Settings** allow you to adjust the **Brightness, Contrast, Hue** and **Saturation**. You can hide the **Video Settings** and **Playlist** by clicking on the two leftmost icons in the block of three towards the top of the media player and also shown left.

The Media Guide

Clicking this button on the media player connects you to the Internet and onto a Web page hosted by WindowsMedia.com. On this page are links to topical films, music and video.

Some of these multimedia clips can be downloaded to your hard disc and played whenever required in your media player. Other pieces of music and video can be broadcast directly to your computer for immediate listening or viewing. In this process, known as "streaming", the multimedia files are not recorded on your hard disc. Currently, if you connect to the Internet via a modem, the quality of streamed video is very basic. Broadband connections such as ADSL and cable modems produce better quality streamed video.

The Radio Tuner

When you select the **Radio Tuner** button, you will be automatically connected to the Internet, assuming you have a modem and Internet connection set up and working correctly. Your media player will display a set of Internet radio stations from around the world. In addition you can search for a particular station using a range of search criteria such as the **Format** (Oldies, Rock, etc.) the **Frequency** and the **Location**.

When you have found the radio station, while listening to the music, click **File** and **Add to Library** and **Add Currently Playing Track**. This provides a link at the bottom of the **All Audio** playlist in the **Media Library**. Now highlight the entry for the radio station in the **All Audio** playlist and click the **Add to Playlist** button. A drop down menu appears from which you select the playlist in which the link to the radio station is to appear. In future, to tune in to the station, highlight its name in the playlist and click the **Play** button. If necessary, the computer will connect to the Internet and then tune in to the Internet radio station.

MP3

Currently the term **MP3** is highly topical for a number of reasons. MP3 is an abbreviation for MPEG 3 or Motion Picture Experts Group Layer 3. This refers to a group which lays down international standards for audio and video files, of which MP3 is an audio standard. MP3 allows audio files to be saved in a very compact, compressed format. MP3 files occupy only about a tenth of the disc space taken up by conventional audio files. This compression is achieved when the music is recorded by removing audio data which may not be essential, such as sound which is drowned by louder sound. MP3 files are saved on disc with the extension **.mp3** and can be managed like other types of data file.

Windows Media Player has its own format for compressed audio files, saving files with the extension **.wma** (Windows media audio). This format is used when you copy music from an audio CD to your hard disc. However, Windows Media Player can also play files in a range of formats, including MP3 files. In order to play MP3 files in your media player, check that it's been ticked in the **Options** window of the media player, accessed from **Tools**, **Options...** and the **Formats** tab.

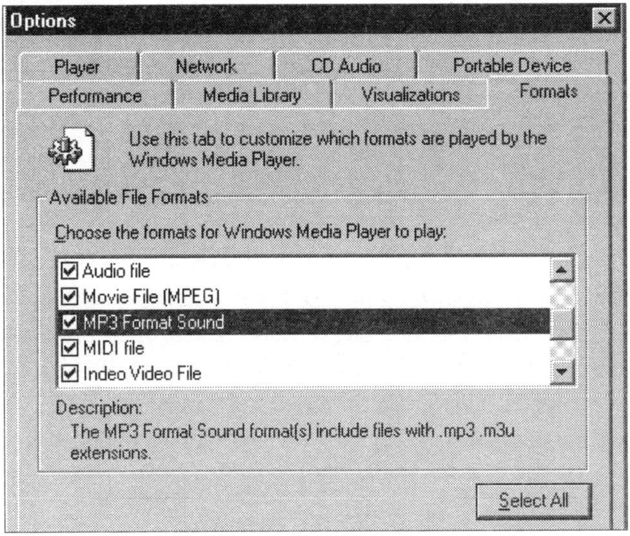

Downloading MP3 Files from the Internet

The compact size of MP3 audio files makes the format ideal for transmitting music across the Internet. Now it's possible to download music from thousands of Web sites around the world, although there's considerable argument over the legality of some of these activities. This has led to courtroom battles between the music industry concerned about loss of revenue and those hosting the music Web sites. However, there are many sites providing copyright-free music for downloading and others where the music can be bought legally. You can find these sites by entering MP3 in your Internet search engine. One such site is **www.mp3.com,** which lists thousands of records covering all types of music.

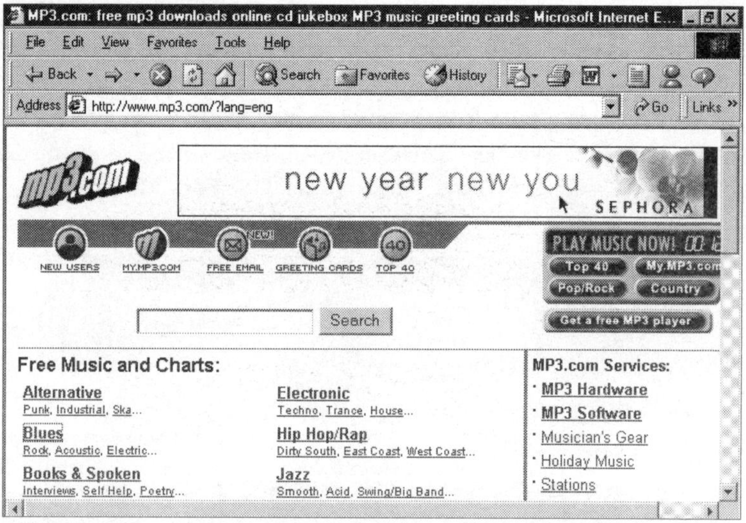

Once you have selected the music, there is usually a choice between playing the music directly across the Internet or downloading it onto your hard disc for playing later. If you have not already acquired the program RealDownload, this enhances the download process and can be obtained free from the Internet. The downloaded MP3 files are added to your Media Library from where they can be played whenever required, using Windows Media Player.

MP3 Players

A further consequence of the downloading of highly compressed music files from the Internet has been the emergence of portable MP3 players. These are small hand-held devices dedicated to playing MP3 files and, since they contain no moving parts, are ideal for people on the move. The MP3 is powered by a small battery and can provide several hours of music.

First the required tracks are downloaded to your Media Library from the Internet. Then the MP3 player is connected to the PC by a cable and the music is copied to the memory of the MP3 player ready for use. The Windows Media Player has a built-in **Portable Device** button as shown below. You may need to scroll down to see **Portable Device** under **Radio Tuner**.

You can see a list of devices compatible with the Windows Media Player by selecting **Tools**, **Options...**, **Portable Device** and clicking **Details...**. This connects you to the Internet where there are several pages listing portable devices supported by the Windows Media Player. The Rio model is stated as the original MP3 player and can hold one hour of music in 32MB of memory. The latest S3 Rio uses the Windows Media Audio file format and this is stated to store twice the amount of music in a given memory size compared with the MP3 format.

The Sound Recorder

If your computer is fitted with speakers and a sound card, you can record and play back sound from an external source such as a microphone or radio. **Sound Recorder** is a software component of Windows Me and is launched from the menus by selecting **Start**, **Programs**, **Accessories**, **Entertainment** and **Sound Recorder**. You may need to install Sound Recorder from your Windows Me CD, as follows:

Select **Start**, **Settings**, **Control Panel** and double click the icon for **Add/Remove Programs**. Now select **Windows Setup**, scroll down and click **Multimedia** and **Details....** Now scroll down until **Sound Recorder** is visible and place a tick in the adjacent box.

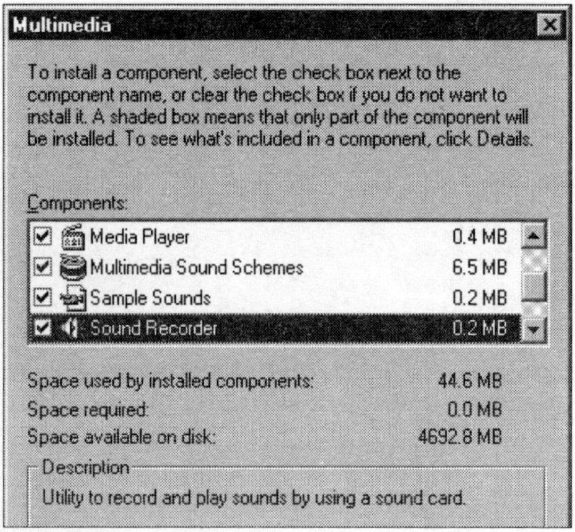

After clicking **OK** and **Apply** you will be asked to insert your Windows Me CD so that the necessary files can be copied.

Launch the Sound Recorder using **Start**, **Programs**, **Accessories**, **Entertainment** and **Sound Recorder**.

The Sound Recorder opens in its own window with the usual Seek and Play controls and a small menu across the top.

The **Record** button is marked with a solid circle and the **Stop** button is next to it. If you want to save a recording in a folder of your choice select **File** and **Save As....**

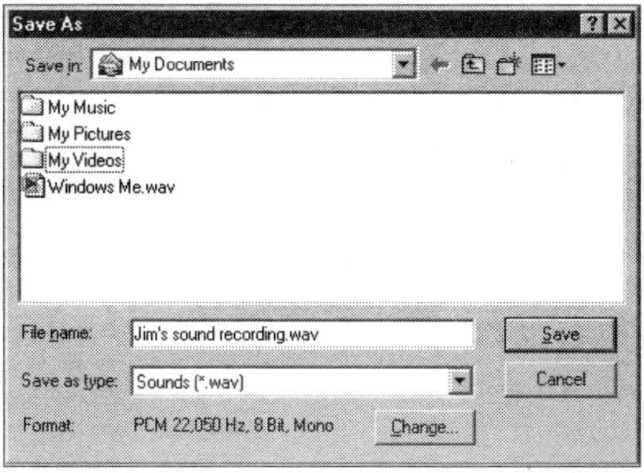

Sound Recorder files are saved with the **.wav** extension. They can be opened in the Windows Media Player by selecting **File** and **Open...** and selecting the required file from the saving location, similar to the one shown above. The sound file is automatically added to the Media Library at the end of the list for **All Audio**.

You can include sound files as attachments to an email, perhaps to send a greeting or personal message to a friend or relative.

Windows Movie Maker

This is a component of Windows Me which allows you to edit your own videos. These may have been copied from your video camera or obtained by a Web Cam attached to your computer. Windows Movie Maker allows you to integrate still shots and video and to add sound tracks and music.

You can experiment with Movie Maker using a sample video included with Windows Me. Launch the program from **Start**, **Programs**, **Accessories** and **Windows Movie Maker**.

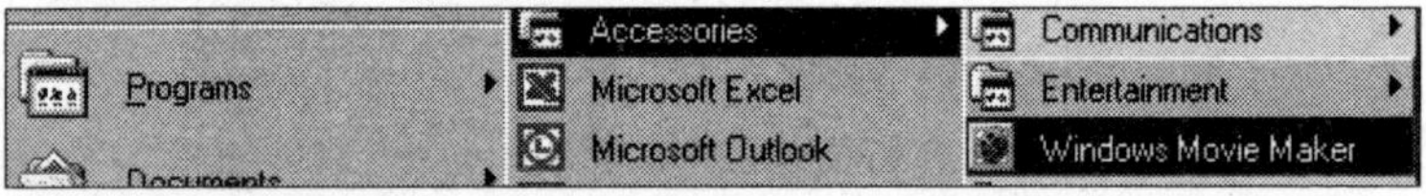

The sample video file is in the folder **My Videos** within **My Documents**, on the **C:** drive. To retrieve this file, select **File** and **Import...** and then select the **My Videos** folder. Highlight the file **Windows Movie Maker Sample File.wmv** and select **Open**.

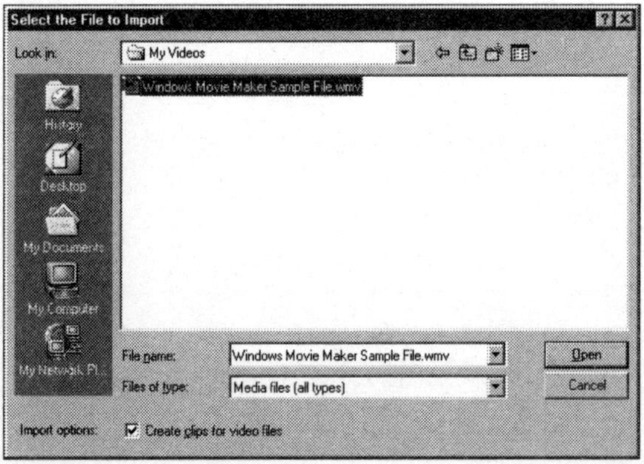

The main Movie Maker window opens and announces that clips are being created as shown on the next page.

The video is divided into a number of clips, for ease of editing. The clips are shown as thumbnails on the left of the Movie Maker window. Once all of the clips have been created, they can be viewed independently by highlighting the clip and clicking the **Play** button.

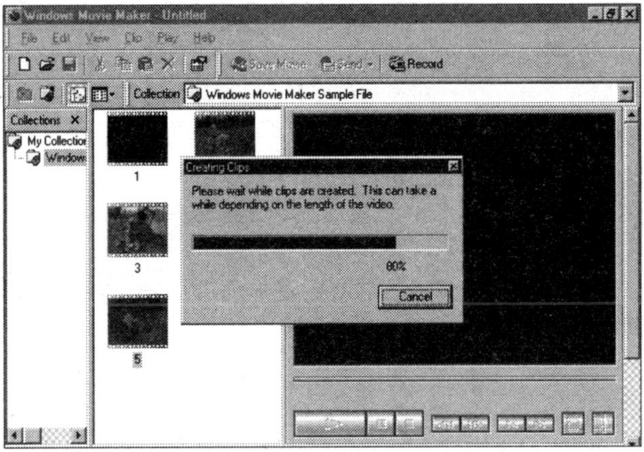

Along the bottom of the Movie Maker window is the "timeline", which looks like a piece of video film. You can drag and drop some or all of the clips onto the timeline to create a film in a particular sequence. The entire film can then be played using the menu command **Play Entire Storyboard/Timeline**, accessed from the **Play** menu at the top of the Movie Maker window.

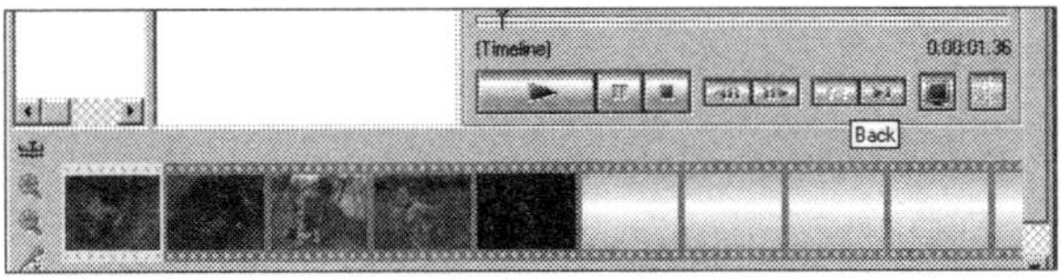

The finished movie can be saved using the **File** and **Save Movie...** menu and opened later in the Windows Media Player, where it can be added to your Media Library. Alternatively, you can use **File** and **Send Movie To...** if you want to email the video to a friend or relative. (Or use the **Send** icon on the top right of the Movie Maker window).

Summary: Windows Media Player

- Windows Me introduces Windows Media Player 7, enabling audio and video files to be played and managed.
- Audio files are played accompanied by a choice of visualizations. These are coloured displays which move in time with the music. Visualizations can fill the whole screen.
- CDs are catalogued in the Media Library. Details of Albums and Tracks can be obtained automatically from the Internet.
- Music CDs can be copied to a hard disc in a highly compressed format, providing a convenient music collection with personalized playlists.
- When music or video is played, the Now Playing feature enables you to cycle through a comprehensive range of audio and video controls including a Graphic Equaliser.
- The Windows Media Player has a number of alternative designs, known as skins, which simulate physical media players. Additional skins can be downloaded from the Internet.
- The media player can search hard discs for any existing audio and video files. These can be added to the Media Library and played.
- The Media Guide connects to a Web site which allows topical music and video clips to be streamed or broadcast directly to the PC, or downloaded and saved on the PC's hard disc.
- The Radio Tuner connects to Internet Radio Stations throughout the world, via a comprehensive search facility.
- Windows Media Player can play the popular MP3 files, the format for compressed music files downloaded from the Internet. The Portable Device button on the media player allows files to be copied to a range of hand-held MP3 players.
- Windows Me provides a Sound Recorder and Windows Movie Maker. These allow sound and video clips to be created, edited and saved then played in the Windows Media Player.

Appendix A: The Universal Serial Bus

Your computer(s), if they are of recent design (later Pentiums) may already be fitted with USB ports. To make sure, look at the back of the machine near to the connectors for devices such as the mouse and printer, etc. The USB ports are small rectangular slots about 12mm by 5mm.

If your machine doesn't already have any visible USB ports, all is not lost - it should be possible to fit the connectors at a modest cost. The basic requirement is for a Pentium or equivalent computer running Windows Me. If no USB ports are visible externally, it's still possible that your computer is equipped with USB ports on the motherboard but simply requires a cable and backplate to provide a connector on the back of the machine. In this case a USB backplate can be bought for a few pounds from local specialist computer suppliers or by mail order from companies such as Maplins.

Even if your machine is supplied with USB ports you still need to check that USB is **enabled** in the BIOS settings of your computer. The BIOS is usually entered as your machine is starting up, by responding to a message on the screen such as "**Press DEL to enter SETUP**". If you have an early Pentium there may be no USB support at all on the motherboard. You can overcome this by fitting a USB PCI Adapter Card. This is an expansion card which plugs into the motherboard and provides two USB connectors on the back of the machine. Before buying a USB Adapter Card you should remove the cover of your computer and check there is a vacant (white) PCI slot, not to be confused with the longer (black) ISA slots.

A number of major companies involved with USB technology have set up a USB Web site containing useful information. You can find the site on the Internet at:

www.usb.org/

Apart from news about peripheral devices designed to utilise the latest USB technology there's also a piece of software which you can

download, called **USBREADY.EXE**. Although this originates from **www.usb.org/**, last time I downloaded it from:

www.softseek.com/

USBREADY.EXE examines your system and reports on the level of USB support which your system already provides.

When you run the testing software, if your machine is already equipped for USB, a message will be displayed saying "**This system has support for USB.**"

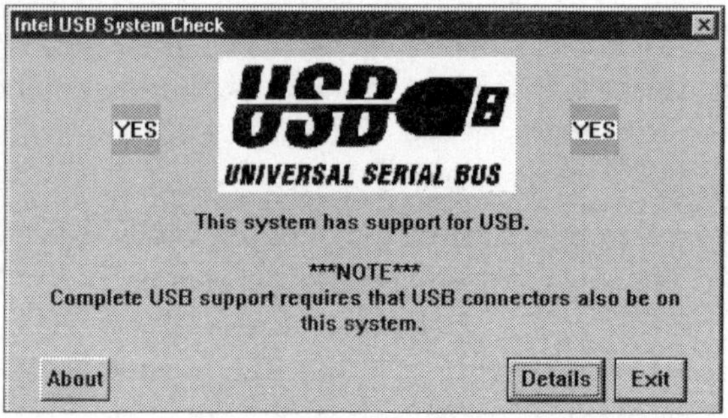

(You may still need a cable and ports on a backplate to provide the connections on the outside of the machine). One of my computers had the USB pins already in place on the motherboard - it just needed a cheap ATX Form Card to be plugged in. This gave two USB sockets and two PS/2 mouse sockets on the back of the machine. The manual for your computer's motherboard should give precise details of what connectors are available. However, if the system check states that the system does not have USB support, you will need to fit a USB PCI Adapter Card as described in the next section. These can be bought for under £20 from local computer repair/upgrade specialists.

Fitting a USB Adapter Card

This section assumes you have checked there is a spare white PCI slot available in your computer and you have obtained a suitable USB Adapter Card.

Switch your computer off at the power point but leave the power cable plugged in at the wall. From time to time while working, earth yourself by touching the metal chassis of the computer. Remove the casing of your computer, usually by taking out several screws at the back or side of the machine. Remove the blanking plate adjacent to a spare PCI slot and firmly press the USB Adapter into place. Fit the retaining screw to secure the card, replace the computer casing and restart the machine.

As PCI expansion cards should be truly "Plug and Play" compatible, all being well you will see a message announcing that new hardware has been found.

New Hardware Found
OPTi 82C861 PCI to USB Open Host Controller
Windows is installing the software for your new hardware.

Then you are asked to insert the Windows Me CD so that the necessary software can be installed.

After the software has been copied, your new USB ports should be ready for use. You can check this by looking in the **Device Manager** obtained by selecting **Start**, **Settings**, **Control Panel** and double clicking **System**. Select the **Device Manager** tab and then **Universal Serial Bus controllers**. You should see the name of the USB Adapter displayed, in this case the **OPTi** model, as shown on the next page.

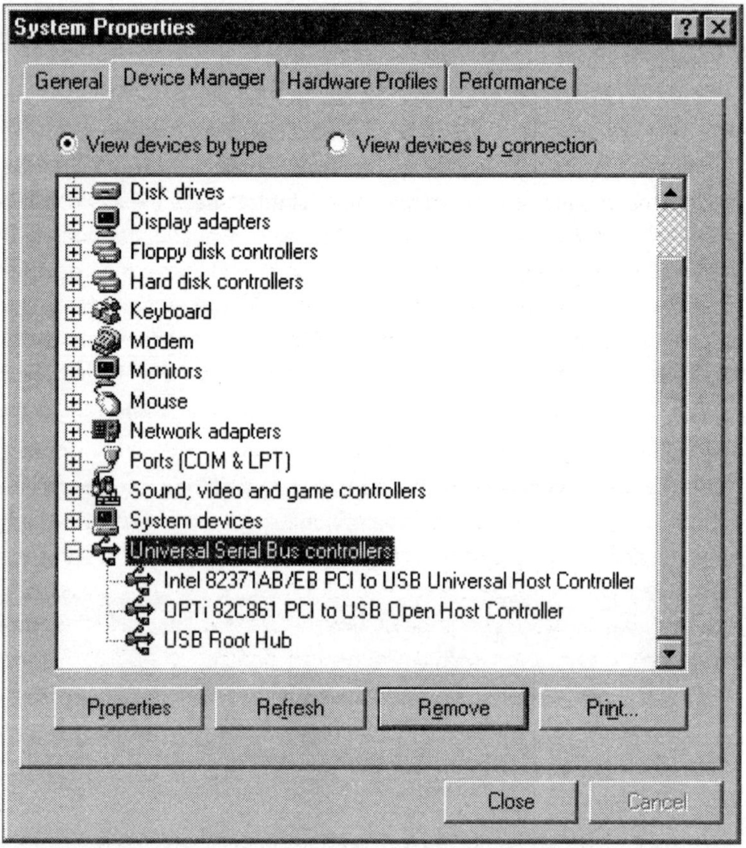

The USB port should now be ready to use. (A fault with the device would be indicated by an exclamation mark in a yellow circle.) You will need to obtain a special LapLink USB cable before you can use the new USB ports to link two computers for data transfer work. You can buy these for LapLink from the Web site at:

www.laplink.com/

The cable package also includes a floppy disc containing the LapLink USB driver. This must be installed on both of the computers to be connected.

Appendix B: Fitting a Parallel Port Expansion Card

The parallel port is a 25 way female socket on the back of the computer, commonly referred to as the Printer Port and LPT1. By design the parallel port is much faster than the neighbouring serial port. The parallel port is generally used for connecting scanners, Zip drives and data transfer software and cables, apart from its primary function as a printer port. Nowadays the USB port is becoming a popular alternative, with its high performance and the way it simplifies the installation of peripheral devices.

Unfortunately, although it's technically possible to have more than one device sharing a single parallel port, this does not give optimum performance. Also, for data transfer work between computers with a program like the Direct Cable Connection or LapLink Professional, you will probably need to disconnect any other devices already using the port. Clearly if you want to use a parallel link on a regular basis - say to back up your laptop computer onto a desktop machine, it's very inconvenient to have to keep disconnecting printers and other devices. The only solution is to fit one or more extra parallel ports to each machine as required. (Up to 4 parallel ports designated LPT1-LPT4 may be fitted to a modern PC.)

Extra parallel ports can be bought on expansion cards which plug into slots on the *motherboard*, the main printed circuit board inside of your computer. Cards designed for the older ISA standard are cheaper than the newer PCI standard. The ISA cards fit into long black slots on the motherboard while the PCI slots are white and shorter. Before buying any expansion card you should check that you have a spare slot of the right type on the motherboard. Expansion cards are available from computer dealers and mail order companies such as Maplins.

If you can afford a PCI card it will be easier to set up under Windows Me than an ISA card. The procedure is similar to that for a USB Adapter as described in Appendix A. It's just a case of removing the case of the computer and inserting the card in a vacant PCI slot.

Fitting an ISA Parallel Port

When you restart the computer Windows Me should, in theory, detect new hardware and complete the installation. However, the ISA card, although relatively cheap, is harder to install since it's not Plug and Play compatible. First you need to set some jumpers on the card to match the available IRQs in your computer. These are the Interrupt Request settings, numbered 0-15 and refer to lines of communication between the device and the central processor of the computer. Two devices can share the same IRQ number but only if they will not be used simultaneously. First you need to find the available IRQs by looking at **Start**, **Settings**, **Control Panel**, **System**, **Device Manager** and **Computer**. Some apparently unused IRQs may in fact be reserved for use by the system.

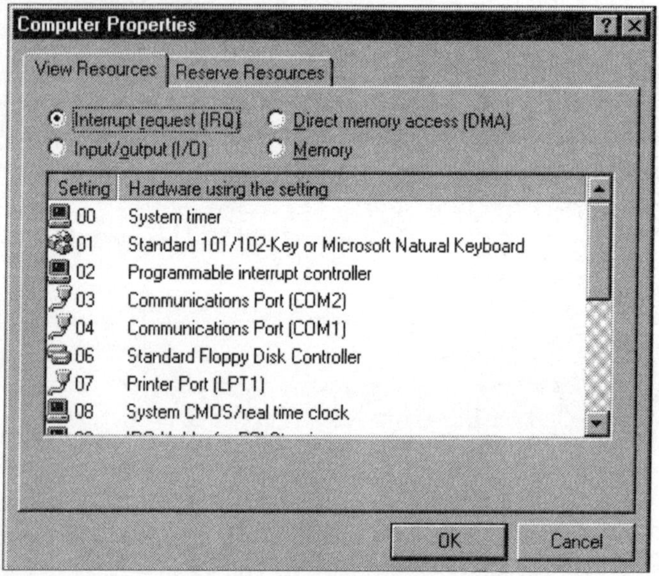

You can see from the above that IRQ7 is used for the first parallel port LPT1. IRQ5 is not listed above, so this is available for our new parallel port LPT2. (IRQ5 is commonly used for a second parallel port.)

Now look at the instructions supplied with the parallel port expansion card and locate the *jumpers*. These are small push-on connectors used to bridge pairs of pins on the card.

The instructions should explain how to set the jumpers to give the appropriate IRQ number (IRQ5 or whatever). Next, with your computer switched off, remove the case and carefully but firmly insert the parallel port expansion card in an available ISA slot. Then replace the retaining screw which secures the card to the chassis and fit the case to the computer.

Now restart the computer and run the **Add New Hardware** applet accessed from **Start**, **Settings** and **Control Panel**. The parallel port should be detected and assigned the name LPT2.

Add New Hardware

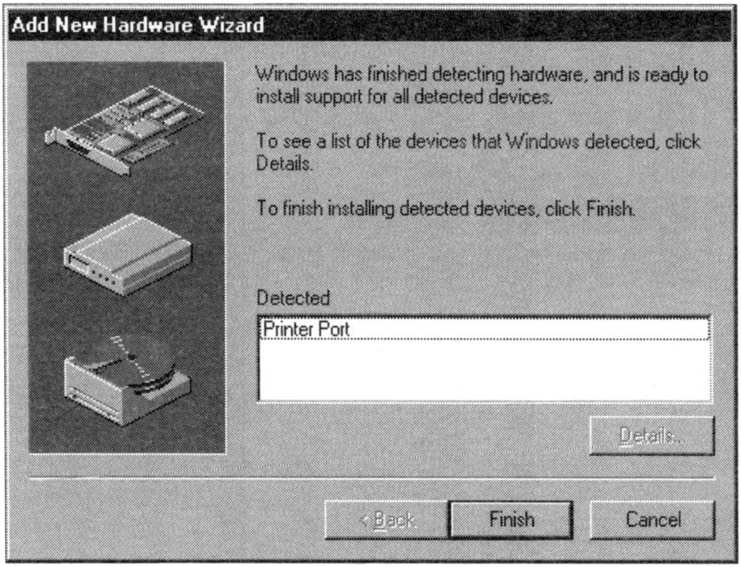

Click **Finish** to complete the installation. You can check if the port has been installed by looking for LPT2 in the list of ports in the **Device Manager** (**Start**, **Settings, Control Panel and System**).

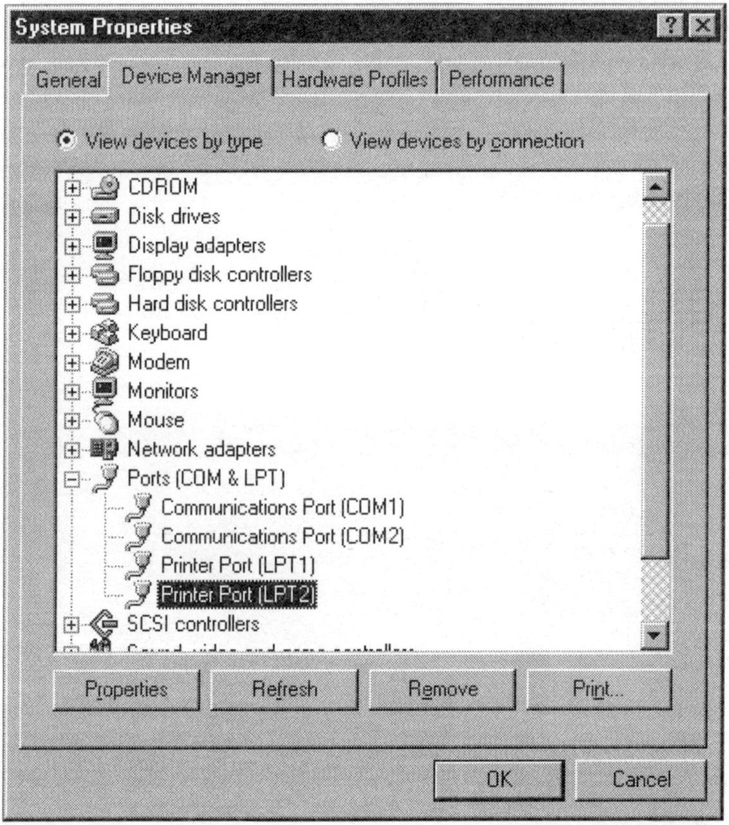

Any problems with the card are likely to be with the Interrupt Setting or possibly because the card itself has not been properly seated in the ISA slot on the motherboard.

You can examine the interrupt settings in Windows Me by double clicking on **LPT2** in the **Device Manager** then selecting **Resources**.

To make changes you need to remove the tick from **Use Automatic Settings** then select the **Change Setting...** button as shown in the **Properties** window on the next page.

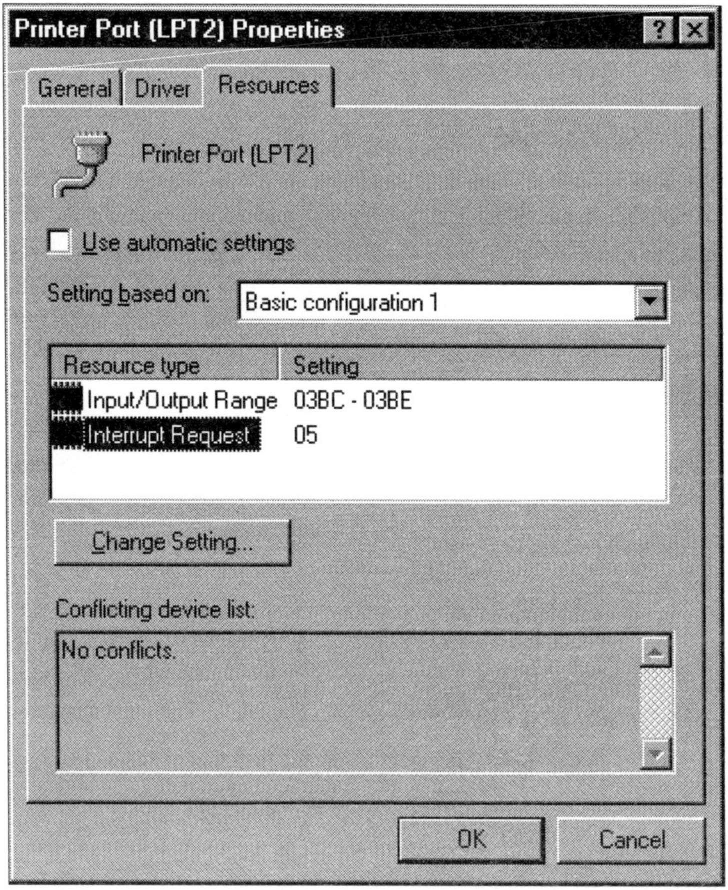

Try to complete the LPT2 setup with the **Use automatic settings** check box ticked. If this is not possible, experiment with the **Basic Configuration** by scrolling down in the **Setting Based on:** bar. You should highlight each of the settings **Input/Output Range** and **Interrupt Request** in turn and check that **No Conflicts** appears in the panel under **Conflicting device list:**. Any alterations you make using the **Change Setting...** button above should correspond to the physical jumper settings on the ISA expansion card. Typical settings for LPT2 are **IRQ5** and **0278-027A** for the **Input/Output Range**.

Notes

Index